AMERICA SINCE 1920

Daniel Snowman

HEINEMANN EDUCATIONAL BOOKS LTD
LONDON

Heinemann Educational Books Ltd
22 Bedford Square, London WC1B 3HH
LONDON   EDINBURGH   MELBOURNE   AUCKLAND
HONG KONG   SINGAPORE   KUALA LUMPUR   NEW DELHI
IBADAN   NAIROBI   JOHANNESBURG
PORTSMOUTH (NH)   KINGSTON   PORT OF SPAIN

ISBN 0 435 31776 8

© Daniel Snowman 1968, 1978
First published 1968 as
U.S.A.: The Twenties to Vietnam (Batsford)
Revised, updated edition first published
by Heinemann Educational Books 1978
Reprinted with revisions 1980, 1984

Printed by
Richard Clay (The Chaucer Press) Ltd.
Bungay, Suffolk

ACKNOWLEDGEMENTS

The author and publishers wish to thank the following for permission
to reproduce extracts on the pages indicated: Mrs. Ellen Wright and
Jonathan Cape Ltd. (Richard Wright, *Black Boy*) on p. 10. Constable
and Co. Ltd. (Robert S. Lynd and Helen Merrell Lynd, *Middletown: A
Study in Contemporary American Culture*) on p. 12. Harper and Row Inc.
(F. L. Allen, *Only Yesterday*) on pp. 17–18. William Heinemann Ltd.
(John Steinbeck, *The Grapes of Wrath*) on pp. 39–40. Hodder and
Stoughton Ltd. (Cordell Hull, *The Memoirs of Cordell Hull*) on p. 78. Da
Capo Press (Jack Goodman (ed.), *While You Were Gone*) on p.115.

CONTENTS

DIAGRAMS, MAPS AND TABLES

NOTE: The statistics quoted in this book, including those incorporated into diagrams and tables, are generally (unless otherwise stated) from US Government publications. Of greatest value have been the *Historical Statistics of the United States* and various editions of the *Annual Statistical Abstract of the United States*.

PREFACE

Many books have already been written on modern American history. It may be appropriate, therefore, to offer a few words of explanation for the appearance of yet another.

Every historian has to make judgements. Moral judgements he should perhaps try to avoid (although his very choice of language will be bound on occasion to suggest approval or disapproval). But he certainly has to make judgements about what is and what is not important. No history book—and certainly not one of this length dealing with a sixty-year period in the history of a great nation—can pretend to contain what are sometimes loosely referred to as 'all the facts'. The historian must be selective and must decide which facts to emphasize.

Many history books (not least those on recent American history) tend to give particular emphasis to institutional and political events and to the roles played by individual leaders. They are often filled with details about who was elected by what sort of majority, what statutes were passed, what wars and battles won and lost. Sometimes, in an effort to take account of the results of recent research, they will include special sections on 'Social Developments' or 'Cultural Developments'. In addition, since histories of the United States are sometimes intended to serve a socializing as well as a purely educational function, they often tend to give more emphasis than is warranted to the apparent unity and flow of American history. Such books can give a misleading picture to the students whose ideas are formed by them.

In the first place, while it may be easier for the historian to write about dramatic events or notable men than about gradual tendencies, students do not always bear in mind that the former are usually symptoms rather than causes of the latter. Pearl Harbor, to take an extreme example, was not so much *the* cause of America's decision to enter the Second World War as the last straw that broke the camel's back. In the same way, writers of 'personalized' history sometimes use the name of an authority figure such as the President as though he ruled by fiat. 'Roosevelt passed the Social Security Act' is occasionally to be seen, or, to take a classic example from earlier American history,

'Teddy Roosevelt destroyed the Northern Securities Company'. This sort of phraseology is quite acceptable if it is recognized that the name of the President (and the verb following his name) is used as a short cut, almost as a metaphor. But not all students—or, I fear, all authors—fully realize this.

A student might also not know, after reading some of the standard textbooks, what life was really like for a member of the society being described. It is quite reasonable, of course, for a historian to write a narrow monograph; but a general book must try to give a general picture. This is not given if the official actions of the nation's élite are given undue prominence.

Then again, the gullible student might be led to assume, from the isolated nature of the 'social' and 'cultural' sections in some of the texts, that these aspects of history can be seen in watertight compartments, separated from other aspects of history. This, of course, is far from the case. Conversely, there are some writers who go to the other extreme and generalize too much about America as a whole. One comes across phrases (such as 'America decided that . . .' or 'public opinion was in favour of . . .') that assume a degree of unity and intellectual consensus the very absence of which has often been one of the most important characteristics of modern American history.

The institutional and personal approaches to history represent a theory of society that can be regarded nowadays only with the greatest caution. They presuppose that the men at the top make decisions relatively unencumbered by any interests other than their own and that everybody else goes ahead and carries them out. In fact, of course, the relationship between the 'governors' and the 'governed' is far more complex than that, and no purely 'output' theory is adequate. It would be foolish to go to the other extreme and claim, with the classical democratic theorists, that all decisions derive from 'the people'. But the historian should try to understand the complex interrelationships that exist within a modern industrial society.

In order to try to avoid some of these pitfalls, I have concentrated on the general social developments of the period and have relegated many of the more dramatic political events to the chronological table at the back of the book. By the same token, the main theme is a social rather than a political one: the constant tug-of-war between those forces making for social conflict and those making for social stability in the United States. American society is, by any standards, extraordinarily diverse. In some ways that diversity has been disruptive: it has expressed itself from time to time in the form of tensions, rivalries, intolerance, and violence. In other respects, however, it has been conducive to a more balanced society: it helps to explain, for example, the high level of religious toleration generally found in the nation. In some periods, the stabilizing (or centripetal) aspects of America's social diversity have tended to be in the ascendant, whereas at others the more disruptive (or centrifugal) aspects have predominated. In the 1920s and 1960s, American society showed signs of major social tensions; some of the interests and social groups within the United States came, or threatened to come, to blows with one another. In the middle 1930s, the 1940s and the early 1950s, the differences within American society were largely submerged in the face of a series of common dangers — the Depression, the Second World War, and the onset of the Cold War.

This approach has helped us to see the often wayward and maverick facts of modern American history as pieces in a reasonably comprehensive jigsaw puzzle. But it was also necessary, while writing this book, to beg a number of important questions. Lack of space has, for instance, forced us to assume rather than to argue that social diversity can make for social tension; similarly, it has been necessary to avoid discussion of the extent to which social and personal tensions rise and fall together. Even more seriously, it has proved impossible in a book of this length to attempt any serious international comparisons. But although this book deals almost exclusively with the United States, the author is not of the opinion that American experience is necessarily different in some qualitative way from that of other societies.

Despite these limitations, and others that will doubtless suggest themselves, it is hoped that this book will prove interesting and even stimulating and that it might provoke some of its readers into furthering their researches into modern American history.

I am grateful to Tribune Publications Ltd., Messrs Methuen and Co., Maurice Temple Smith Ltd., and the Danbury Press for permission to reproduce short passages of my own text previously published by them.

Fig. 1.1 Map of continental United States

One

THE 1920s:
AN AGE OF
ROSE-COLOURED NIGHTMARES

America's 'normal' society

Throughout the 1920s, many Americans in positions of authority spoke of the pleasantly relaxed nature of their society. They were confident that they and their society were, in the words of Dr Coué, the popular French exponent of the theory of autosuggestion, 'getting better and better'. This comfortable serenity was anticipated right at the beginning of the decade by Senator Warren G. Harding of Ohio, soon to be nominated by the Republican Party as their presidential candidate.

On 14 May 1920, Harding outlined America's needs as he saw them:

> America's present need is not heroics, but healing; not nostrums, but normalcy; not revolution, but restoration; not agitation, but adjustment; not surgery, but serenity; not the dramatic, but the dispassionate; not experiment, but equipoise; not submergence in internationality, but sustainment in triumphant nationality. . . .

America, Harding hoped, was to become a calm and stable society. But this meant that it would also have to become a prosperous one. A second theme that was repeated again and again by America's leaders between 1920 and the Great Crash nine years later was that the United States was and would ever continue to be the most economically advanced society the world had ever seen. As late as New Year's Day 1929, as sober a newspaper as the *New York Times* was able to burst into raptures concerning the economic achievements of the past year:

> It has been a twelvemonth of unprecendented advance, of wonderful prosperity. . . . If there is any way of judging the future by the past, this new year may well be one of felicitation and hopefulness. . . .

In many ways, of course, the rosy picture painted by US leaders was not unwarranted. During the decade between the end of the First World War and the Great Crash, American society was apparently a great deal more stable than at many other periods in her history. There were no major revolutionary or radical movements, no sustained or recurrent riots, fewer lynchings than at any other time since Reconstruction, and, after the first couple of years or so, few serious industrial disputes. Economically, too, the optimistic 'boosters' had a great deal of evidence for their case, for, by and large, the years 1922–9 saw a period of uninterrupted economic progress. Throughout all this colossal economic boom, prices remained remarkably stable, so that the new scientific innovations – the automobiles, the telephones, the radios, the refrigerators – were available to an increasingly large proportion of upper- and middle-class Americans.

But the well-documented cheerfulness of America's leaders does not tell the whole story of the 1920s. The decade may have appeared to be one of relative social stability, but it was also one that witnessed a good deal of vicious fanaticism; it may have been a period of unprecedented economic development and of widespread economic well-being, but it was also one that was snuffed out by the sudden and devastating Depression. All was not quite as well as the real-life Hardings and the fictional Babbitts liked to imply.

'Normalcy' could have meant almost anything – except, perhaps, what Harding wanted it to mean. If there were any qualities that had *not* normally been characteristic of American society in the past, they included serenity and equipoise. On the contrary, in almost all periods of previous American history some group or other had vociferously held and agitated on behalf of nostrums of one sort or another. The American norm (if, indeed, there was one at all) was not the relaxed stability that Harding had in mind, but restlessness and social instability.

This social instability was a result, to some extent at least, of the fact that the United States, throughout its history, lacked an established and, above all, a homogeneous social structure. Indeed, the more heterogeneous the elements that had composed American society at any given time, the greater had been the likelihood of nostrums, agitation, and experiment. For instance, one period in which American society had been extremely diverse was the 1840s and 1850s. This was a period not only of massive immigration, but also of frantic westward expansion, a period when one part of the country was industrializing and the other was not — and, of course, it was a period that culminated in the Civil War. Another great wave of immigration came to an effective stop at the outbreak of the First World War. In terms of the various countries in which her inhabitants were born, the United States was, in 1920, as mixed a multitude as she had ever been before; indeed, American society was probably, in the decade following the Treaty of Versailles, composed of more colours and religions and speaking more languages than had ever before been the case in any nation-state in history. One graphic illustration of this is that in 1920 more than two-thirds of the 3,000 or so American counties contained more than 1,000 foreign-born or non-white inhabitants. Fig. 1.2 shows the composition of the American population in 1920.

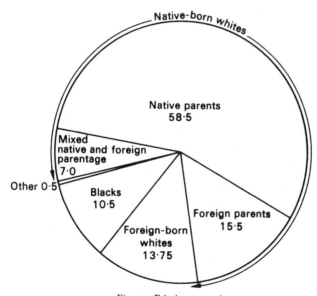

Fig. 1.2 Ethnic groups in 1920

But it was not only in the multiplicity of its ethnic and religious groups that American society in 1920 was extraordinarily heterogeneous. Another important division is revealed by a glance at the income figures. The decade was one of the very rich and the very poor: the top 1 per cent earned almost 15 per cent of all earned incomes (by 1948, they were earning only about 8 per cent). In 1929, one-third of all personal income was being earned by the top 5 per cent. Gross fortunes were made and inherited, particularly in the big

cities. In 1924, 4·6 per cent of all stockholders owned 76·9 per cent of
all stock. In 1926, 207 individuals — the highest number on record —
paid taxes on 1 million dollars or more in a single year. F. Scott
Fitzgerald writes ambivalently about the rich. They are, he says
wistfully, 'different from us', but he knows that the perfect girl of the
period — the ideal 'flapper' — should be not only 'lovely' and 'nineteen' but also 'expensive'. He is critical of the undeserved wealth of a
poseur like Gatsby, but he knows that only the man with wealth can
really have the opportunity of enjoying all that life has to offer.
Fitzgerald — who was very far from being poor — compensated for his
lack of real wealth when he was a young man by inventing problems
for his rich heroes. 'All the stories that came into my head,' he later
recalled, 'had a touch of disaster in them — the lovely young creatures
in my novels went to ruin, the diamond mountains of my short stories
blew up, my millionaires were as beautiful and damned as Thomas
Hardy's peasants.'

But for all his ambivalence and even resentment towards the wealthy, Fitzgerald — in company with most other writers of the time —
gave hardly a thought to the indescribable poverty that afflicted some
sections of American society despite the general affluence of the age.
'Show an American citizen with means and a disposition to be generous an individual in distress and he will invariably be moved to aid,'
said a perceptive writer in *The New Republic* in 1926. But, he went on,
'show this same citizen a group and he will find the greatest difficulty
in visualizing distress.'

One of the groups most in need of generous help in the twenties, but
which received very little, was the farming community. The income of
the farm labourer, even in the most affluent years of the decade, was
generally only about half that of coal miners and usually not much
more than a quarter that of clerical workers.

American Indians who were farmers — as most of them were now
forced to be since they were living on reservations — were in an even
more parlous state. A commission study on the Indian, submitted to
Secretary of the Interior Hubert Work in 1928, said that most Indians
lived on land so poor that, even if the government were to give them
proper assistance — which it did not — they would not have been able
to make a decent living out of it.

The economic diversity of the period can also be illustrated by
looking at the distribution of the labour force among various industries. As recently as the 1870s, half the national labour force had still

been engaged in agriculture, with manufacturing a very poor second. By 1920 manufacturing had outstripped agriculture, and the proportion of the labour force in professional and clerical jobs had risen sharply. These trends were to continue as the decade progressed (Fig. 1.3).

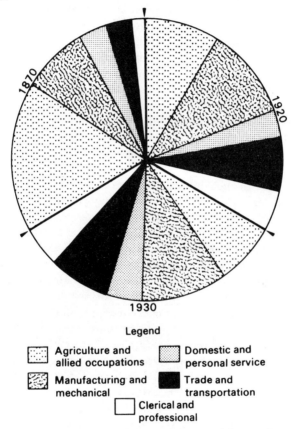

Legend

- Agriculture and allied occupations
- Domestic and personal service
- Manufacturing and mechanical
- Trade and transportation
- Clerical and professional

Fig. 1.3 Percentage distribution of gainfully occupied persons (16 years of age and over)
SOURCE: *Recent Social Trends*, 1933, p.284

The eclipse of agriculture as the nation's largest industry is one manifestation of what was, perhaps, the most important fact about American society in the years after the First World War. The 1920 census showed that, for the first time, more Americans were living in towns (defined by the Bureau of the Census as communities of 2,500 inhabitants or more) than in the country. The urban majority was as yet a very small one not yet able, as it was in later decades, to swamp the occasional *cri de cœur* from the rural minority. Consequently, the 1920s saw a constant battle on many fronts between the almost equal forces of countryside and town. The countryside was seen by its inhabitants as being the rightful home of white, Protestant America, the repository of the old Puritan virtues of thrift, hard work, and self-denial. To these people the new industrial cities, swarming with recent, as yet un-Americanized immigrants, epitomized all that was sordid and ungodly. Rural America gained some dramatic victories in the 1920s: the manufacture and sale of intoxicating liquor was outlawed by the Eighteenth Amendment to the Constitution; a Tennessee schoolteacher, John Scopes, was successfully indicted in 1925 for breaking a state law forbidding the teaching of 'any theory that denies the story of the divine creation of man as taught in the bible and [teaching] instead that man has descended from a lower order of animals'; and in the 1928 presidential election a Protestant millionaire born in the Midwest trounced a 'wet' Irish-Catholic from New York. But the rural victors were enjoying nothing more substantial than a noisy swan song. The continuing migration from the farms to the cities and the increasingly widespread distribution of the new urban-based mass media made it clear to those who cared to read the signs that the rural—urban conflicts of the 1920s were certain, sooner or later, to be resolved in favour of urban America.

A less obvious but equally significant rift within American society was that between the generations. American youths had just fought what, at first, some of them had romantically and rather naïvely thought would be the war to end all war. Many of them were injured, some killed. Those who survived — men like Ernest Hemingway and John Dos Passos — were quickly disabused of any optimism that they might have felt earlier with regard to the fighting. As soon as the First World War was over, many of the most sensitive and articulate of them thought of it as having been a pointless and destructive holocaust in which they had been forced to participate as a result of the ineptness of their parents' generation.

But if the war had given young people a glimpse of blood and horror, it had also enabled many of them to see, for the first time, some of the more attractive aspects of Europe. Many a survivor of the trenches returned to his parochial, inbred, and cultureless Midwestern township bursting with enthusiasm for the undisturbed individualism that, in his mind's eye at least, characterized the capitals of

Europe. Some of the young men went back, and their presence attracted others who had never been to Europe before. Paris in the 1920s contained a sizeable colony of young expatriate American writers, among them Ernest Hemingway, F. Scott Fitzgerald, Louis Bromfield, and Glenway Wescott. Others, although not going to Europe, at least took the step of getting out of their small Midwestern towns — Sherwood Anderson's 'Winesburg, Ohio'; the 'Zenith' caricatured by Sinclair Lewis; the 'Spoon River' satirized by Edgar Lee Masters; or Muncie, Indiana, disguised by the sociologists Robert Lynd and his wife as 'Middletown' — and taking off for the big city, sometimes Chicago, more often New York. In the big cities the young men and women of the Jazz Age often lived the vigorous and unconventional lives described so poignantly in the work of Scott Fitzgerald.

The representative symbol of the age was, perhaps, the 'flapper' with her bobbed hair and pudding-basin hat, her rouge and lipstick, her flattened breasts, her waistless short skirt, her flesh-coloured stockings, and her undergraduate escort. The two of them went — in a car if the young man could afford one — to movies and to parties where they probably danced the Charleston and Black Bottom. As likely as not, some strong illegal liquor was served and, by late evening, the couple might well have been conducting a spirited wordless debate as to the amount of 'necking' and 'petting' that 'nice' girls permitted. To some extent the energetic *joie de vivre* of these young people was a natural expression of youthful high spirits. But there was often, also, a strain of resentful rebellion running through the apparently flippant high jinks of the twenties: rebellion against the values of the generation that made the war and was satisfied with the quality of life in Winesburg or Zenith.

America in the 1920s, then, was full of sharp social contrasts and, latently at least, tense rivalries. But over and above these social divisions that made America smoulder like a restless volcano at this time there were other respects in which it was obvious even to the most superficial observer that America was undergoing a whole host of radical changes. In 1920 35 per cent of the American population had their homes lighted by electricity; by 1924, for the first time, this figure went up to more than 50 per cent. In 1910 there was one telephone for every $14^{1}/2$ people in the United States; by 1920 there was one for every $8^{1}/2$ people. In 1910 there were fewer than half a million passenger cars registered; by 1920, in spite of a major falling off of production during the war years, there were more than 8 million

(a figure that had leapt to almost 23 million by the end of the decade).
Although the national death rate was, throughout the twenties, falling
off at all age groups, the proportion of Americans killed in automobile
accidents shot up every single year.

Unequal slices of a very rich pie

This was the raw material out of which Harding and his Ohio cronies
intended to mould 'normalcy'. But what of the economic optimism
voiced by the cheery business moguls of the period? We now know,
and they were to find out, that all was not well with the stock market
towards the end of the decade. There were even a few prophetic souls
(such as Bernard Baruch) who at various times during the late
twenties warned that the industrial boom was doomed to end. As
early as the autumn of 1926 Baruch wrote to Mark Sullivan:

> Now let me make a prediction to you. Business has undoubtedly reached its zenith,
> and what we see in motors, steel, and railroad statements, is evidence of what has
> gone by and not of what is before us. There has been a stimulation of business by
> high-power salesmanship on the partial payment plan of homes, radios, auto-
> mobiles, etc. Whereas it is wise to buy things on the partial payment plan that will
> result in time in increased economies and better living, at the same time it can be
> overdone. I am afraid it has now been overdone.[1*]

By March 1929, Paul M. Warburg, the chairman of the International
Acceptance Bank, was quoted as saying:

> If orgies of unrestrained speculation are permitted to spread too far, . . . the ultimate
> collapse is certain not only to affect the speculators themselves, but also to bring
> about a general depression involving the whole country.[2]

However, most businessmen had no difficulty finding answers for the
few Cassandras like Baruch and Warburg. Almost any index of
economic growth between the end of 1922 and the autumn of 1929
showed a massive improvement (so long as you looked at the national
aggregate and did not break down your figures by region, race, or
profession). During those seven years of plenty, industrial production
went up by about a half and wages by a third. Prices, particularly of
industrial goods, were remarkably stable, once the immediate postwar inflation had played itself out. Corporate net profits went
up, according to one study of the period, by 76 per cent and
dividends to stockholders by 108 per cent.

But the apparent health of the economy was misleading. There is

---

*Superior numbers throughout relate to the references listed on pp. 238–9.

no doubt of the productivity, the price stability, and the resulting prosperity of the middle years of the twenties. Nevertheless, America's foreign policy seemed, in those respects that touched on international finance, as though it had been specially designed to bring that prosperity to an end. The United States insisted that the victorious Allies repay every penny that they had borrowed during and after the war. At the same time, America was lending money to Germany with which the latter could pay the enormous reparations that she was obliged to give the Allies. With this money, the Allies began to repay their war debts to the United States, thus creating an absurd financial triangle. 'It would have made equal sense', says William E. Leuchtenburg, 'for the United States to take the money out of one Treasury building and put it into another.'[3]

But America's economic policies towards her erstwhile allies were not only foolish; they were self-defeating. Although France and Britain would pay back their debts with money gained from German reparations, the Americans — by means of the Dawes Plan and later, the Young Plan — devised ways of enabling German reparations to be paid off over a longer and longer period. The Dawes and Young plans were well intentioned and ingenious, but they did not help the United States to collect her debts from Britain and France. The ability of these latter to pay was impeded, too, by the high tariff barrier (the Fordney—McCumber Act) that Congress enacted in 1922. This Act had many effects — one of which was to make it harder for Britain and France to obtain the dollars with which eventually to make their repayments to the United States. By the end of the 1920s very little of the German reparations and Allied debts had been paid off; and once the Great Depression arrived, there was no real question of the various payments ever being made.

During the pre-Depression decade, as we have seen, domestic production was going up and up, and almost all industries had a desperate need for enlarged foreign markets. But American producers were forced by the economic isolationism of the governments of the decade to try to sell most of their goods in the home market. If one looks carefully at that home market and, in particular, at some of the very large but relatively inarticulate elements within it, further objections emerge to the blanket optimism of Harding and others.

A tenth of the population was made up of blacks, a group that was living in almost unrelieved squalor and misery. Most were still living in the South (in 1920, the population of two states — Mississippi and

South Carolina — was still predominantly black), and the South was overwhelmingly the poorest part of the country. Living conditions in the remote cotton areas were wretched by any standards but, when seen in the context of an extraordinarily prosperous nation, they were atrocious. Richard Wright was more fortunate than many southern blacks, but even he was able to remember, in his autobiography, *Black Boy*, the pangs of hunger when his father left home:

> Hunger stole upon me so slowly that at first I was not aware of what hunger really meant. Hunger had always been more or less at my elbow when I played, but now I began to wake up at night to find hunger standing at my bedside, staring at me gauntly. The hunger I had known before this had been no grim, hostile stranger; it had been a normal hunger that had made me beg constantly for bread, and when I ate a crust or two I was satisfied. But this new hunger baffled me, scared me, made me angry and insistent. Whenever I begged for food now my mother would pour me a cup of tea which would still the clamour in my stomach for a moment or two; but a little later I would feel hunger nudging my ribs, twisting my empty guts until they ached. I would grow dizzy and my vision would dim.[4]

Another important but largely inarticulate element within the American domestic market in the 1920s was the new industrial worker. The Lynds found that three-quarters of their sample of 100 working-class families in Middletown in 1924 were earning less than the $1,920 considered by the Bureau of Labor to be the minimum annual cost of living for a standard family of five people in that year. The Middletown industrial worker could generally get a job, but 'when times were bad', such as during the middle six months of 1924, there was a very serious danger of sudden unemployment. The Lynds interviewed 165 working-class families in Middletown and discovered that 'during the first nine months of 1924 . . . only 38 per cent of the 165 lost no time [through unemployment], another 19 per cent lost less than a month, and 43 per cent lost a month or more'. It is true that by the 1920s the Middletown worker had a marginally greater chance of promotion than had his father in the 1890s and was less likely to suffer a serious vocational injury, but he was still far from confident that, a year or even a few months hence, he would continue to hold at least as good a job and take home at least as big a wage as at present. The relative poverty and economic uncertainty of the Middletown industrial worker were repeated, in patches, throughout the United States. Coal miners in Pennsylvania and Kentucky had similar problems; so did textile workers in Massachusetts. It was not that America was poor; as a nation, she most decidedly was not. But her economy was largely unregulated and in consequence its overall benefits were very unevenly distributed.

In immediate terms, of course, the uneven nature of the American economy — the existence of pockets of poverty and of unemployment — did not do the economy as a whole much harm. Labour was plentiful and cheap and profits were high. Labour disputes and union activities generally were, after the immediate postwar period at least, minimal. One reason for this was that the man who was lucky enough to get employment in industry felt that he was thus enabled to enjoy the prevailing affluence and had no grounds for complaint; another, however, might well have been that the man who was poor and unemployed was in no position to bargain with a potential employer.

In the long term however, the bonanza of the 1920s could not last — and it was likely to come to an end partly because of the existence of the very pockets of poverty upon which it had earlier been built. Manufacturers continued to produce goods (including large quantities of new luxury goods) at an unprecedented rate, but the extent to which they could seek foreign markets was severely limited by the economic isolationism of the decade. Many of them were, therefore, forced to try to sell most of their products in the glutted domestic market. As the decade progressed, the home market showed signs of reaching saturation point. High-pressure advertising techniques were developed; the public was cajoled into buying more and more. Real prices fell; production continued to increase. So did consumption among some — and poverty among others. The men who were producing the goods seemed to have forgotten that they must also maximize the buying power of their market. Since wages were low and unemployment not infrequent, a sizeable body of potential consumers was simply not equipped to join in the spending spree. Prices fell and advertising increased; but the black, the farmer, the Middletown factory hand, the New England textile worker, the Pennsylvania coal miner, and many another could still not afford a car or a radio or the latest style of dress for his wife or a doll for his little girl. So long as the poor were a small minority, the economy would continue to thrive. Most wealthy Americans thought that this would happen, and they optimistically spent much of their surplus cash on shares in big business companies. But American producers over-extended themselves, the number of those who were relatively poor increased, and, as we shall see at the beginning of the next chapter, the whole edifice was to come crashing down in the last months of the decade.

Contrasts and tensions

America in the twenties, then, was far from being the homogeneous, stable and universally prosperous society that those who benefited from it sometimes liked to imply. The slogans of the day were those of health, progress and optimism (Babbitt, talking about 'the Real He-man, the fellow with Zip and Bang', says that these are the fellows who have 'hair on their chests and smiles in their eyes and adding-machines in their offices'[5]); those who were successful spoke aggressively of their society as though it were a perfect example of uninhibited social mobility. But the social facts were, not infrequently, characterized by appalling poverty and frustratingly unachievable expectations. Nor was this the only paradox of the age. William E. Leuchtenburg, towards the end of his study of the decade, writes:

> It was . . . an age of conformity and of liberation, of the persistence of rural values and the triumph of the city, of isolationism and new internationalist ventures, of *laissez-faire* but also of government intervention, of competition and of merger, of despair and of joyous abandon.[6]

Contrasts and rivalries were not new to American history. What was peculiarly true of the twenties was that so many of the divisions were so evenly poised. Another way of putting this is to say that American society was right in the middle of a number of very important transitions: no longer rural, but not yet dominated by either industry or the white-collar professions; no longer overwhelmingly either Anglo-Saxon or Protestant, but not yet resigned to the idea of becoming a genuinely pluralistic society. America was in a state of precarious balance between the old and the new. Professor Lynd and his wife noticed this in the concluding pages of their sociological analysis of *Middletown*:

> . . . Middletown . . . may be observed to employ in the main the psychology of the last century in training its children in the home and the psychology of the current century in persuading its citizens to buy articles from its stores; it may be observed in its courts of law to be commencing to regard individuals as not entirely responsible for their acts, while in its institutional machinery for selling homes, failure to pay, whether due to unemployment, sickness, or other factors, is regarded as a deliberate violation of an agreement voiding all right to consideration; a man may get his living by operation of a twentieth-century machine and at the same time hunt for a job under a *laissez-faire* individualism which dates back more than a century; a mother may accept community responsibility for the education of her children but not for the care of their health; she may be living in one era in the way she cleans her house or does her washing and in another in the care of her children or in her marital relations.[7]

The period was one of uneasy equilibrium, a period of apparent social truce, a period when the 'haves' thought that life would always remain the way it was and the 'have nots' seemed, by and large, to be resigned to not having.

But the equilibrium and the truce were at best temporary and at worst illusory. In the 1920s almost all elements within American society were repeatedly being bombarded with the forces of radical and speedy change. Under these circumstances many of the latent tensions with which America had been living uneasily for several decades pressed their way, every now and then, to the forefront of the nation's consciousness.

During the period of America's participation in the First World War, American society had been relatively united; there was an external threat to overcome, an external enemy to hate, an external victory to achieve. Some of the aggression of war spilled over into the domestic society; some Americans of German origin, for instance, were made to feel acutely uncomfortable and, in some circles, *Sauerkraut* was renamed Liberty Cabbage. But internal tensions were, as is so often the case in wartime, at a minimum. The end of the war, however, liberated, within the United States itself, all sorts of aggressions that could no longer be conveniently externalized. To foreign immigrants were ascribed many of the vices of the defeated enemies. If the immigrants were from Eastern Europe, they were, as likely as not, thought to be potential Lenins, plotting day and night to overthrow the political system of the very country that had been so good as to give them a home. 'Isolationist' Republicans blamed President Wilson for leading the country into a pointless involvement in European affairs. 'Internationalist'* Democrats looked askance at what they considered to be the unnecessarily selfish patriotism of their critics. And there were moderates who considered both elements to be misguidedly dogmatic. Sons rebelled against the values that they had been taught by their fathers. Religious intolerance flourished.

During the twenties these aggressions gave rise to two types of behaviour pattern. In the first place, American society responded to the tensions within it by making use of a number of equilibrating devices — attempts, in effect, to reduce the strains and stresses within society and to maximize the stability of the social system. Some of these devices (such as the development of spectator sports and team loyalties) served the function of canalizing aggression into socially acceptable directions, while others (such as the immigration-restriction laws) were really ways of avoiding an apparently insoluble problem. In the second place, however, many of the aggressions and

*For a discussion of these terms see pp. 96 *et seq.*

latent tensions in American society continued, on and off throughout the twenties, to manifest themselves in a depressingly wide range of times, places and forms. For the rest of this chapter we will examine some examples of these two behaviour patterns.

Attempts to reduce social tensions

What were the equilibrating devices available to America in the 1920s by means of which she could liberate herself from the divisive effects of social tension? There were, of course, a great many traditional institutional devices. In the political field, for instance, there were the much-vaunted checks and balances, the basic elements of which had been invented by the Founding Fathers in order to prevent one governing element from becoming too dominant at the expense of the others; but these were not of much help in the twenties, since the tensions did not generally take the form of rivalry between contending power structures. Occasionally there was such a clash: the Senate refused to ratify the Treaty of Versailles and, in consequence, to accede to President Wilson's wish that the United States become a member of the League of Nations; President Coolidge twice vetoed the McNary–Haugen Bill, which was designed to help the farmers by offering them subsidies in return for crop restriction; Coolidge's nominee for Attorney-General in 1927 was twice rejected by the Senate. But, by the standards of both earlier and later American history, clashes between the major branches of government were rare and unimportant in the 1920s. Within the Democratic Party, all was not quite so harmonious. The conventions of 1920, 1924 and 1928 were all bedeviled by the divisive issue of Prohibition, and the latter two by the Catholicism of Al Smith. At the 1920 and 1924 conventions the Democratic Party saved itself from the possibility of considerable harm by the two-thirds rule, whereby no man could be nominated as candidate for the presidency unless he obtained the votes of two-thirds of the delegates. By this device – an annoying one to the impatient delegates who had to poll more than one hundred times in 1924 – the eventual nominee and his running mate represented views that were sufficiently vague or middle-of-the-road that the party was able to go, more or less united, to the polls. If the two-thirds rule had not been in operation in 1924, the Democratic Party might conceivably have split into two viciously antagonistic factions and even, in the long run, into two parties – an eventuality that could have given the Republicans an almost indefinite period of essentially unchallenged power. That the political system was able to remain on an even and traditional keel, with two major parties contending regularly for most electoral prizes, might well have been due in no small measure to such infuriating little political checks as the two-thirds rule.

Some of the institutional equilibrating devices of the 1920s were new. There were Acts of Congress, for instance, like the immigration laws of 1921 and 1924. The first of these declared that no more than 357,000 immigrants could enter the United States each year. This figure (little more than a third of the annual totals in the years just before the First World War) was broken down into national quotas. Each quota represented the proportion of the people originating from that particular country who happened to live in the United States in 1910. The 1924 Act cut the maximum figure to about 164,000 and pushed the base year for the quota proportions back to 1890. The net result of these laws was to reduce drastically the number of foreign immigrants who were able to enter the United States and also to make sure that those who could come in relatively greater numbers were from precisely those countries (notably Britain) in which the desire and the need to emigrate to the United States was fairly low. Conversely, those countries that had, since the late nineteenth century, been sending the greatest number of immigrants – Russia, Poland, Italy, Turkey, Greece – were, by the 1924 law, given by far the smallest quotas. These laws were not simply the cruel and vicious enactments of a handful of reactionary xenophobes. Some of these, of course, there were in Congress; many more, nationwide, welcomed the laws when they were passed. But these Acts were also favoured by many of the progressives of the twenties; even the more restrictive 1924 Act passed the Senate without the adverse vote of the progressive senators. These men welcomed immigration restriction not so much because they disliked foreigners (though they all represented western states and had little first-hand knowledge of the real conditions and needs of the poor masses of newcomers huddled in the tenements of New York), but because they felt that many of the problems of American society could be solved, if at all, only if the composition of that society were kept at least relatively static for a while. Also, they were anxious to create and maintain a political alliance with the unions (particularly the American Federation of Labor) which tended to consider large-scale immigration – and the cheap and unskilled labour that it brought in its wake – as a threat to the

American working man.

But it was not only national statutes that were passed in an attempt by American society to alleviate the tense divisions within it. At a local level, too, all sorts of official political actions can be seen, in their intentions at least, in this light. Some of the defenders of the Tennessee anti-Darwin law, for instance, saw the measure chiefly as an attempt to reduce the likelihood of violent verbal — and even physical — argument. A New York statute designed to bypass the Prohibition Amendment was passed during the governorship of Al Smith in 1923 and had a similar intention.

If there were plenty of formal, institutional devices whereby American society tried to remain on an even keel in the 1920s, there were more informal ones too.

One classic example is the widespread lack of interest in politics. There were, as the first half of this chapter has shown, a great many social and economic problems that cried out for at least some attempt at solution by political means. But an age that has enormous problems that only the political system is properly equipped to solve is also, not infrequently, one that ignores politics for fear that the process of solving problems might be more painful than the temporary ignoring of them. Fitzgerald said that 'it was characteristic of the Jazz Age that it had no interest in politics at all.' His judgement is borne out by the turn-out figures for presidential elections for the period. In 1920 and 1924, for the only times in the whole of American history, less than half the electorate bothered to vote (see Table 1.1).

Table 1.1. Percentage turn-out of eligible voters in presidential elections since 1860

1860	84·2	1924	49·1
1864	84·9	1928	57·4
1868	79·4	1932	57·8
1872	74·9	1936	61·9
1876	85·8	1940	62·1
1880	78·4	1944	55·1
1884	76·7	1948	53·5
1888	78·7	1952	63·6
1892	76·4	1956	60·4
1896	79·2	1960	64·0
1900	73·5	1964	63·0
1904	65·8	1968	60·2
1908	66·3	1972	55·7
1912	60·0	1976	54·4
1916	63·7	1980	54·0
1920	49·3		

Part of the explanation of the low turn-out in the early twenties is that women, who were enfranchised by the Nineteenth Amendment to the Constitution only a few weeks before the 1920 election, needed some time to get used to the idea that they were permitted to vote. A further explanation is that there were many immigrants who by 1920 had been in the United States long enough to obtain citizenship but not long enough to feel sufficiently involved in the political processes of their adoptive country to want to vote in its elections. But these considerations hardly explain why the turn-out went down still further in 1924, four years after the Nineteenth Amendment and three years after the first immigration restriction Act.

When the turn-out began to creep up again in 1928, many of the tensions and divisions within society that had been successfully swept under the rug at the previous two elections had burst into the open. The result was that the 1928 campaign was one of the most bitter and divisive in history.

But let us, like so many of the men and women of the 1920s, look away from politics for the moment and, instead, at the way Americans spent their leisure time. The age was one of absurd high jinks, of flagpole-sitting sessions and marathon dances; one year, crossword puzzles were all the rage, another year it was Mah-Jongg. In the summer of 1925 every car owner in the country seemed to be racing off to Florida to buy cheap land. The ballyhoo, of course, was directly experienced by only a small percentage of the total population. But the overall affluence of the age and the development of the media of communication enabled even those with merely average incomes to get at least vicarious — and often first-hand — pleasure from the pastimes of the day. The decade saw a great increase in the popularity of spectator sports — in which the participant was investing his emotional capital in the victory of one side against the other, while the observer, as well as sharing the emotions of his favourite participant, was also able to indulge in that gloriuos opiate, hero-worship. ' . . . 67,000 people jammed into the new $1,700,000 Illinois Memorial Stadium,' according to the *New York Times* on 19 October 1924, to see Red Grange and the Illinois team beat Michigan. In 1921, we are told by F. L. Allen, 'nearly 75,000 people paid over $1\frac{1}{2}$ million dollars'[8] to see Jack Dempsey defeat Georges Carpentier. In 1926 the same author writes:

> . . . 130,000 people watched Tunney outbox a weary Dempsey at Philadelphia and paid nearly 2 million dollars for the privilege; 145,000 watched the return match at

Chicago and the receipts reached the incredible sum of $2,600,000. Compare that sum with the trifling $452,000 taken in when Dempsey gained his title from Willard in 1919 and you have a measure of what had happened in a few years. So enormous was the amphitheatre at Chicago that two-thirds of the people in the outermost seats did not know who had won when the fight was over. Nor was the audience limited to the throng at Chicago, for millions more — 40 millions, the radio people claimed — heard the breathless story of it, blow by blow, over the radio.[9]

Sporting heroes could, for the first time, spring up overnight; the decade is full of the exaggerated adulation afforded to Babe Ruth, Bobby Jones, Bill Tilden, and many another.

The nation's need for partisanship and mass idolatry was not confined to the world of organized sport. The decade was the great age of Hollywood, the age of the Vamp, the 'It' girl, the great lover and, inevitably, the tycoon. If the films were silent, this meant only that the celluloid sex idols had to exaggerate their romantic movements and gestures and, as a result, the emotional responses of their suggestible audiences. It was the age of the fabulous stars, of Rudolph Valentino, of Theda Bara, of Clara Bow, of Mary Pickford. These stars and many others had their 'fans' — and very aggressive fans they could be, too. No Valentino fan could permit words of praise for Ramon Navarro to be uttered in his presence; debate raged as to whether Ben Turpin was funnier than W. C. Fields — or whether Chaplin outdid them all. The movies, like the spectator sports, were developing, very quickly, a large nationwide audience. By the middle of 1926, according to a report in *The New Republic*, America had some 17,000 'film houses' which formed no less than 97 per cent of all amusement houses in the United States. The other 3 per cent included not only all theatres offering legitimate drama, but also those devoted to vaudeville and burlesque.

The age had a passion for heroes wherever it could find them. Some, like most of the sporting and movie stars, had, through a combination of luck and judgement, made their own way to what was considered 'the top'; others, like the young Prince of Wales, or Queen Marie of Rumania, were lucky enough to have been born there. And there was another type of hero, the person who did something grotesque or bizarre or both. Ruth Snyder, the murderess, who was photographed illegally while dying on the electric chair, became a posthumous heroine of sorts; the two college boys who committed a 'rational' murder, Leopold and Loeb, also caught the attention of an at least semi-sympathetic public; people who broke endurance records by sitting for days on top of flagpoles or by doing marathon dances also found that they could become popular heroes. But the greatest hero of them all was Charles A. Lindbergh Jr, 'Lindy', the 'Flying Fool', the first man to fly solo across the Atlantic. Lindbergh took off from New York on the morning of 20 May 1927 and, thirty-three hours later, landed at Le Bourget Airport, Paris. The adulation accorded to Lindbergh when he returned from his trip was extravagant in the extreme. He was given the greatest tickertape parade in New York's history. After the Lindbergh parade, the New York street-cleaning department estimated that 1,800 tons of paper had been torn up and thrown out of windows; 55,000 telegrams were sent to Lindy (one of which, according to F. L. Allen, 'was signed with 17,500 names and made up a scroll 520 feet long, under which ten messenger boys staggered'). He had dinner with President Coolidge, was promoted to the rank of Colonel, and was awarded the Distinguished Flying Cross. So extravagant was the hero-worship accorded to this young man that it requires some sort of explanation beyond, simply, the admiration normally given to somebody who achieves some daring and unusual feat. After all, others had flown the Atlantic before, though, admittedly, not alone and not all the way to Paris.

The explanation of Lindbergh's incredible popularity lies in the fact that his achievment was one of very few that managed to wed the dazzling scientific advances of a self-consciously progressive age to the nostalgically recalled values of the past. On the one hand, he had obviously done something that required, both in himself and in the many other people who had helped to make his trip possible, great technological skill. On the other hand, Lindbergh himself epitomized for many people — in his healthy and rugged appearance, his self-effacing charm, his physical courage — all the legendary American virtues which seemed in the 1920s to be at such a premium. In an age when the young were the constant butt of parental disapproval, Lindbergh appeared as a reassuring breath of fresh air, a sign that the virtues of past generations might yet be perpetuated.

Another person who managed to combine the scientific achievements of the 1920s with the putative glories of Old America was Henry Ford. As the first great mass-producer of automobiles, Ford might be said to have done more than any other person to alter out of all recognition the society into which he had been born. There were obvious quantitative changes: the number of cars shot up astronomically during the 1920s, as did the number of roads on which they ran.

By the middle years of the decade the automobile industry as a whole
was overwhelmingly and in all respects the largest in the country. But
the reverberations of the rapid rise of this giant industry were felt in
every little corner of the nation's life. In the purely industrial field, a
great many lesser industries came to depend more and more on the
automobile. John B. Rae writes of the middle twenties that

> ... the motor vehicle was now consuming annually 90 per cent of the country's
> petroleum products, mostly in the form of gasoline, 80 per cent of the rubber,
> predominantly tyres, 20 per cent of the steel, 75 per cent of the plate glass, and 25
> per cent of the machine tools.[10]

In Washington the nation's legislators passed the Federal Highway
Act (1921) to encourage roadbuilding, while as the decade progressed
every state legislature passed laws taxing gasoline. The nation found
that its entire living pattern was changing as a result of the multiplicity of horseless carriages that were now invading the length and
breadth of the country. Many middle-class Americans, hitherto living
in overcrowded cities or isolated rural areas, began to move into new
suburbs. Summer holidays in remote corners of the continent became
the vogue. Old people and invalids found themselves less cut off from
their families and friends; young men with a little money and a flair for
adventure found in the automobile a new weapon in their arsenal of
courtship. There were films and plays about cars; newspaper car-
toonists (such as the creator of *Gasoline Alley*) were mesmerized by
them. Motor-car metaphors turned up in the most unexpected places,
ranging from sermons ('Solomon, A 6-cylinder Sport') to gangsterism
(a rival would be 'taken for a ride'). The automobile, said some of its
critics, broke up families and helped to create unwanted ones,
reduced church attendances, made possible much of the bootlegging
and gangsterism of the period, and led to a new and undesirable order
of priorities whereby, in Middletown at least, ownership of an automobile was usually more important than ownership of a bathtub and,
to some people, more important than adequate food. But the defenders of the automobile pointed out that its opponents should have
fired their critical arrows not at cars but at people. The car, after all,
could take people *to* church as well as away from it, it could be used by
policemen as well as gangsters, and it could enable young and old
alike to enjoy far more of their beautiful country than had ever been
possible before.

Henry Ford did not make any valuable contribution to this debate;
his chief preoccupation was simply with turning out cars. This he did

with astonishing success. When the twenties began, one car in two throughout the world was a Ford Model T. The success of Ford's assembly-line technique ensured that these 'Tin Lizzies' would continue to pour out of the Ford factories at the breathtaking rate of one every three minutes. So successful was Ford that he was able to offer his men a guaranteed five-dollar day, thus effectively preventing any major unionization (to which he was dogmatically opposed), attracting good workers, and, incidentally, giving himself and his product another huge advertisement. But Ford did have other interests. Indeed, he claimed in his avuncular way to have opinions about a great range of subjects. Most of these were decidedly conservative. He was a fanatical believer in unfettered economic *laissez-faire*, politically something of an élitist, and morally rather a prig. He was a rabid anti-Semite. And even his ideas about industrial management, something of which he had had enormous experience, were little more than feudal. By the late twenties his autocratic and eccentric approach to the industry that he had built up was seriously impeding its progress. So wedded was he, for instance, to the Model T that he refused to discontinue it. When he eventually succumbed to sound advice in May 1927, and the assembly lines producing the Tin Lizzie stopped for the first time in twenty years, Ford had given no real thought to producing a genuine alternative. By this time Ford Motors, so long without peer in the field of automobile manufacturing, was slipping into second place. General Motors, under the brilliant management of Alfred P. Sloan, was outselling Ford by the end of the 1920s. Henry Ford himself gave more and more vent to his crotchety conservatism and by the end of the decade, when the country was plunged into the Depression, began to think about turning the area around his Dearborn factories into an 'old-time' park, complete with transplanted log cabins and colonial cottages, rustic glades, babbling brooks, and − irony of ironies − horse-and-buggy tours.

A third extraordinary combination of traditional America and the self-consciously mechanical postwar world was Aimee Semple McPherson. Sister Aimee provided a splendid diversion for the bewildered folk of Los Angeles. An attractive and authoritative woman with a classic hardluck story, she built up a colossal following and a large fortune as a preacher. Her gaudy theatrical performances at the Angelus Temple at which she preached her vacuous but reassuring 'Four-Square Gospel' attracted huge numbers, and in time her services were broadcast; millions were then able to hear the calculatedly purple prose of this shrewd hot gospeller. Aimee's theatricality led her into trouble in 1926. She 'disappeared' from a Pacific beach (had the Lord whisked her off so as to enable so saintly a soul to keep more spiritual company?); but after her reappearance more than a month later, it became clear that, in all probability, she had disappeared in order to spend a blissful time in the arms of the radio operator who had broadcast her services. Sister never quite repeated her earlier triumphs, but the disappearance and a rather sordid court case notwithstanding, she continued, as long as the prosperity of the carefree twenties continued, to attract great numbers of people — most of them looking desperately for a way of returning to the simpler faith of yesteryear — to her neon-lighted, electronically amplified Four-Square services.

In their different ways, Lindbergh, Ford, and Sister Aimee each represented both modern America and the myths of America's past. Each was turned into something of a hero precisely because he or she enabled the American to observe a person who, while making conspicuous use of all that was new and daring, seemed to be operating in the name of the cosy traditional values that America held dear. Lindbergh, Ford, and McPherson (or rather, the fact that so much attention was paid to them) reflected the uneasy equilibrium of the twenties. All three were adventurous; each caused the nation to hold its breath with awe because what they were doing was, in its own way, revolutionary. But they were all revolutionaries in the name of tradition, and, as the later career of each was to show, decidedly conservative in their political and moral position.

Intellectuals tended to look askance at the Lindbergh fuss and to regard Henry Ford as a rather despicable eccentric who happened to produce cars. Sister Aimee was, to them, little more than a passing subject of gossip. But, in spite of this condescending viewpoint, the intellectual, too, had his heroes, his diversions, his ways of escaping from the tensions that were threatening to engulf his world no less than everbody else's. For the intellectual the period was one of frustrating relativism. The certainty of the past, whether in physics, biology, religion or morals, was being gravely undermined. Indeed, serious doubts had been cast on the attainability or even the meaningfulness of rational certainty by Einstein, with his theory of the interrelationship of the observer and the subject under observation, by Freud, with his hypothesis of the unconscious, and, above all, by Heisenberg, with his uncertainty principle.

There were a number of ways out of these intellectual dilemmas. One could plunge happily into the waves of the future, proclaiming with satisfying certainty that, paradoxically, nobody could ever know anything with real certainty. To this predisposition, the works of John B. Watson, the founder of 'behaviourism', appealed. Watson took Freud, diluted him and simplified him, and came up with the theory that man is merely a machine responding to external stimuli. If we knew enough about a man's experiences and about the stimuli acting upon him, Watson claimed, we would be able to predict his thoughts and his actions. The implications of Watsonianism coincided very conveniently with the predispositions of many a young man at college in the Jazz Age. For if morality was relative and a man was merely the morally neutral machine that his experiences made him, why should he not have all and any experiences that he might wish? Indeed, if he had also been reading his Freud, he would have known that civilization was repressive and, consequently, unhealthy so that, if one could be reasonably certain of anything, it was that the way to keep oneself psychologically healthy was to indulge one's libido and encourage one's flapper friends to do likewise. And it just so happened, conveniently enough, that the national economy, glutted with luxury items at easy prices, also gave every encouragement to the favoured young man to pursue his fancies.

Another way of dealing with the relativism of the age was to lower one's sights and look for certainty within an avowedly limited sphere. The great exponent of 'contextual relativism' was John Dewey, philosopher, educationalist, humanist. Dewey accepted that man's mind was limited, but held that it could and should be used, experimentally and with appropriate humility, in an endless quest to ameliorate the details of human life. The thing to do was not to go to absurd intellectual extremes — Dewey had little time either for the monumental system-builder or for the verbal quibbler — but to apply all the intellectual force at one's disposal to definable but socially important problems. In particular, Dewey was interested in education; his belief that the learning process is essentially one of practical experimentation, that the student should be not a passive receiver but an active doer, has been an important influence on education in the United States and elsewhere.

Dewey was writing in a great age of scientific invention and discovery. Men like Edison, Carver, or Admiral Byrd were all, in their different ways, popular symbols of the scientific inventiveness of the age. To Dewey and the Pragmatists, the value of scientific knowledge was that it equipped you to achieve limited but worthwhile aims. Science, he felt, was not a key with which to open a door marked Truth; it was, rather, a method of experimentation, a means of minimizing one's doubts about practical matters.

The attitude of the intellectual filtered down throughout society in the 1920s faster, perhaps, than at any previous period of American history. The development of the radio and the vast increase in the cirulation of the daily and periodical press saw to that. In no time, it seemed, unlettered men were using Freudian jargon and quoting Einstein or Planck. Even the most absurdly mundane products were being feverishly advertised as 'scientific' (one popular advertisement claimed that the 'somnometer', a device attached to bedsprings, showed quite scientifically that Union Masterpiece Bedspring mattresses gave more perfect nightly comfort than did any competitor). A Dr Miller was giving lectures on psychology and science in 1920 that were advertised in *The Chicago Tribune* in part as follows:

> Lecture 1. Scientific living, embracing scientific breathing, sleeping, feeding, speaking, thinking, exercising, etc. . . .
> Lecture 2. Re-education of the subconscious mind. In the subconscious mind of every man and woman there is a genius asleep. Dr Miller teaches you how to awaken and make practical use of this concealed power – how to utilize it to reach your highest goal.

The ballyhoo continued and the country seemed fat, affluent, and happy. We have looked at some of the more successful devices whereby society managed in the 1920s to come to terms, at least temporarily, with the latent tensions within it. Some of these devices, such as Aimee McPherson's escapades or the adulation of Valentino, for instance, may seem to the serious-minded to have been unhealthy and bizarre exaggerations of emotion. But these were all successful devices in the sense that they made, on balance, for an alleviation or a socially acceptable release of tensions.

The failure to reduce social tensions

But American society in the 1920s has another side, a darker side; for the decade also saw, with alarming frequency and in a horrifying number of guises, clear evidence that society could not cope with all the potential conflicts within it, and that the rivalries and the tensions that were smouldering just beneath the surface could not always be kept there. Many of the most famous or infamous of the events and personalities of the twenties, consequently, are associated with the more vicious and dysfunctional manifestations of social tension during the period. These manifestations took two major forms: intolerant extremism and anti-social self-indulgence.

The decade got off to a very lugubrious start. Once the First World War was over, many Americans began to look upon the whole thing as a repugnant nightmare and regretted that their country had become involved in European affairs. The Senate refused to ratify the Treaty of Versailles, and, consequently, refused to make the United States a member of the League of Nations — the brainchild of her own President. In the 1920 election, the party of Wilson was overwhelmingly defeated. The naïve but well-meaning 'isolationism' that set in towards Europe and other areas of the world was merely one aspect — and, in itself, arguably a rational aspect — of a more general xenophobia. By 1920 many otherwise humane and broad-minded Americans just did not like foreigners. In the decade preceding the war, something like a million foreigners a year had arrived in the United States. This meant an annual increase in the overall population of as much as 1 per cent by immigration alone. Often these newcomers were dirty and unskilled, knew little or no English, and had no home to go to and no money with which to buy or even rent one. They tended to stay in the city of disembarkation, usually New York, and live in atrocious conditions, eking out a living only by making every member of the family slave at some tedious and often unhealthy manual job. As has been seen, the massive prewar immigration was reduced to a trickle by the immigration acts of 1921 and 1924.

The lot of the foreign-born American was not easy. If you were born in any of the Central Powers countries you were immediately suspected as a sympathizer with the recent enemy. If you were born in Ireland, you might be suspected as a dangerous anti-British and potentially anti-American saboteur; the fact that you would also have been a Catholic did not help. Above all, if you were from Eastern Europe, you were in grave danger of being suspected as a red, a Bolshevik, a communist, an anarchist, or any of the other vague and often mutually contradictory epithets that were, in the hate jargon of the day, used as synonymous blanket descriptions of the undesirable immigrant.

The pre-war immigration and the horrors of the war were two of the main reasons why many Americans, even otherwise liberal ones, succumbed to xenophobia in the third decade of the century. There were other reasons as well. Dislike of foreigners had been a traditional plank of American conservatism throughout much of the history of the Republic. Precisely because the nation was composed almost exclusively of people who were at one time or other immigrants, there had developed a rigid pecking order according to which status was derived from the length of time that any given group had resided in the United States. At times of social tension, these rivalries and jealousies had regularly come to the surface, to this extent, the nativism of the twenties was one more manifestation of a traditional American prejudice.

But, more immediately, there were economic reasons why this particular brand of hate should emerge at the time and in the form that it did. The war had provided the American economy with a splendid stimulus and converted the country from a debtor nation into a creditor nation. But once the war industries had to slow down and reconvert to the demands of peacetime, once the troops began to return from abroad and seek jobs in an already saturated labour market, much of the economic stimulus of the war looked, for the moment at any rate, like waning. The year 1919 saw the first signs of a recession which was to last until late in 1921, and it also saw a considerable amount of industrial discontent. These economic troubles came, it must be remembered, very soon after the Russian Revolution, and in 1919 the American press was full of the civil war, the exploits of the White Russians, and the monstrous excesses of the Bolsheviks. It was against this background that the American political and economic élite viewed the outbreak of strikes and incidents of violence that occurred in 1919.

The year began with a strike of shipyard workers in Seattle — a strike denounced by the mayor of Seattle, who crushed it, as having been an embryonic Bolshevik revolution. As the year wore on, there were a number of bombing incidents; on one occasion, part of the house of Attorney-General A. Mitchell Palmer was blown up. In September the Boston police went on strike and unrestrained violence broke out in the city. The taciturn governor of Massachusetts, Calvin Coolidge, contributed one of his few memorable comments when he sent a wire to Samuel Gompers, the labour leader, saying: 'There is no right to strike against the public safety by anybody, anywhere, anytime.' Before the year was out there were also major strikes by the steel workers and the coal miners. Many of these indications of major social discontent were widely dismissed as being directed from Moscow or, at the very least, as being the work of some dangerous clique of anti-American immigrant anarchists.

It was in this tense atmosphere that Attorney-General Palmer – a man with presidential ambitions, be it noted – set to work rounding up 'reds' (real or imaginary). He would rid the nation of the red menace and, hey presto, there would be no more strikes, no bomb outrages, no more rising prices. Hundreds of aliens, many of them without trace of a criminal record or even any known political views, were rounded up by Palmer's men and, in many cases, peremptorily deported. Palmer celebrated the arrival of 1920 by arresting, in a single night, somewhere between 4,000 and 6,000 suspected communists in thirty-three different cities. These people, and many others, were kept in jail without cause in cruelly uncomfortable conditions. Some were then subjected to the indignity of a fixed 'trial'. Palmer's denial of civil liberties came ill from an American Attorney-General, but his actions were consistent with the mood of the times, because the age was one of hyperbolic expressions of loyalty to America and of superabundant patriotism. Palmer later overplayed his hand by preparing the nation for a vast red plot on May Day 1920, but the day passed without incident. Palmer's presidential ambitions and his red-baiting were now things of the past.

But xenophobia did not leave the national scene with Palmer. In one guise or another it reappeared throughout the decade, like variations on a macabre musical theme. And the refrain was the constant recurrence before the national conscience of the Sacco–Vanzetti case. Two Italian-born Americans, Nicola Sacco and Bartolomeo Vanzetti, both of whom were known to have anarchistic leanings, were arrested in the summer of 1920 for a murder in Massachusetts, and were condemned to die despite only the flimsiest evidence against them. Appeal after appeal was lodged on their behalf. The liberals of the day, men like Felix Frankfurter and John Dos Passos, devoted long articles and even books to the injustice of the case. It was clear that both judge and jury were hopelessly biased from the start against these very Italian-looking Italians. Judge Thayer is reported to have referred to them out of court as 'dagos' and 'sons of bitches'. The case and its various appeals dragged on for no less than six years – and then, in mid 1927, the two men were, absurdly, executed. Half a century later, the Governor of Massachusetts formally acknowledged that a mistrial had occurred.

To some extent, the revival in the 1920s of the Ku Klux Klan was occasioned by the anti-foreign sentiments of the day and, of course, by their obverse: arrogant American self-righteousness. In 1926, in a Kansas newspaper, the Klan listed among those whom it was fighting:

> every criminal, every gambler, every thug, every libertine, every girl-ruiner, every home-wrecker, every wife-beater, every dope-peddler, every moonshiner, every crooked politician, every pagan papist priest . . . every K of C* . . . every Roman-controlled newspaper, every hyphenated American, every lawless alien . . .[11]

– and of course, the Klan was also dogmatically anti-Semitic. The Ku Klux Klan of the 1920s was named after the similar movement that flourished in the Deep South at the time of Reconstruction, but its scope was wider. It can be interpreted primarily as a last-ditch effort by the poor rural redneck to assert himself within a society in which he was becoming more and more irrelevant. The Klan considered itself to be patriotic, righteous, and justifiably aggressive. In fact, it was born more out of fear than of anger, a nervous reaction against the invincible forces of modernity. It was only occasionally violent (the number of recorded lynchings in the 1920s was down, on average, to forty-five per year, less than half the number of some pre-war years; in 1928 there were only eleven recorded lynchings in the United States). But the depths to which some of those whom the Klan attracted could sink when the occasion seemed ripe is illustrated by the following description (from *The Washington Eagle*) of the death of a black man convicted of murdering a white woman in Georgia in 1921:

> The Negro was taken to a grove, where each one of more than five hundred people, in Ku Klux ceremonial, had placed a pine knot around a stump, making a pyramid to the height of ten feet. The Negro was chained to the stump and asked if he had anything to say. Castrated and in indescribable torture, the Negro asked for a cigarette, lit it and blew the smoke in the face of his tormentors.
> The pyre was lit and a hundred men and women, old and young, grandmothers among them, joined hands and danced around while the Negro burned. A big dance was held in a barn nearby that evening in celebration of the burning, many people coming by automobile from nearby cities to the gala event.

Extremism breeds extremism. It was during this very period, the years just after the First World War, that the first large-scale urban race riots took place. These were the years, too, during which flourished one of the few black separatist organizations, Marcus Garvey's 'Back to Africa' movement. Garvey, like Malcolm X and Stokely Carmichael forty years later, preached that the black man's only hope of salvation lay in separation from the white man.

*Knights of Columbus, an organization of Catholic men.

If the Klan did not encourage wholesale ritual murder, it did develop extremely effective methods of harassment and intimidation in the twenties. As a result of a calculated application of all the new techniques of high-pressure salesmanship (in conjunction with the usual Klan methods of huge and hooded rallies and cross-burning ceremonies), the Klan came close to taking over the state of Indiana under the leadership of an unscrupulous megalomaniac who eventually went to prison for murder and seduction.

Elsewhere, too, the Klan had its successes, feeding on the frustrations of those elements in small-town and rural America that resented the fact that life seemed to be passing them by and making them obsolete. These people developed a gloomy and ultra-conservative approach to life, their minds became inflexible and authoritarian, and they sought their comforts increasingly in their usually erroneous interpretation of a mythical American past. What they were essentially trying to do was to impose their own tradition-rooted values on to a rapidly changing society, a society that was becoming increasingly well equipped to resist the onslaught. This was soil in which fanaticism and extremism could flourish.

Every now and then the extremists had a field day. The Scopes 'Monkey' trial was one. Millions of people throughout the nation followed the trial very closely, many of them in a most partisan fashion. Scopes and Darwin were defended by one of the nation's leading advocates, Clarence Darrow, and the forces of God were led by no less a champion than William Jennings Bryan, thrice Democratic candidate for the presidency. The climax came when the two famous men confronted each other, Darrow incredulously asking a series of questions about the Bible, Bryan nervously answering them from an extreme fundamentalist position. Scopes was, technically, proved to have broken the law and fined a nominal sum (which was paid by the American Civil Liberties Union); his conviction was later overturned by the state Supreme Court. But, for the time being at any rate, the anti-Darwin law remained on the Tennessee statute book.

A more serious triumph for the narrow and extremist forces of rural and small-town America came with the Eighteenth Amendment to the Constitution, that banning 'the manufacture, sale, or transportation of intoxicating liquors within ... the United States'.

This amendment was the law of the land from January 1920 until the end of 1933, but it was one of the most abused and ignored laws in history. Its main effects were to encourage the manufacture, sale and consumption of vile home-made brews of various sorts (which often contained industrial alcohol that had been deliberately poisoned by smug and overzealous drys) and the widescale practice of smuggling, and to give rise to an era of violence and lawlessness that called into disrepute the whole corpus of American law and the very concept of law enforcement. While alcohol was banned, it became all the more attractive; since the federal government made no serious attempt to enforce the amendment (until the end of the decade, at any rate), alcohol was a very readily available forbidden fruit. The Eighteenth Amendment effectively put an end to widespread beer-drinking in the United States; beer was associated with Germans and big cities and all the other things that pure, rural America objected to, but it also happened to be harder to make in one's own bathtub — and harder to bootleg — than gin. The latter drink, on the other hand, received a great boost from Prohibition; America's reputation as the great land of the mixed drink, the gin-and-something, dates largely from the twenties, the days when gin was plentiful but when, in order to make it palatable, you had to dilute it with something else.

The more militant defenders of the amendment were recruited from a wide range of elements within American society; the one thing that they had in common other than their obsession with banning liquor was a frustrated resentment at the direction that was being taken by their country. Many of them were from rural areas, and most of them were, or pretended to be, of the oldest and most respectable Anglo-Saxon stock; some of the more vociferous were also ostentatiously religious — often fundamentalist Protestants; some, though this became a rarer phenomenon as the decade wore on, thought of themselves as progressive reformers. The alcohol issue served to effect a temporary alliance between various groups within American society that had some real or imagined reason for resenting society, and also, for a while, between these groups and the ranks of the moderate progressives. But the law that they had united to pass broke down; so did the alliance. By the end of the decade there were increasingly loud and persuasive voices begging for repeal. In 1928 the Democrats nominated the wet Irish-Catholic governor of New York, Al Smith, as their presidential candidate. Smith, epitomizing all that dry America stood against, was badly defeated by Hoover, but — and this was an omen for the future — he did remarkably well in many of the large and growing cities. The presidential campaign, in which alcohol and religion were the biggest issues, produced some of the most bigoted and intolerant speeches in election history, although the candidates themselves behaved with dignity.

But intolerant extremism was not the only form in which the discontents of the twenties burst out of the socially acceptable bounds that had been created for them. The decade was also characterized by a widespread disregard for law and order; for religious, conventional, and even prudential morality; and for the rights and wrongs of society's underprivileged. The more sophisticated expressions of these selfish sentiments came from the great men of the day. The official emphasis on unfettered *laissez-faire,* rugged individualism, and self-help were all, in effect, ways of encouraging society's elephants to dance on its chickens if they felt like it. The chickens were blacks, Indians, Jews, Catholics, farmers, foreigners – and, not infrequently, the private, law-abiding, white, Anglo-Saxon, Protestant inhabitants of the major cities. Chicago, in particular, was virtually run throughout much of the decade by bootlegging gangs (notably that of Al Capone) which bribed, shot, and drank their way to political dominance in a way that would have been inconceivable in any decently organized democratic state. But the Chicago of Mayor Bill Thompson and Al Capone was not such a state.

Nor was the country as a whole when Harding and his Ohio Gang were in charge of it. A year or two after the death of that unfortunate President in 1923, several important members of his administration were shown to have been using high office to enrich themselves and their friends at the public expense. When the corruption of the Harding years was revealed to an incredulous public in the mid 1920s, the most commonly heard reaction was one of regret that muckraking congressmen and journalists should have displayed the bad taste to publicize these abuses and so weaken public respect for the federal government. But by that time, when a mere 2,000 underpaid and easily bribable liquor agents were 'enforcing' a constitutional amendment that few people wanted and even fewer obeyed, respect was not very high in the first place.

Despite the intolerance and the self-indulgence of the 1920s, however, American society survived the decade. Before long, Americans would, once again, have something far bigger than their own internal squabbles to worry about. But in 1928 and the beginning of 1929 few were able to guess that the country's unprecedented prosperity had less than a year to run. So the more leisured Americans continued to idolize sporting heroes and film stars, to sit on flagpoles and play

Mah-Jongg, to drive all over the country in their flivvers, or, if these pastimes did not satisfy them, to concoct and consume poisonous hooch, to make vitriolic speeches about their less fortunate neighbours, and to shoot one another. The great majority of Americans, who were now equipped as their parents had never been to know what the wealthy and the powerful were up to, had no option but to work hard, to exist as best they could, and to dream that all this talk about self-help and enterprise and rugged individualism and God helping those who helped themselves might, one day, prove true in their case too.

Two

THE 1930s:
THE DEPRESSION, THE NEW DEAL
AND FRANKLIN D. ROOSEVELT

Crash and Depression

Nobody is quite sure when the Jazz Age began; some people would put it at the end of the First World War, while others suggest that it was not really inaugurated until the end of the 1921–2 recession. There is far more agreement about when it ended: 24 October 1929, the day the stock market crashed. America had had her seven fat years; she was now to enter the most devastating and prolonged depression in her history.

Why is the stock market crash considered so significant a watershed? Was the Wall Street disaster a cause of the Depression or a symptom – or merely a coincidence? To answer these questions, we must look at the stock market itself. Throughout the 1920s, when credit was readily obtainable, more and more Americans had been putting more and more of their savings into investments. This habit was encouraged by the widely publicized successes of those who had been lucky at the time of the Florida land boom of 1925 and by the generous policies of the all-important New York Federal Reserve Bank, which cut its discount rate from 4 per cent to 3·5 per cent in 1927, thus making credit even easier to obtain than before. The nation went Wall Street crazy in the late 1920s. The volume of trading increased in large (but significantly irregular) leaps and bounds through much of 1928. Fortunes were gained and lost overnight. Radio shares, which withstood the violent fluctuations of 1928, went up during the year from 85 points to 420, Du Pont from 310 to 525. In 1929 the leaps and bounds of the previous year became even larger – both upward and downward. Buying and selling took place at a more frantic pace than ever before. During a single day in March, more than 8 million shares changed hands. Businesses put their profits into investments, employees were encouraged to spend their savings on buying up stock in the company for which they worked, and an army of 'experts' arose who made a fortune by advising people about the market (and, in some cases, taking full charge of people's money and investing it for them).

What was happening was, in essence, that an increasing number of people were living off credit. 'A' would borrow, say, $1,000 and buy a series of shares which he would then sell to 'B', who would give him a credit note for $1,300. 'B' would then sell the shares for $1,500 to 'C', who had borrowed money especially for this purpose. Everybody, it seemed, stood to gain. Those who wanted to lend money found plenty of takers; those who wanted to borrow for investment found plenty of lenders. An enormous credit circle was created: everybody lived on the profits that somebody else was expected to make.

But what if somebody should suddenly refuse to play the game and demand not credit but cash? This began to happen, occasionally, in 1928 and early 1929. A few shareowners, suspicious of the severe market fluctuations, quietly sold stock while the going was good. By late 1929, selling became the rage, and signs of panic appeared. People were, essentially, asking for 'money now' rather than more credit in the future, and it soon became obvious that the money was not there. Belated and confused steps by the Federal Reserve Board in Washington and at the eleventh hour by a group of prominent American bankers failed to halt the feverish trading. On 24 October the market plummeted disastrously. Like a dying old man, it made sporadic efforts in the next few days to breathe again and to relive the energetic activities of its prime. But, unlike previous selling panics, this one went right on. And it inaugurated the Great Depression.

But it would be foolish to attribute the Depression entirely to the stock market crash. It is true that the sudden transformation from a period of easy credit to one of severe credit restriction played an important part in bringing to an end the furiously expansionist economy of the twenties. But there had been economic recessions before – one as recently as 1921–2 – and none of them had been followed by such widespread and prolonged misery as was to follow the 1929 crash.

The seeds of the Great Depression were being sown during the previous decade. We have seen that industrial production was increasing rapidly but that the purchasing power of the industrial worker (and, even more so, the farmer) was advancing much more slowly. For this, the employer was often to blame: he put his profits into further investments (often in capital goods) instead of reimbursing his employees. By the beginning of 1929, 5 per cent of the population was earning between a quarter and a third of all earned income, but 60 per cent of all families were earning less than the $2,000 per year considered by a Brookings Institution study to constitute 'sufficient to supply only basic necessities'. And this unequal distribution of wealth was increasing.

Despite the limited purchasing power of most Americans, however, the big industries continued in the late twenties to pour out all sorts of items, notably durable consumer goods such as automobiles and luxury home appliances, which could be bought only by the middle and upper classes. They could not easily be exported, either, for the high tariff walls with which Europe and America menaced each other meant not only that American goods were extremely dear abroad, but also that most countries lacked the dollars with which to buy them. Inevitably, the domestic market became glutted towards the end of the twenties; producers were faced with the option of reducing output or selling at low prices — either of which was likely to bring in its train the layoff of workers.

How had this economic impasse been allowed to come about? The men officially in charge of American society were, with exceptions, neither stupid nor cruel. But they were, for the most part, inflexible apostles of the dogma of *laissez-faire*. America had become a great nation, argued people like Presidents Coolidge and Hoover and Secretary of the Treasury Andrew W. Mellon, because her governments had wisely refrained from interfering in the free interplay of economic forces. The great men of America were 'rugged individualists' who, neither greatly helped nor greatly hindered by any factor other than their own drive and initiative, had met untold success. The Depression, said the members of the Hoover school of thought, must presumably have been caused by America's involvement with other countries; if the United States had not been so generous as to help Europe to end its war and get out of its subsequent financial difficulties, the worldwide economic depression would never have reached the United States. They were sure, nevertheless, that the Depression would soon be over and, to help it on its way, they severed America's commercial links with Europe still further by pushing the tariff higher than it had ever been before (by the Hawley—Smoot Act of 1930). This action simply caused the angry European nations to retaliate, and America's dangerous economic isolation was exacerbated.

Because of their complacence and their failure to understand the domestic causes of America's economic plight, Coolidge and Hoover and their subordinates have been widely blamed not only for the occurrence of the Depression but also their failure to alleviate its worst effects. Hoover, in particular, hailed as the 'Great Engineer' when he was elected in 1928, is blamed for having done nothing to halt the Depression once it had started. More generous commentators, pointing to the relief and public works programmes that he initiated and to the creation, in mid 1932, of the Reconstruction Finance Corporation, whose job was to lend federal money to needy states, would agree with the 1935 judgement of Walter Lippmann that 'most of President Roosevelt's recovery program is an evolution from President Hoover's'. Furthermore, in the early days of the Depression, very few people — and Governor Franklin D. Roosevelt of New York was certainly not one of them — were advocating any of the more drastic steps that were later to be taken by the New Deal administration.

But however well intentioned and whatever the lack of alternative suggestions, Hoover's policies (not to mention his sunny statements about voluntary help and the Depression being over in a matter of weeks) made hardly a dent in the iron hand of the Depression. A glimpse at some figures will give an idea of how devastating the Depression had become by the winter of 1932–3. A quarter of the entire labour force was unemployed (see Fig. 2.1); the national income was down by more than half; the production of durable manufactured goods fell by 77 per cent between August 1929 and March 1933; private savings were down to an eighth of their 1929 level, personal investments down to less than a sixteenth. More ominous still, there were signs that not only the national economy but also the social fabric itself was beginning to crumble; the suicide rate in 1931 was as high as it had ever been before — and was easily overtaken in 1932.

Figures, however, cannot tell the whole story; they cannot communicate the intense personal tragedy that, as the weeks turned into months and the months into years, the Depression visited upon countless anonymous households up and down the country: the old man who sees his life's savings vanish, the ragged child surviving on the one 'meal' a day of dough fried in last week's bacon dripping, the

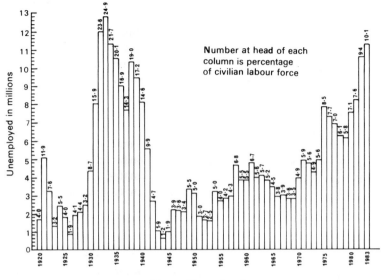

Fig. 2.1 Unemployed

young wife who watches her energetic and handsome husband become, by degrees, idle, then irritable, then scared, then just listless. No amount of statistics can communicate what it felt like when the money ran out. Sometimes a little could be borrowed, but this was unusual. Mortgages were foreclosed and evictions became common. As the Depression passed its second winter, the army of unemployed and destitute grew. They congregated on the outskirts of the big cities, living in a grotesque assortment of scrap-iron and corrugated cardboard shacks and do-it-yourself gunny-sacking tents. If their city could afford to, it would keep alive the wretches on its outskirts by providing them with soup and bread: if it could not, then the inhabitants of Hooverville, as the squalid camps came to be called, would fish around in garbage cans and street gutters for food.

Nobody knew in the early thirties when or even whether the tumbling Depression would ever be halted, and level-headed men began to feel desperate. There was talk of violence and revolution. An 'army' of First World War veterans from many parts of the nation, all now in desperate economic straits, set up a Hooverville just outside Washington in the summer of 1932 and demanded that they be paid there and then the bonuses that Congress had promised to pay them by 1945. For their pains, these former soldiers were branded as revolutionaries, criminals, and communists by a panicky administration and were dispersed — and their temporary dwellings burned — by a full-scale military operation, complete with tanks, machine guns, tear-gas bombs, and bayonets.

The veterans did not get their bonus, and when they went home in the autumn of 1932 they did not get jobs. That winter the school-teachers of Chicago did not get paid. By February 1933, the nation's banks were closing their doors, one by one.

Those early weeks of 1933 saw, perhaps, the nadir of the Depression. Things never seemed quite so bad again, partly, no doubt, because of the remedial actions of the Roosevelt administration, but partly, too, because people adjusted themselves to the ordeal of living in poverty and deprivation.

They had to, for the Depression was the one constant, ubiquitous fact of life throughout the rest of the decade. It affected the entire style of life. The nation's diet consisted increasingly of concentrated foods (such as condensed milk) and conspicuously wholesome ones (such as oranges), whereas some of the slightly less nutritious old staples, such as cereals and potatoes, were neglected. Clothing styles changed: women's fashions were more feminine and less boyish than in the twenties (dresses emphasized female curves, nail polish became popular, toeless shoes made their appearance, and long hair replaced the flapper's 'bob'), but materials were, inevitably, shoddier, and more and more women resorted to making their own clothes and, in time, those of their children and menfolk as well.

When the Depression first hit America, it seemed to vent its wrath with particular vehemence against the big cities. This was partly, of course, because the farmers, who had long been struggling for a living on account of the uneconomic surpluses that they produced, were more casual about the fact that the national prosperity had ended; it was also, no doubt, an economic as well as a psychological fact that the worst immediate effects of depression — unemployment and food shortage — were felt in the teeming cities. Unemployed and hapless town dwellers, believing the countryside to be relatively immune from the effects of the Depression, left their homes by the thousands and went to look for work on the farms or to live with their no doubt embarrassed rural cousins. As a result, there was in the early 1930s, for almost the only time in American history (except during periods of

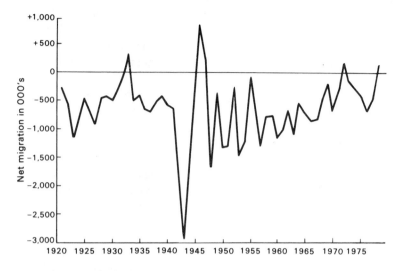

Fig. 2.2 Net migration to farms

rapid military demobilization), a net migration from the towns to the countryside (see Fig. 2.2). By 1934, therefore, rather more people were dependent upon America's economically precarious farms than previous figures would have led one to expect. But in 1934, too, there was a disastrously dry summer which turned much of the Midwest and South-West into a huge bowl of dust. Very rapidly the net migration from town to countryside reversed itself. Those farmers who owned land in Oklahoma, Arkansas, and the surrounding states found that it would produce not too much, as previously, but nothing; those who were tenants were frequently pushed off the land by owners who had run out of credit. Nowhere, it seemed to many farming families, could be worse than home; so they would sell what they could, pile the rest of their belongings on the back of an old truck, and take off — probably for fertile California. This mammoth migration from the Dust Bowl to California is described in poignant terms by John Steinbeck in *The Grapes of Wrath:*

> And then the dispossessed were drawn west — from Kansas, Oklahoma, Texas, New Mexico; from Nevada and Arkansas families, tribes, dusted out, tractored out. Carloads, caravans, homeless and hungry; twenty thousand and fifty thousand and a hundred thousand and two hundred thousand. They streamed over the moun-

tains, hungry and restless — restless as ants, scurrying to find work to do — to lift, to
push, to pull, to pick, to cut — anything, any burden to bear, for food. The kids are
hungry. We got no place to live. Like ants scurrying for work, and most of all for
land.... They were hungry and they were fierce. And they had hoped to find a
home, and they found only hatred.[1]

There were other migrants, too. More than 300,000 blacks moved
from the poorest area of all, the Deep South, to the marginally less
impoverished northern cities, though this was only half the number
that had made the trip a decade earlier. The state of Pennsylvania,
with its sick coal-mining areas, lost, during the decade, a net population of more than 300,000 people (though the state's overall black
population increased by more than 20,000).

One way or another, the 1930s was a period of great restlessness. It
was not so much that everybody went to live somewhere else; most
people did not dare run the risks involved in moving. But there were
probably fewer families than ever before who were really happy and
contented to live in the area in which they found themselves. Hope
springs eternal, and while the sale of expensive new cars was unre-
markable throughout the 1930s, the sales of old and barely serviceable
jalopies continued to rise throughout the decade. The upper-middle-
and middle-class American family could do without its electric
toaster, its washing machine, its electric egg-beater; but the last thing
it wanted to do was to get rid of its car.

But if the Depression had the effect of disturbing traditional patterns of life, of making people restless and discontented, it also had, in
a number of ironic and poignant ways, a stabilizing effect. Families
spent — had to spend — more time together than they did a decade
earlier. The representative family of the twenties was splitting up; the
children were taking off for the big city (possibly, if they were lucky,
for college) and were consciously adopting attitudes that were at
variance with those held by their parents. But in the thirties the
prodigal son often found it necessary to return to live with his parents.
Not infrequently, he found that his uncles and his aunts and his
cousins had already moved in as well.

As though to compensate for the 'doubling up' of families, the
population increase in the thirties was far and away the slowest up to
that period in American history. This was due very largely to the low
birth rate (every year from 1932 up to 1940, the birth rate was for the
first time in the whole of American history less than twenty births for
every 1,000 people — a record not to be paralleled until the years
following 1965; see Fig. 5.5, p. 167). Children were (except, perhaps,

in the Deep South, where they could pick cotton for a pittance) an economic liability* and, because men often had to accept even the most inconvenient jobs, they were forced to spend long periods — or, at best, long and irregular hours — away from their tired and hungry wives. But the low birth rate was due above all to the triumph of what was now called 'planned parenthood' but what, in the virile days of Theodore Roosevelt, had been dismissed as 'race suicide'.

One significant phenomenon to which the low birth rate contributed was the fact that by the end of the Depression decade more than 6 per cent of the American population was sixty-five or older — a higher proportion than at any previous time in American history (and more than double the 1890 figure). These old people were hurt by the Depression more perhaps than any other large segment of the population. A few of them had contributed to voluntary state or business pension schemes; the great majority had no pension at all and were either staying on at work long after they should have retired or, more commonly, were the first workers to be laid off. Life for the elderly was often at best pathetic and at worst intolerable; some of them could live off savings for a while, others could go to relatives. Many simply begged, rummaged, and stole.

But the old were not the only people to suffer by the onset of depression. The farmer, who was used to a persistently low standard of living, seemed in the early thirties to have no option but to continue to produce more crops and cattle than the depressed market could absorb. The young man, leaving school full of hopes and aspirations, often found it impossibly difficult to enter the labour market. Craftsmen who were idle forgot their skills; hungry writers, painters, and musicians, forced to sweep public parks in order to keep alive, were becoming cynical and uncreative. Honest and efficient business leaders found their prestige ruined as a result of the chicanery and the bad luck (ruthlessly exposed in the early thirties by the Pecora Committee) of some of their more adventurous colleagues. Labour leaders, who had not been very successful in their efforts to organize the workers in the twenties, found with the onset of depression that men

---

*The outlawing of child labour by the federal government had been declared unconstitutional by the Supreme Court in 1918 in *Hammer v. Dagenhart*, 247 US 251, but, under the NRA codes (see below, p.46), most industries agreed not to employ children. There was an increase in child labour immediately after the Supreme Court's invalidation of the National Industrial Recovery Act in 1935, 295 US 495 (see below p.46) but it was finally banned by the Fair Labor Standards Act three years later.

with jobs would take one pay cut after another rather than join a union and run the risk of being fired. Rickets and pellagra were increasing; so were suicide and insanity. There were even cases of people dying from starvation. And the farmers outside the Dust Bowl continued to produce surpluses.

Roosevelt and the New Deal

This was the gloomy backcloth against which the presidential election of November 1932 was fought. By that time it was becoming quite clear that, Hoover's public optimism notwithstanding, the Depression was not simply going to disappear. Intelligent men could no longer sit back and leave the nation's problems to the Great Engineer, for it seemed his engineering had its limitations. Ideological attitudes began to harden. Many of those who were on record as having accepted Hoover's philosophy in time of prosperity found themselves manœuvred into a fanatical defence of it when it was attacked by victims of the Depression; other people, never wild about *laissez-faire* in the twenties, were now using 'I-told-you-so' arguments to buttress their vehement advocacy of large-scale government direction of the economy. If you liked or disliked *laissez-faire* capitalism before the Great Crash, you were, as likely as not, loving it or hating it by 1932.

Governor Franklin D. Roosevelt of New York was one of those people who did not fall easily into either camp. To some extent, this was due to his undogmatic mind and his predilection for compromise; it was also good sound politics. As governor of the Empire State, Roosevelt was clearly a possible Democratic candidate for the presidency and during his four years at Albany he studiously avoided alienating important groups of potential voters. Even after he had been made his party's official nominee, Roosevelt's appeal lay far more in his energy, his good cheer, his vague but reassuring promise of a 'new deal', than in particular policies. He did not know in any detail what he would do to try to end the Depression should he become President, nor did the electorate greatly care. What they wanted was simply somebody new, with new ideas, somebody who could inspire them with new hopes. So, not without misgivings, they elected Roosevelt by a colossal margin and were excited — it was the excitement of desperation — by his bold inaugural address on 4 March 1933:

This is pre-eminently the time to speak the truth, the whole truth, frankly and boldly. Nor need we shrink from honestly facing conditions in our country today. This great nation will endure as it has endured, will revive and will prosper. So, first of all, let me assert my firm belief that the only thing we have to fear is fear itself. . . .

When the new President spoke these bold words, the Depression was, as we have seen, at its worst. All eyes turned anxiously to Washington; in the opulent twenties people were not generally very interested in politics, but once they were hit by the Depression politics became very central to the nation's consciousness. They looked to their President for action and were not disappointed.

The first hundred days of the Roosevelt administration, in particular, during which the newly elected Congress sat in special session, were crammed with an unprecedented volume of activity and sustained excitement. Decrees were issued, reports ordered and delivered, speeches made, appointments announced, press conferences given. Young men from the universities descended upon Washington and would talk, bright-eyed, about their plans for saving America. Eager journalists sniffed hungrily around Capitol Hill and the White House for news and they were frequently rewarded. Above all, a barrage of new laws was passed.

The first preoccupation of the new President in 1933 had been emergency relief; America's destitute millions had to be given something to eat. Among the innovations of the Hundred Days, therefore, were the establishment of the widely popular Civilian Conservation Corps, which in the next six years gave healthy open-air work plus a small wage to nearly 3 million young men, and the Federal Emergency Relief Administration, headed by Harry Hopkins, which had half a billion dollars to distribute (half on a matching basis and half in the form of direct grants) to the states for relief. At first these measures were criticized as looking too much like a government dole, and many people in the administration (including Roosevelt and Hopkins) were anxious to set up a programme of economically justifiable jobs. This was done by Title II of the National Industrial Recovery Act (NIRA), which established the Public Works Administration (PWA). The purpose of the PWA was to set up projects, such as the building of bridges, dams, civic buildings, etc., which would provide work for some of America's unemployed and, at the same time, be of permanent value to the community.

The PWA was administered by Secretary of the Interior Harold L. Ickes, a far more cautious and punctilious man than the tense and constantly active Hopkins. Ickes vetted all proposed projects very carefully and took extreme measures to eliminate any suggestion of patronage or pork-barrel corruption from PWA operations. But caution does not solve immediate problems. As the winter of 1933–4 approached, well over a fifth of the labour force was still unemployed. In order to avoid a repetition of the misery of the previous winter, the administration set up a huge crash programme of jobs known as the Civil Works Administration (CWA) under Hopkins. The function of CWA was to provide temporary jobs to help some 4 million otherwise destitute families to survive the hardships of winter. Hopkins knew that this would be an expensive task; tools and transportation and temporary residences had to be provided at government expense. But by the spring of 1934, it was clear that the emergency relief and job programmes – FERA, PWA, CCC, and CWA – had helped millions of Americans to survive the worst afflictions of the Depression. Furthermore, these collective measures had gradually increased mass spending power, a fact which in itself would act, in time, as a stimulus towards the creation of still further jobs.

The disbanding of CWA in the spring threw 4 million men back on the labour market. Some of the lucky ones were absorbed by other government job programmes such as PWA. The rest went back to the dreary routine of Hoovervilles, soup kitchens, and the FERA dole. The government was deeply dissatisfied with the FERA which, it seemed, was increasing rather than decreasing the number of people living off public charity; the CWA, on the other hand, had shown (as the painfully slow PWA had not) that it was possible to have a job programme by means of which millions of workers could receive an adequate wage from the federal government without their dignity and morale being impaired. After 1935, therefore, the limelight fell increasingly on a new agency – essentially a perpetuation of the ideas of CWA – called the Works Progress Administration (renamed in 1939 the Work Projects Administration) and also on what was really a kind of junior equivalent, the National Youth Administration.

The WPA, which was directed by the tireless Harry Hopkins, was different from Ickes' PWA in several ways. For one thing, Ickes was pre-occupied with the beauty or, at any rate, with the practical usefulness of any given project, while Hopkins' chief concern was to provide people with jobs – with the result that Hopkins' WPA was sometimes accused of 'boondoggling', or creating pointless and wasteful jobs and then paying men to perform them. Ickes, wrote

Robert E. Sherwood, 'was proud of the amount of heavy, durable materials that went into the PWA projects ... whereas Hopkins boasted of the small percentage of the WPA dollar that went for materials and the consequently large percentage that went directly into the pockets of the workers on relief.'[2] The PWA was supposed to cover the bigger projects, WPA those costing less than $25,000; but the expansionist Hopkins frequently undertook projects costing millions — and obtained the necessary funds by sub-dividing them into several 'separate' small enterprises.

Not surprisingly, there was considerable tension between Ickes and Hopkins, the former, in particular, feeling that the existence of the other was almost a personal insult to himself. But Roosevelt thrived on rivalries within the official family, and throughout his career he was blithely prepared to let two different people carry on closely similar or even overlapping jobs. This was partly because he hated to sack anybody, but partly, too, because he knew that rivals try to outpace each other, with the result that each often becomes more productive. In the field of public works, the two rival administrations, the PWA and the WPA, both achieved many magnificent monuments to the hard work and dedication of their respective chiefs. The PWA is best remembered for the great projects that it built or helped to build: the Texas port of Brownsville, the Kansas City auditorium, the road and bridge system linking Key West to mainland Florida, New York's Triborough Bridge, and the Boulder, Grand Coulee and Bonneville dams. The WPA was more celebrated not only for the thousands of hospitals, schools, libraries, and courthouses, the hundreds of miles of road and air strip that it built, the millions of school lunches it served, the clothes that it made, but also for the sheer number of people (some 8 million) to whom it gave employment. Some of its most famous employees were artists, writers and musicians who, although economically not very productive, were felt by Hopkins to have an essential part to play in the life of any modern and progressive society.

Not everybody, of course, was unemployed in the early days of the Depression. But even those sectors of the economy where the employment level was high were not without their problems. The labour-relations experts in the Roosevelt administration found themselves faced from the start with two major difficulties, the solution to either of which seemed to rule out a solution to the other. On the one hand, workers (including women and children) were frequently earning extremely low wages and working in appalling conditions. Both humanitarian and long-term economic considerations seemed to suggest that employers should abolish the child and female labour and then build up the purchasing power of their male employees by giving them decent working conditions and a reasonable wage. But the second problem was that most of the nation's industries were sick, grinding to a halt through lack of capital and credit — and the last thing they could afford to do was to pay higher wages or sack their cheap labour.

The first steps the new administration took to alleviate these apparently intractable problems were contained in Title I of the NIRA, in which important concessions were made to both sides of industry. Employers were asked to write codes guaranteeing fair working conditions for their employees and to submit the codes to the newly established National Recovery Administration (NRA) in Washington, which would, after due investigation and negotiation, give the codes to the President for his signature. Once an industry had had its code accepted, it was entitled to display the coveted Blue Eagle sign, which included the words 'We Do Our Part'. Any Blue Eagle industry was likely to be smiled upon by both labour and the administration and — the final carrot — was exempted from various anti-trust actions. Labour, of course, had much to gain from the codes, but even more from the famous Section 7a of the Act, which guaranteed the right of labour to organize and to bargain collectively with employers.

The NRA had a short and chequered career. Launched with great flamboyance and drive by its sensitive and imperious chairman, General Hugh Johnson, it soon became bogged down in the impossible task of trying to give a code to every industry in the nation. Johnson overworked himself and his staff, became bad-tempered and ill, and in September 1934 was persuaded to resign. Eight months later the Supreme Court unanimously declared Title I of the NIRA to be unconstitutional*, partly on the grounds that it gave the President powers that were essentially legislative and partly because it had given rise to the regulation of industries that were not, strictly speaking, involved in interstate commerce. The NRA had always been intended as only a temporary emergency measure (though Hugh Johnson seems to have thought otherwise), and it had in any case been subjected to increasing attack from both sides of industry. On the other hand, it had been the embodiment of an important new

*Schechter v. United States, 295 US 495.

principle — that the government should and could act as a sort of honest broker between management and labour; this principle, it seemed, the Supreme Court could effectively shatter. The chief importance of the NRA lay not so much in what it did as in what it made possible. Frances Perkins, Roosevelt's Secretary of Labor throughout his years in the White House and the first woman Cabinet member, was to write later that the great significance of the NIRA was 'the degree to which [it] educated the country to the feasibility of wage and hour regulation'.

But the principles of the NIRA did not, after all, die in May 1935 with the Act. Six weeks after the Act was invalidated, the principles of Section 7a were expanded in the famous National Labor Relations Act, known, after its chief sponsor, as the Wagner Act. Roosevelt himself had not been terribly interested in Senator Wagner's Bill, and many sympathetic members of the administration never thought that it would get through Congress. The Bill was essentially remedial; it proposed giving the National Labor Relations Board powers to eliminate some of the unfair practices that management had been using, despite Section 7a of the NIRA, to interfere with the process of unionization and collective bargaining. The NLRB, under the Bill, would be able, among other things, to abolish employer-dominated company unions; to order elections among employees to determine whether they wished to belong to a union and, if so, which; and to eliminate the 'yellow-dog' contract whereby an employee had to commit himself not to join a union. The Bill, largely as a result of the tireless efforts of its sponsor, was passed by both Houses and signed by the President. 'The aspirations of Section 7a,' writes Arthur Schlesinger, 'at last had the promise of becoming enforceable realities.'[3]

The Wagner Act ensured the American working man the right to unionize but it did not ensure that, even if he were represented by a union, he would obtain a reasonable contract from his boss. Under the NRA the industrial codes had usually contained clauses about hours and wages, but these codes had been swept away by the Schechter judgement. A number of people in Washington, among them Senator Hugo Black of Alabama (later to become a distinguished justice on the Supreme Court) and Secretary of Labor Frances Perkins, spent much time and effort trying, year in and year out, to obtain a comprehensive wage-and-hour Bill, but it was not until 1938, after many a tussle with the Supreme Court, the Congress, and the leaders of industry and labour, that such a Bill was passed. The Fair Labor Standards Act established a minimum hourly wage of 25 cents (to rise to 40 cents over a 7-year period) and a maximum 44-hour week (to fall to 40 hours over a 4-year period).

Under the New Deal organized labour was clearly receiving friendly encouragement from the federal government that contrasted sharply with the cool disdain and even open hostility with which it had been regarded by the Republican administrations of the previous decade. In the more encouraging atmosphere of the thirties, labour unions expanded, and did so very rapidly. In 1930 there were $3^{1}/_{2}$ million union members, a number that had remained almost static throughout the twenties; a decade later, there were nearly 9 million (see Table 2.1). The most remarkable expansion of the first years of the New Deal had taken place in the Union of Mine Workers, headed by the vast and fiery John L. Lewis. The UMW, which had a membership of about 75,000 in the early days of the Depression, rocketed to half a million under Lewis' powerful leadership within a very short time of Roosevelt's accession to power.

Table 2.1. Union membership (in thousands)

1930	3,401	1941	10,201	1952	15,900*	1964	17,976
1931	3,310	1942	10,380	1953	16,948	1965	18,519
1932	3,050	1943	13,213	1954	17,022	1968	20,258
1933	2,689	1944	14,146	1955	16,802	1970	20,752
1934	3,088	1945	14,322	1956	17,490	1972	20,893
1935	3,584	1946	14,395	1957	17,369	1974	21,643
1936	3,989	1947	14,787	1958	17,029	1976	21,171
1937	7,001	1948	14,300*	1959	17,117	1978	21,784
1938	8,034	1949	14,300*	1960	17,049	1980	22,351
1939	8,763	1950	14,300*	1961	16,303		
1940	8,717	1951	15,900*	1962	16,586		

* to nearest 100

Lewis' phenomenal success with his own union led him to want to organize labour everywhere and anywhere that it could be found. To this end he tried to pursuade the gentle President of the American Federation of Labor, William L. Green, to undertake a huge organizing campaign, and, in particular, to try to unionize the enormous and largely unorganized steel and automobile industries. But here Lewis came slap up against one of the AFL's sacred principles, one that had been particularly dear to its founder, Samuel Gompers. The AFL was to be a respectable organization of skilled craftsmen and was not to encourage the unskilled riff-raff to apply for membership. The great majority of the AFL's affiliated unions were therefore craft unions such as the bricklayers, the masons and the barbers. There were very few — Lewis' UMW was the one big example — that represented not a craft but an industry. What Lewis was really asking Green was that the AFL should lower its sights a little and embark upon the organization of industries as such. He had several powerful arguments on his side. For one thing, modern industrial techniques had made many crafts obsolete but had increased immeasurably the proportion of workers who were unskilled. Then again, America's millions of recent immigrants (the flow, it will be remembered, had been reduced as recently as the early 1920s) — to whom the AFL had maintained an almost scornful attitude — had for the most part had to take unskilled jobs in large new industries. Finally, if craft unionization was still to rule the day, the workers in a huge company like, say, Ford would have to be members of 40–50 separate unions — the welders, the cutters, the painters, and so on — and labour's ability to bargain effectively would be grossly impaired.

Lewis failed to persuade the AFL to change its craft-union policy and, with a number of supporters, stalked dramatically out of the 1935 AFL convention. The new splinter group formed what they called the Committee for Industrial Organizations (later renamed the Congress of Industrial Organizations), and after a few months of bitter and fruitless correspondence with the AFL set out on its own to organize the industrial workers. The civil war within the ranks of labour, which was to last until 1955, when the AFL and CIO at last combined, was on.

During the first weeks of 1936 workers in a number of General Motors plants in Michigan, copying a technique first used by Akron rubber workers a year before, embarked on a 'sit-down' strike. The men were striking not so much for better pay and hours as for the right to join a union of their own choosing and to have that union bargain on their behalf. For several weeks the men, in shifts, simply stayed in the plants but refused to work. This technique had the great advantage for the men that it effectively prevented the management from employing 'scabs'. But it had its disadvantages. The general public felt that the sit-down strike was an unfair way of making a point — particularly when it became known that sympathetic outsiders were occasionally helping the strikers by entering the plant on a union pass and doing a sit-down stint. There were demands that Governor Murphy use the National Guard to drag out the strikers by force. Meanwhile, Lewis, who had doubts about the sit-down method but was straining every nerve to get GM unionized, negotiated on behalf of the strikers. The impasse was broken, suddenly and unexpectedly, when, as a direct result of prodding from the White House, GM capitulated. On 11 February 1937, the company agreed that the men could join a union (the new CIO Union of Auto Workers) and agreed to bargain with that union. They promised to take back all the strikers and to allow their employees to wear union badges and discuss union matters on the plant premises during lunch breaks. And they even gave the men a 5 per cent pay rise.

Three weeks after GM acceded to Lewis' demands, another of the great giants of the economy, US Steel, went down almost without a fight. Generous pay increases were given to the steel workers, and their new CIO union, the Steel Workers' Organizing Committee, was recognized by US Steel's chairman, Myron C. Taylor.

Within a year of its existence the CIO had built up a membership of $3^3/4$ million (300,000 more than the AFL). Eventually even the Supreme Court seemed to give its official blessing to Lewis' organizing drive when, in May 1937, it made its dramatic turnabout and declared that the Wagner Act, with its machinery guaranteeing the right to unionize, was constitutional*.

But there were great numbers of needy people whom unions could not help, among them many of the nation's aged. In California, where people of sixty-five or older numbered a record 8 per cent of the population, it was not uncommon to see numbers of embarrassed old people scrounging around in a garbage bin looking for left-over scraps of food. Francis Townsend, a retired physician, moved by just such a sight, concocted a disarmingly simple scheme to alleviate the suffering of the nation's aged. He wanted the federal government to give $200 each month to every citizen over the age of sixty on the sole condition that the money be spent within the month. The plan would be financed by the imposition of a 2 per cent sales and transactions tax. Townsend explained that his scheme would increase the amount of money in circulation, would push up mass purchasing power, and would accordingly increase the number of jobs. The doctor's economics were preposterous, but his idea attracted millions of ardent sup-

*National Labor Relations Board v. Jones & Laughlin Steel Corp. 301 US 1.

porters throughout the nation. It was partly to pre-empt Townsend's growing popularity that the administration decided to introduce what became the 1935 Social Security Act. There were other reasons. Most European nations were already operating old-age pension programmes and, in any case, the Crash and Depression had acutely sensitized America's social conscience. The new Act, something unprecedented in American history, set up a scheme of nationwide old-age pensions (graduated according to previous earnings), and it also contained a plan for unemployment insurance.

The Act had its critics. Those of the Left regretted that old-age pensions were not going to be equal and, above all, were disappointed that the Act did not tackle the problem of health insurance. Conservative critics objected to Congress promising to pay out money that had not yet been collected and feared that the new Social Security Board in Washington would absorb some of the very money that was to be earmarked for the unemployed and the aged. Finally, there was the point that any Bill requiring money to be put aside for future use was taking that money out of current circulation and thus slowing down further the still dangerously stagnant economy.

But the principle of Social Security was widely popular; by 1938 a Gallup poll revealed that nine out of ten Americans approved of the idea of compulsory old-age pensions. Roosevelt himself, according to Frances Perkins, was deeply interested in the details of the Social Security Act and 'took greater satisfaction from it than anything else he achieved on the domestic front.'[4]

America's farming community, while benefiting from some of the New Deal measures, had special problems of its own. In particular, the farmers had long been producing more crops and livestock than the market could absorb. Crushed between the relatively high cost of necessary equipment and the rock-bottom prices of his own products, the farmer, like almost every other element in American society in the early days of the New Deal, looked anxiously to Washington for help.

Henry A. Wallace, Roosevelt's idealistic Secretary of Agriculture, thought that he knew how to solve the problem of farm surpluses and low prices. Even when his father was Secretary of Agriculture in the super-conservative days of Harding and Coolidge, young Wallace was recommending that the government encourage farmers to reduce their output in return for federal subsidies, which could be raised by a tax on the food-processing industries. This approach was embodied in the Agricultural Adjustment Act, one of the most sweeping measures of the entire New Deal. But it was a measure that puzzled and upset many of the farmers whom it was designed to help. The small-time cotton or corn producer needed a lot of convincing before he would agree to reduce his acreage and it tended at first to be the big farmer who, although least in need of help, understood the scheme and signed up. The sad confusion of many of America's cotton growers was exacerbated when, in August 1933, they were asked to plough up a quarter of that season's crop in return for a government subsidy. Wallace, of course, had issued this order with the greatest reluctance, but could think of no other way of preventing the dangerously low price of cotton from sinking still further. With even greater revulsion — but again in order to save a huge farming area from the nightmare of rock-bottom prices — he had the government buy up and slaughter some 6 million pigs.

The AAA was invalidated by the Supreme Court in 1936* on the grounds that the processing tax applied to industries not involved in interstate commerce, but the principle of restriction and subsidy was by that time widely accepted. It might be distasteful in the abstract to bribe a farmer into reducing his output (or, as was done later on, to buy his surpluses at an artificially inflated price). But these ideas saved millions of farmers from bankruptcy and starvation in the 1930s — the restriction principle was incorporated into a new and slightly altered AAA in 1938 — and have been an important feature of American agriculture ever since.

A few of the congressional critics of Wallace's original plan objected outright to governmental interference with the free economy; many more, however, particularly in the Senate, accepted the need for government-induced inflation, but could not see why there should be a measure exclusively concerned with farm prices. The Senate inflationists were placated, however, when Roosevelt and Wallace agreed to accept an amendment to the AAA which empowered the President to inflate the currency by various techniques, including the reduction of the gold content of the dollar — a power of which Roosevelt proceeded to make considerable use (much to the consternation of America's trading partners who accused her of trying to gain unfair trade advantages). In January 1934, Roosevelt stabilized the dollar at 59·06 per cent of its old value.

Roosevelt himself did not have a profound understanding of economics, and in this field as in many others he surrounded himself

*United States v. Butler, 297 US 1.

with advisers who disagreed among themselves. But they were all in agreement about one thing: the circumstances that produced the Depression must never be allowed to recur. To this end a number of steps were taken. In 1934 a new agency, the Securities and Exchange Commission (SEC), was established to administer a series of measures designed to regulate the transactions of the stock market. These measures were eventually to include: the Securities Act of 1933, which required anybody issuing securities to the public to disclose all the essential facts concerning the issue; the Securities and Exchange Act of 1934, which set up the SEC and regulated the actual operations of the stock market itself; the Holding Companies Act of 1935, which liquidated all public utilities holding companies not of demonstrable economic benefit to the general public; and the two Investment Acts of 1940 which required the registration of all investment trusts and all individuals earning money by advising people how to invest.

Like the stock market, the banks had failed the nation in the darkest days of the Depression. The Glass–Steagall Act separated commercial from investment banking so that a depositor's money could no longer be breezily invested, and empowered the federal government to insure deposits of up to $5,000 (a figure that was later doubled). Other measures (such as the Farm Mortgage Foreclosure Act, the Home Owners and Loan Act, and the Farm Credit Act – all passed in the Hundred Days), as well as the generous policies of the Reconstruction Finance Corporation, tried to ensure that credit would be readily available to those groups in most desperate need of it, and in particular to enterprises likely to make the most productive use of it.

Appraisal

What, in retrospect, was the New Deal, and what did it accomplish? Some see it as a single movement, a series of measures designed by men who shared the general philosophy that the government had the right and duty to try to establish, in Roosevelt's words, 'a sense of community within a huge democratic industrial society'. The New Dealers, according to this interpretation, found that their work fell into three (sometimes overlapping) phases: *relief* – the immediate need to feed the hungry and house the homeless (PWA, FERA, CWA, Home Owners Loan Corporation, etc.); *recovery* – the attempt to put the nation's economy back on to a sound footing (NIRA, AAA, etc.); and *reform* – the enactment of more permanent measures designed to help particular elements within society (Tennessee Valley Authority, Securities Act, Social Security Act, NLRA, Fair Labor Standards Act, etc.). These three phases logically succeeded each other; phases two and three each presupposed the achievement, sooner or later, of the preceding one. Some would go further still in this pattern-building and assert that, by and large, phases one and two (relief and recovery) were the preoccupation of the First New Deal (March 1933 – Summer 1935) but that the Roosevelt administration, moving further to the Left in mid 1935, spent the Second New Deal (1935–40) building up a series of permanent reforms.

There is some substance to the 'pattern' theory of the New Deal so long as it is remembered that it presents no more than a general and formalized picture of what happened. It is important to remember that the New Deal's greatest achievements arose out of the fact that it was experimental, flexible, and essentially unplanned. Roosevelt, certainly, had no fixed ideas about how to solve the nation's problems. Indeed, one of his greatest assets was his cheerful accessibility to new people and new theories. Roosevelt's advisers and the American people as a whole felt that he would always be prepared to listen to a new idea, and he had a genius for making every visitor leave the White House firmly convinced that *his* were the ideas that were going to be accepted.

Roosevelt's extraordinary capacity for seeming to be constantly accessible accounted for much of his political appeal. In Hoover's day, one man used to deal with the presidential mail; but so many felt that FDR would listen to what they had to say that, with 5,000 to 8,000 letters pouring in every day, the White House press staff in the 1930s often numbered fifty people. When Hoover was President, he held only infrequent press conferences (at which journalists heard formal replies to written questions); Roosevelt, who held two a week almost without fail throughout his tenure of office, would invite the journalists into his study, chat to them informally and often, in confidence, discuss with them some of the secret matters of state that were currently on his mind. Roosevelt's radio manner, too, inspired not only admiration but also personal affection. Frances Perkins has described 'men and women gathered around the radio, even those who . . . were opposed to him politically, listening with a pleasant, happy feeling of association and friendship.'[5] Not all the letters were from friends, of course, and many of the newspaper editorials (but very few of the reporters!) were critical; one or two of the 'fireside chats' (such as the one outlining the plan for expanding the Supreme Court) left much of Roosevelt's audience unconvinced and unmoved. But, by and large, FDR — whose paralysis kept him from travelling as much as he might have wished — made constant and masterful use of all the means whereby the President and the people could keep in touch with one another, with the result that, for the first time since his cousin Teddy had been in the White House, millions of anonymous Americans felt that they knew their President and that he was really interested in them.

Partly as a consequence of this great personal appeal, Roosevelt was able to establish a huge new political coalition, one that was to help to keep the Democratic Party in power in the White House for all but eight (and in Congress for all but four) of the next thirty-six years. The backbone of this coalition was the lower-class and lower-middle-class city dweller. Millions of the young immigrants who were brought to America in the early years of the century voted for the first time in 1928, and in that year, despite the Hoover landslide, an overall majority in the nation's twelve biggest cities voted for the Democratic candidate, Al Smith. This trend, just visible to the perceptive few in 1928, asserted itself powerfully throughout the 1930s and 1940s and is still one of the major factors in any political calculation in the 1970s. The Democratic Party had traditionally been the party of the Deep South, and this area remained loyal to Roosevelt. But it was really the New Deal that fixed the Democratic Party in the public mind as the party of the immigrant, the 'hyphenated' American. It was in the 1930s, too, that the black American began to vote Democratic — if he was able to vote at all. For it was only under the New Deal that the black, traditionally indebted to the party of Lincoln, began to perceive the Democratic Party as being the one more likely to devote its attention to ameliorating the lot of the underdog. 'In 1932, most Negroes in the country were still Republicans,' writes Samuel Lubell.[6] 'In 1936, in many cities two out of every three Negro voters were for Roosevelt.' Roosevelt's hold on the underprivileged urban citizens was so powerful that they have tended to vote for his party ever since. To the extent that American elections are fought on class lines, the line-up largely dates from the thirties.

But there were some respects in which the Roosevelt coalition was to prove less than permanent. America's desperate corn and hog farmers voted for Roosevelt in 1932, and many of them, grateful for federal subsidies and electrification, turned out for him again in 1936.

But their locally elected officials tended (and have continued) to be Republicans almost to a man. In 1940 the Corn Belt backed Willkie and, with the single exception of 1964, has voted Republican in presidential elections ever since. A similar pattern is seen among many of America's bankers and financiers. Despite their traditional Republicanism, says Lubell,[7] 'in 1932, one-fourth of the Democratic campaign funds was contributed by bankers'. But, with 1964 again the exception, Wall Street has never again shown such enthusiasm for a Democratic national ticket. Finally, while most state office holders in the South have continued to be Democrats, parts of the area have bolted the party or threatened to do so in every presidential election since the death of Roosevelt. Despite subsequent defections, however, the political coalition of the New Deal era was not the least of Roosevelt's achievements. This coalition created a new political alliance that has been the basis of American national politics ever since.

But the New Deal was very much more than the creation of a political alliance, and its effects on history are to be seen not only in subsequent voting patterns.

In the first place, Roosevelt's administration did much to alleviate the unprecedented suffering with which the country was faced. Food, money, and medical supplies were distributed to many people who desperately needed them, and various federal housing and job programmes were set up. The administration also took a number of significant steps to try to ensure that, once the Depression was ended, there could never be another of similar proportions. The emergency measures (FERA, CWA, WPA, etc.) were all allowed to lapse as the fight against the Depression seemed to be making ground; but the more permanent reforms, such as the regulation of the stock market, the old-age pensions, the principle of crop restriction and subsidy — these achievements have long since been recognized by political leaders of all shades of opinion as having a permanent place in the American political system.

Along with these reforms came an enormous increase in the size of the federal government. In the 1920s the number of its civilian employees went up from 560,000 to 601,000; by 1940 the figure was well over a million. Except during the Second World War, the number has never again risen at quite the New Deal rate, but the expansionist tendencies of the thirties have tended to continue and the current figure is close to 3 million (see Fig. 2.3). Federal expenditure,

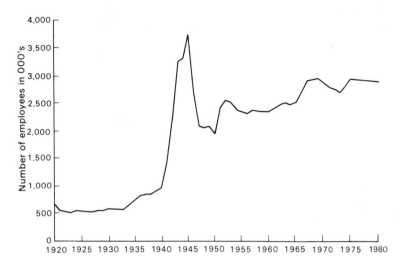

Fig. 2.3 Paid civilian employees of the federal government

too, shot up at a record rate in the 1930s. With the exception of 1918 and 1919, when America was paying for her war effort, there had never been a billion-dollar deficit. Then, in 1932, there was a deficit of $2·7 billion, a figure that had by 1936 leaped to $4·4 billion (see Fig. 2.4). The idea expressed most authoritatively by Lord Keynes, that the federal government might be able to stimulate the economy

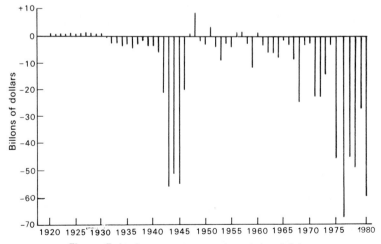

Fig. 2.4 Federal government annual surplus or deficit

beneficially by deficit financing, was one that was introduced by the
New Deal administrations. It has been adopted (though not always
deliberately!) by many administrations at both federal and state
levels since that time.

The scope of the federal government, especially the executive
branch, has grown enormously in recent decades, and this trend too
really began in the 1930s. The presidential practice of sending to
Congress not only messages and recommendations but also actual
drafts of Bills is one that was first made common by Roosevelt. The
list of presidential appointments now includes a whole host of offices
(e.g. the members of the Securities and Exchange Commission) that
never existed before the New Deal. The expansion of the size and
scope of the federal government had necessitated considerable reorganization, and the most important structural change was also a
direct product of the New Deal experience. By the Reorganization Act
of 1939 the President was empowered to set up the Executive Office, a
collection of White House agencies whose sole and common purpose
is to help the President discharge his duties more effectively. The
Executive Office today incorporates several vital agencies created
after the Second World War, none of which could have been established without the Act of 1939.

This growth in the size and scope of the American federal government has been both praised and damned with great heat. Nobody
likes the idea of bureaucratic red tape and remote, interfering government officials. But neither Roosevelt nor his advisers thought of
the growth of the federal government as an end in itself or even, for the
most part, as a particularly desirable means. Rather, it was seen by
them as the *only* means whereby it would be possible, in the darkest
days of the Depression, to save American society from further devastation.

That devastation was not only material. Many people felt in the
early days of the Depression that America was on the brink of political
ruin as well. Italy was already a fascist state and Germany was shortly
to fall under the spell of Hitler. Many thoughtful Americans, despair-
ing of their country's democratic and capitalistic tradition, felt that
communism might be the only answer. Others began to idolize fiery
dictatorial reformers like Huey Long of Louisiana. As we have seen,
political feeling had begun to polarize by 1932. Many people were
asking not whether or how America's traditions would be saved, but
whether and when America would succumb to dictatorship or, alter-

natively, break up in revolution. One of the greatest achievements of the New Deal, or so Roosevelt himself was to feel, was that it saved America from political extremism and not only salvaged but actually strengthened America's cherished traditions — personal liberty, private property, and the profit system. The fact that America survived her great ordeal with buoyant good spirits and without seriously discarding her political traditions is widely accepted as a triumph, not only for America and Roosevelt but also for democracy.

In this sense, therefore, the New Deal was a conservative development, a huge effort to prevent a going concern from undergoing a qualitative change. Roosevelt himself, aware as he was of the unprecedented nature of his reforms, justified them with the phrase 'To preserve we had to reform.' But many of his more conservative critics could not understand why the government had bothered with the 'Second' New Deal reforms. These measures, they felt, made little difference to the Depression (and had nothing to do with the preservation of democracy). Oddly enough critics on the Left used a similar argument — that many of the New Deal reforms (even the more dramatic and unusual ones) did nothing, in the words of Benjamin Stolberg and Jay Vinton, 'that could not have been done better by an earthquake'.[8] On the other hand, of course, there are both conservative and liberal critics of the New Deal who have said that its policies were not so much irrelevant as excessive. Critics on the Right have not been slow in pointing out that measures like the 1935 wealth tax flew directly in the face of the traditional American belief that individual initiative should be encouraged. Those on the Left regret that the New Deal was at such pains to resurrect a palpably rotten capitalist system. But those critics of Left and Right have remained in a minority. For the most part, the New Deal has received a good press and the main measures of the 1930s have long since become permanent features of the American political landscape.

Many commentators on the New Deal, friends and foes alike, have assumed that it was something qualitatively new and that although its basic aim might have been to bolster up a series of wilting traditions, the actual means used by the Roosevelt administration of the 1930s were quite unprecedented. This question of the extent to which the New Deal was a qualitatively new experience in American history has become one of the major contemporary historiographical battlegrounds. Many leading scholars have spent much time and energy trying to prove that the New Deal was revolutionary, or that it was merely an extension of the ideas of the Progressives, or of the emergency practices of the First World War, and so on.

If there is one denominator that is common to all writers on the subject, it is that the New Deal did represent a significant Leftward tilt in American politics. The question arises as to why this happened when it did. Why, for instance, was there not a substantial continuation of progressivism during the buoyant twenties and a return to cautious conservatism during the Depression? It is not enough to say that economic crisis makes for political adventurousness; previous economic setbacks — those, for instance, of 1837, 1873, 1893, and 1921 — had been dealt with in a largely orthodox fashion, and the first and fourth had *followed* rather than preceded periods of progressive politics. Nor can one say more generally that crisis — any sort of crisis — tends to produce major political reorientation, for the 1873 and 1893 economic crises both occurred in the middle of a series of economically orthodox administrations, while the Second World War and the urban riots of the 1960s both occurred in the course of a series of progressive administrations. The change, in other words, from conservative to progressive government that occurred in 1933 cannot, therefore, be attributed exclusively to the exigencies of the Depression.

A clue to the timing of the New Deal has been put forward by Arthur M. Schlesinger Jr, one of the most eminent of the historians of this period. Schlesinger, elaborating on a theory first propounded by his father, has suggested[9] that modern American history tends to unfold in a series of fairly regular liberal and conservative waves. The progressivism of Theodore Roosevelt and Wilson was followed by what was, in effect, a continuation of the conservatism of the late nineteenth century — and was followed inevitably by what was in essence a progressive, or liberal, revival. The pattern of the 1920s and 1930s has been repeated in the 1950s and 1960s.

Schlesinger's cycle theory may sound like a far-fetched whim, but there is much evidence to show that, although such a cycle does not necessarily have to unfold, it has in fact often done so. It follows that, with or without the Depression, America was due for a resuscitation of the progressive tradition sometime in the 1930s. Far from denying the Depression any significance, Schlesinger considers that it gave the New Deal its dramatic and unique characteristics. But he insists that there would have been growing pressure on the political system for progressive reform in the 1930s even if the general prosperity of the previous decade had continued unabated. Indeed, it is even arguable that without the Depression the politics of the 1930s might have been rather *more* progressive than they were. After all, the New Deal was, as we have seen, a holding action, an attempt to salvage and perpetuate certain American values. The most radical reforms in American history, on the other hand, have usually been brought about when American society is comfortable and relatively stable. The reformist tradition, says Hofstadter, 'was chiefly concerned not with managing an economy to meet the problems of collapse but simply with democratizing an economy in sound working order'.[10] If Hofstadter is right − and if Schlesinger with his cycle theory is also right − then America might well have seen a rather more radical shift to the Left in the 1930s had there been no Depression than, in fact, it did. The Depression, in other words, acted as a brake on the reformist tendencies of the era and ensured that those in positions of official responsibility would have to move heaven and earth in their efforts merely to perpetuate an existing but threatened social system.

This of course was frustrating for the idealists and planners among the New Dealers. These radical critics of the New Deal were not slow to point out, at the time and subsequently, that it left almost untouched great chunks of American life and that in particular almost nothing was done to ameliorate the lot of the black American. Nor, despite the dynamic political involvement of the President's wife and the presence for the first time of a woman in the Cabinet, did the New Deal administrations take any important steps towards securing social and civil equality between the sexes. A third criticism of the New Deal was that American education, having been inspired by the optimistic pragmatism of Dewey earlier in the century, was left to flounder as best it could during the thirties with little help from Washington. What these criticisms amount to is that, despite the WPA projects for artists, the idealism of the CCC, and so on, the New Deal was primarily preoccupied with material and economic matters and only marginally with the quality of American life. This overall assertion is valid − but it is valid not only for the New Deal but also for most of American history. Most Americans have never expected or wanted their political leaders to take the initiative in shaping the values of American society. The major shifts in those values have tended to occur as a reaction to technological change, and the shifts have only belatedly been recognized by governmental institutions. Take, for instance, the question of minority rights. As we shall suggest in Chapter 5, the black revolt of the 1960s was fundamentally made possible by the revolution in communications that immediately preceded it and that it was only *after* the movement had begun to make its case widely known that the Civil Rights Acts were passed.

While it may be possible, therefore, to criticize the New Deal for worrying too much about quantitative reforms and not enough about qualitative ones, it is only of an unusually progressive era that such a criticism would be worth making at all. For the New Deal, while not infusing into American society any brand-new set of values and ideals, did make possible a vigorous dialogue about the values of existing society, about their shortcomings, and about how to improve them. By the end of the 1930s America's social conscience was more sensitive than it had ever been before, and the old catchwords like 'rugged individualism' were coming to be dismissed more and more widely as another name for selfishness. By 1940 Americans were more concerned with the communality of their experience and a little less with its individuality than had been the case a decade earlier. Despite the occasional divisive voice – Huey Long attacking FDR in the early years for moving too slowly, Father Coughlin or Colonel Lindbergh condemning his 'interventionist' foreign policies at the end of the decade – most Americans were closing ranks in the 1930s and were becoming increasingly conscious of American life as a shared experience. There were still plenty of problems to solve (unemployment, for instance, remained appallingly high even at the end of the 1930s), but people seemed prepared to face them with something approaching optimism once again.

Which was just as well, for they were soon to be called to arms.

Three

FOREIGN POLICY:
PLUS ÇA CHANGE...

What happened

The United States emerged from the First World War as one of the Great Powers – arguably the greatest. During the 1920s and 1930s she tended to make minimal use of her potential political influence among the other nations of the world; after the Second World War she sometimes seemed to be making up for lost opportunities. The story of American foreign policy since 1920 is long and complicated, a story to which no short narrative could possibly do proper justice. In this chapter we will outline the major political events that occurred and then try to fill in the skeleton with some discussion of the principal debates that have occurred and some of the themes and patterns that are discernible.

Within only a year or two of the end of the First World War, the United States had already signed away some of her potential influence on others. The Treaty of Versailles had failed to gain the necessary two-thirds majority in the Senate and the United States was not, in consequence, to join the League of Nations, the brainchild of its own President, Woodrow Wilson. In 1921, at the Washington Arms Conference, American Secretary of State Charles Evans Hughes amazed and delighted many delegates by recommending that the United States, Britain, Japan, Italy, and France agree to limit the size of their respective navies and keep them to the proportions 5:5:3:1·75:1·75. This proposal was eventually accepted in February 1922 and, on the same day, all the powers with possessions in the Pacific (except the Soviet Union, which was not invited to the conference) agreed to respect the rights and interests of the others in the Far East. In 1927 (at Geneva) and 1930 (at London) there were other conferences, convened largely on American initiative, which tried to take further the principle of international naval disarmament; the first was a fiasco, but the second was moderately successful.

A similar pattern was emerging 'south of the border'. Since 1898 a militant and nationalistic interpretation of the Monroe Doctrine had led the United States to intervene repeatedly in the affairs of Latin American nations. But Hughes inaugurated a period in which America would try to behave towards her sister hemispheric republics in the friendly but correct manner of what Franklin D. Roosevelt was to call the 'good neighbour'. Much of the policy of the United States towards her southern neighbours was devoted, in the 1920s, to the job of bringing home American marines. Occasionally (as in Nicaragua, where a renewed revolt broke out in 1927) the process was temporarily reversed. But, by and large, the policy of the twenties was one of dismantling the armed imperialism (or, as some argued, renouncing the hemispheric responsibilities) of earlier years.

Towards Europe the United States adopted an attitude of benign remoteness. She wished Europe well but did not want to get involved politically in her petty problems. In the 1920 election, after all, the Democrats had been ousted partly because they had seemed to lead the country into what was now perceived as having been primarily a European squabble. This was not to say, of course, that America had not benefited from her participation in the war; indeed, she had gained not only prestige but also money. When the war began she had been a debtor nation; when it ended she was a creditor nation. What she now wanted was to get back the money that she was owed by the European nations, reparations from Germany and war debts from France, Britain, and others. We have seen in Chapter 1 that her policies in this respect were short-sighted and her success limited.* European history did not stop just because America turned her back. The Bolshevik Revolution, having succeeded in defeating its Russian and foreign (including American) assailants continued to consolidate its position; so did fascism in Italy. In Britain and France, meanwhile, there was chronic (though mild) political instability. For the most part, America's attitude towards these developments was to deny that they were any major concern of hers.

In the Far East, too, America's attitude tended to be one of disassociation. This policy was epitomized by a congressional Act of 1924 (which even President Coolidge signed only with reluctance)

*See p. 9 above.

which effectively put an end to Japanese immigration into the United States. Ever since 1907 the United States and Japan had had a 'gentlemen's agreement' whereby the Japanese authorities would severely limit the issuance of passports to people wishing to emigrate to the United States. The 1924 Act, by pushing the formal responsibility for exclusion on to the United States Government, thus constituted a gratuitous insult to the increasingly self-assertive Japanese leaders, an insult to which the Japanese public reacted with considerable resentment and, in some places, violence.

American foreign policy in the 1920s, then, was characterized by a desire on the part of the policy-makers to minimize the extent to which America's fortunes were dependent upon those of the other nations of the world. This general attitude was usually expressed negatively, by attempts to cut the nation off from various types of international commitments. Just occasionally − notably at the Washington Arms Conference − the policy took a more positive turn. Perhaps the most memorable American foray into international diplomacy in the whole decade was the Kellogg−Briand Pact of 1928, whereby the signatories (who, by the mid 1930s, were to include virtually all the sovereign nations of the world, including Germany, Japan, and Italy) agreed to outlaw aggression as a means of furthering their national interests.

The Roosevelt administration that came to power in March 1933 was at first almost totally absorbed in domestic problems. Although it took the long overdue step of recognizing the Soviet Union, its attitude to world affairs was just as much one of 'hands-off' as had been that of the Republican administrations that preceded it. Some international commitments, of course, had to be honoured. There was, for instance, the Geneva Disarmament Conference, which had convened in 1932 and was destined to break up to all intents and purposes (largely because of Germany's refusal to attend the later sessions) in the summer of 1934. Roosevelt sent a delegation to the conference, but seems to have had little faith in the likelihood of the conference achieving anything concrete. Then there was Hoover's promise to send a delegation to the World Economic Conference at London, due to convene in the summer of 1933. If the Conference were to perform its function properly and stabilize world currencies, the United States might well stand to gain. In fact, however, the agreement at which the conference had tentatively arrived was rejected by FDR in a special radio message that, in his own words, 'fell upon [the Conference] like a bombshell'. He said in effect that he wanted the United States to remain free to manipulate its own currency in whatever way it chose. The nations of Europe, already deeply suspicious of America's good intentions towards them, were much more so after Roosevelt's diplomatic clumsiness at the London Economic Conference. The only really productive international initiatives of those years emanated from the soft-spoken, silver-haired Cordell Hull, Roosevelt's Secretary of State. Hull, who had long been an advocate of lower tariffs, was the guiding force behind the Reciprocal Trade Agreements Act of 1934. Once the Act was passed, Hull made full use of its provisions and took a leading part in negotiating many subsequent trade agreements with various nations. But Hull's efforts received little popular attention and the headlines tended to be devoted to America's more obviously selfish policies, such as the rejection in 1935 of American membership of the World Court at The Hague, and the Neutrality Acts of 1935, 1936, 1937, and 1939.

If world events continued to march in the 1920s, they positively hurtled in the 1930s. By the time of FDR's Second Inaugural, the decade (and the impotent League of Nations) had already seen the Japanese conquest of Manchuria (1931), the rise of Hitler (1933) and his seizure of the Rhineland (1936), the Italian invasion of Ethiopia (1936), and the beginning of the Spanish Civil War (1936) — to all of which the United States had retained the attitude of official remoteness that had seemed to benefit her in the more tranquil 1920s. Indeed, the more threatening and potentially dangerous events became in various parts of the world, the more Washington seemed to want to cut the United States off from having to be in any way concerned with them.

But the wicked world just wouldn't go away and leave America alone. In Europe Hitler's demands became excessive and led, in September 1939, to war. The next spring and early summer saw Germany overrun, in quick succession, Denmark, Norway, the Netherlands, Belgium, and France. Hitler's ally, war-hungry Japan, had invaded China — a nation with which America had important and long-standing economic and sentimental ties — in July 1937 and by the end of the decade was at war with Britain and France and was seriously challenging their possessions and economic interests in South-East Asia and American interests in the Philippines.

American policy towards the war in Europe and the Orient was hopelessly confused. The various Neutrality Acts had tied America's hands more and more firmly behind her back, while at the same time various steps designed to help Britain (such as the Destroyer Deal of September 1940) or to hinder Japan (e.g. the embargoes of July, September, and December 1940) seemed to many people to be tailor-made to ensure that the United States would be provoked by the Axis Powers into joining the war. The President and his advisers, eager to play a leading and constructive part in preventing or at least localizing international conflict, felt themselves hamstrung by the isolationism of Congress and the need to appeal — in 1940, of all years — to an ignorant and short-sighted electorate. The Pacific and European wars went on; America's friends continued to succumb to Axis brutality, and America's trade interests continued to be challenged. But even as late as the autumn of 1941 Roosevelt would probably have failed had he asked Congress to declare war on the Axis. However, Japan, worried about her oil reserves and anxious to precipitate what she saw as an inevitable showdown with the United States on terms as favourable as possible to herself, launched a surprise attack on the American fleet at Pearl Harbor on 7 December 1941. American deaths and naval losses were considerable. The day after the attack, Roosevelt had no difficulty in persuading Congress to declare that a state of war existed between the United States and Japan. A few days later, Hitler, busy fighting his erstwhile allies the Russians and probably angry at having to take on another powerful adversary, upheld his obligations to Japan and declared war on the United States.

Churchill, understandably delighted at the turn of events, sped across the Atlantic, made brilliant speeches in Washington and Ottawa, and returned to a war-torn London in early 1942 with the message that the war against the Axis could and would be won. The Anglo-American alliance during the war was a noble epic of comradeship, bravery, and sheer hard work. On the major strategic questions, Churchill and Roosevelt were in basic agreement: the first priority was the defeat of Germany. On details, such as how and when there should be an invasion of Europe, there was endless debate. Churchill and his generals wanted the invasion to come as late as was reasonably possible and, preferably, from North Africa; Roosevelt and his military advisers — notably his brilliant Chairman of the Joint Chiefs of Staff, George Marshall — were in favour of an early invasion from the north of France. The third of the major allies, Stalin, was even more anxious for an early invasion, for this would take some of the pressure off his own beleaguered troops.

In 1943 the tide turned in favour of the Allies and, by 1944, the year of the great Normandy invasion, some thoughts were already being given to the problems that would face the postwar world. In July 1944, a month after D-Day, an international conference was held at Bretton Woods, New Hampshire, which laid the groundwork for the post-war creation of the International Monetary Fund and the World Bank. In October, after two months of meetings between the Allies at Dumbarton Oaks in Washington, DC, agreement was reached regarding most of the principles that were to be incorporated in what became the charter of the United Nations. In February 1945, tentative ideas were exchanged by the Big Three at Yalta on how to end the war and how to distribute the postwar prizes. In April Roosevelt died and his place was taken by his nervous but determined Vice-President, Harry S Truman. In May Germany capitulated; three months later, America's two atomic bombs were dropped on Japan, and, days later, the war was over.

The goodwill between the United States and the Soviet Union that had been necessitated and nourished by their wartime alliance quickly dissolved. American diplomacy, fortified by the American monopoly of nuclear power, displayed a new intransigence and impatience towards the Soviets; Russia, for her part, soon showed signs of entrenching herself irremovably into those areas of Eastern Europe in which FDR and Churchill had earlier agreed that she had a general interest. The United States and the Soviet Union tended to act towards each other independently of the United Nations, that organization in which they had, publicly at least, invested so many of their hopes for a peaceful future.

By 1947 the mutual suspicions of Moscow and Washington had begun to take the form of clearly enunciated policies. In March President Truman announced, in effect, that American military and civil aid would be given to any nation that was threatened by, but made an effort to resist, communist pressure. This new 'Truman Doctrine' became a cornerstone of subsequent American foreign policy. In the next year, in a test of Western will, the Russians cut off the supply roads to West Berlin; the Americans and British responded by dramatically bringing in supplies to the city by air; in May 1949, one month after the Western powers had signed the North Atlantic Treaty, the Soviet blockade was lifted. Throughout the period of the blockade – and this was, no doubt, one of the reasons for its having been imposed – a West German Constituent Assembly had been meeting in Bonn preparing a constitution for an independent (but, it was assumed, basically anti-communist) Western Germany. The German Federal Republic, consisting of the old American, French, and British zones of occupation, was duly set up in September 1949. A month later (and one week after the establishment of the People's Republic of China) the Soviets responded by recognizing the Eastern zone as the German Democratic Republic. And so the Cold War tit-for-tat continued apace.

In the Far East, in Korea, the Cold War actually turned into a shooting war, though the protagonists were, officially, the United Nations and North and South Korean troops. In 1953 both Washington and Moscow acquired new leaders. After three years of heavy fighting, the Korean War was brought to an uneasy end. It was hard to see that anybody had gained very much by either the war or the peace. The Cold War dragged on, always a battle of nerves, sometimes a battle of people, potentially one of nuclear (and, by the mid 1950s, thermonuclear) bombs. Despite the moralistic belligerence of President Eisenhower's Secretary of State, John Foster Dulles, there was a momentary thaw in the Cold War in 1955. Stalin's successors agreed to meet the political leaders of the United States, the United Kingdom, and France in Geneva. For a brief moment — for the first time since 1931 — there was no fighting going on anywhere in the world. The meeting was pleasant enough for the participants, but it achieved nothing concrete and the Cold War soon resumed.

In late 1956 the Soviets brutally suppressed a revolt against communist dominance in Hungary, but the United States (partly as a result of the equally questionable but much less brutal actions of her allies France and Britain at Suez, but above all because of the stern realities of the nuclear age) felt powerless to do anything practical to help the Hungarians. A couple of years later the Middle East was itself the scene of a potential Cold War confrontation; so were Quemoi and Matsu, off the Chinese mainland; so was Laos; and so, always, was Germany. In May 1959 Dulles died. Eisenhower, finding a strength and determination that he had rarely shown when Dulles was alive, received Khrushchev as his guest in September 1959, and then took off, in late 1959 and early 1960, on a series of world-wide goodwill tours during the course on which he no doubt did something to offset the anti-Americanism that had sprouted in many parts of the globe in Dulles' time. But Eisenhower's genial globe-trotting was not a total success. In particular, the 'Summit' meeting that was called in Paris in May 1960 was brought tumbling to a premature halt before it had even begun because the Soviets had shot down a 'U—2' spy-plane over their territory only weeks before the conference was due to begin — and because Eisenhower's reactions to the understandable public accusations and taunts of Khrushchev were a terrifyingly inconsistent cross between the naïve and the untrue. The next month the earnest but bitterly disappointed President had to cancel a scheduled good-will trip to Japan because he was warned that he might run into dangerously hostile crowds.

A few months later Eisenhower was out of public office. His successor Kennedy, inexperienced and unsure, acquiesced in a secret plan whereby the United States was to give tacit help to a group of Cuban *émigrés* who were going to invade their native land and try to wrest it from the grip of Fidel Castro. This invasion, at the Bay of Pigs, was an unmitigated failure, militarily, politically, and morally, and it was a nervous and watchful President Kennedy who went to Vienna to meet Khrushchev in July 1961. The Soviet leader was scornful of the youth and apparent lack of command that he saw in his opposite number; the late summer of 1961 saw the building of the Berlin Wall and a mammoth series of Soviet nuclear tests — and, just as Khrushchev had presumably expected, the United States did little more than raise feeble verbal objections. Khrushchev pushed his luck too far in late 1962, when Kennedy, in a show of cool and courageous strength, insisted that the Soviets remove the missiles they had deceptively placed on their satellite, Cuba. The world held its breath and Khrushchev complied. After this traumatic confrontation, when nuclear devastation seemed to be a matter of days away, there was a sharp de-escalation of tensions on both sides, and something like genuine goodwill between the two super-powers prevailed, its most conspicuous achievement being the Test Ban Treaty of July 1963. In the decade following the death of Kennedy, in late 1963, America's involvement in Vietnam repeatedly prevented the two powers from continuing their dialogue in as constructive a manner as they might both otherwise have preferred.

The Vietnam War was the longest, costliest war in American history, the only one she failed to win, and (with the exception of the Civil War) much the most controversial. It was a major factor — along with America's economic power and her nuclear arsenal — in delineating the way in which the USA would be regarded by the other nations of the world. When America finally withdrew from Vietnam in 1973, the cost in lives, money, equipment, and international respect had been appalling. Two years later, with all of Indo-China effectively in communist hands, the failure was complete. By this time, however, American foreign policy was principally concerned with new areas of activity — notably *détente* with Russia, the first steps towards a *rapport* with China, and attempts at mediation in the Middle East and southern Africa.

When the Carter administration came into office in January 1977, American foreign policy-makers, no longer weighed down by the atrocious burden of their country's involvement in Vietnam, could at last face the world again with a degree of rectitude and dignity. Thus, at the end of our period as at the beginning, American policy around the world was based on an assumption that morality was the best policy and should be the guiding principle of America's relations with the rest of the world.

Major issues

Such, in the briefest outline, is the story of American foreign policy since 1920. Let us now look in a little detail at a few of the more important and significant events and controversies in that story. The story itself can be broken down very conveniently into three periods: the period of inactivity and confusion before the Second World War, the war period itself, and the years since 1945. Each of the three periods — which were separated by two cataclysmic events, Pearl Harbor and Hiroshima — had its peculiar characteristics.

1920–41

It is only a little fanciful to look upon the first of these periods as having had something of the quality of a Greek tragedy. It is not only that it ended with the disaster of Pearl Harbor but also that that disaster looks in retrospect as though it might possibly have been avoided. Furthermore, some historians have claimed to see in Roosevelt a visionary leader to whom nobody listened and in most of the other participants (and, *a fortiori*, the mass public) a total unawareness of the doom that their action — or, in this case, inaction — would inevitably bring upon themselves. It is an attractive analogy but one that it is unwise to press too far. For one thing, the historian who looks for trends and who interprets the past in terms of what he knows eventually happened is likely to be misleadingly selective in his choice of evidence and dangerously one-sided in his interpretation of it. For another, the Greek tragedy analogy overrates the perspicacity of Roosevelt and, on the other hand, the influence of public opinion. We will discuss public opinion later in the chapter, but let us look now a little more closely at the role of President Roosevelt.

As has been seen in Chapter 2, Roosevelt had many great qualities as a leader. He had an acute awareness of the possible, a superb ability to persuade, and a lively sense of humour. Confident of his right and his ability to guide American destinies, he was not slow to take initiatives when they seemed necessary but was not anxious to pursue policies that appeared unachievable. When FDR first became President, these leadership qualities had to be harnessed almost entirely to the gargantuan task of solving America's vast and chronic domestic problems. His own foreign policy initiatives were infrequent, sometimes sensible (such as the recognition of the Soviet Union), occasionally unfortunate (such as his message disrupting the London Economic Conference). The day-to-day conduct of foreign affairs was left largely in the hands of Cordell Hull, who was one of the few thoroughgoing internationalists in the American Government at that time. As the situation in Europe and the Far East deteriorated in the middle and later 1930s, Roosevelt found that more and more of his own time and attention had to be given to foreign affairs. In the United States 1936 was an election year; it was also the year in which Hitler's troops marched into the Rhineland and Mussolini's into Addis Ababa. It was the year that saw the outbreak of the Spanish Civil War, and the year that ended with the signing of the Berlin–Rome Axis and the German–Japanese anti-Comintern Pact. And it was a year that began with the signing, by a reluctant and irresolute Roosevelt, of the first real Neutrality Act, which banned American arms and even cash loans to belligerent nations – an act the intention of which was to keep America out of foreign wars, but the effect of which was to hurt the underdog (the Ethiopians, the Chinese, the Spanish Republicans) in any conflict.

In August 1936, just before getting into his stride for the campaign for re-election, Roosevelt made a major speech on foreign policy at Chautauqua, New York. In the course of it, he praised the Neutrality Act and emphasized his desire to keep America out of international squabbles. His one gesture to the opponents of the neutrality legislation was to state that, in his opinion, discretionary power in foreign policy must always remain not with Congress but with the President and the Secretary of State. Roosevelt, as so often in the years preceding the war, was trying to please all sides of the debate over foreign policy but was, in the end, inclined to come down on the safe side, that of non-involvement. Once the campaign for re-election was properly under way, Roosevelt ran almost entirely on his domestic record and had hardly a word to say about foreign policy at all. He was returned by an unprecedented landslide. Soon afterwards, however, things began to go wrong for the President.

The year 1937 saw the fight over the Supreme Court and a further recession; in 1938 there was the vain attempt to 'purge' unsympathetic congressmen. Roosevelt's judgement, it seemed, was not quite as sound as it had been in previous years. His approach to foreign policy at this time was alarmingly inconsistent. In October 1937, at Chicago, he delivered his famous 'quarantine' speech in which he said, in part:

> It seems to be unfortunately true that the epidemic of world lawlessness is spreading.
>
> When an epidemic of physical disease starts to spread, the community approves and joins in a quarantine of the patients in order to protect the health of the community against the spread of the disease.

Just in case the message did not come across from this homely metaphor, the President ended his speech with a clear commitment to the view of the interventionists:

> . . .the will for peace on the part of the peace-loving nations must express itself to the end that nations that may be tempted to violate their agreements and the rights of others will desist from such a cause. There must be positive endeavors to preserve peace.

This bold new departure was very much Roosevelt's own, and he had made this speech in spite of the doubts expressed by several members of his own official family. Reactions to the speech were mixed, but many of the more responsible newspapers applauded the President's bold stand. But Roosevelt, having taken the initiative, seemed to be at a loss as to what to do next. The day after the 'quarantine' speech, he was extraordinarily evasive and not a little petulant when pressed at a news conference to answer the charge that it represented 'an attitude without a program'. In the days that followed he tended to emphasize to all around him that the speech had been trounced in the press, and used this half-truth as an excuse for not following up his words with actions. The only whiff of a programme to which to apply the implications of the Chicago speech was the suggestion (which apparently emanated not from FDR but from Under-Secretary of State Sumner Welles) that the President consult the leaders of other countries about steps that might lead to a relaxation of international tensions. But this tentative plan came to nothing, thanks largely to the coolness displayed towards it by Britain's Prime Minister, Neville Chamberlain.

This Roosevelt pattern — take a new initiative, and then repudiate it or water it down — was evident again and again in the middle and late 1930s. Sometimes, the opening gambit was in a direction favoured by the so-called isolationists (see pp. 96–8). As early as March 1935, for example, Roosevelt was recommending to a startled group of senators that they consider the possibility of introducing wholesale neutrality legislation. Four months later he wanted nothing stronger than an embargo on the sale of arms to aggressor nations — nothing, that is, that would prevent the United States from being able to proffer aid to victims of aggression. But in August the President, after being told that a 'no-arms-to-aggressors' Bill could not pass Congress, returned to his earlier position of accepting the idea of a wholesale neutrality law. A Bill embodying the latter approach was introduced in the Senate and passed *nem. con.* — immediately after which Roosevelt told a group of congressmen that he disliked the Bill. When the Bill went to the House of Representatives, it was accompanied by a number of changes requested by FDR. The House accepted every one of the President's recommendations, as, a few days later, did the Senate. And then, when the Bill came to Roosevelt for his signature on the last day of August 1935, he issued a strong statement to the effect that the blanket arms embargo contained in the Bill would help aggressors and, in the long run, might 'drag us into war instead of keeping us out' — and then signed the Bill into law!

Another example of Roosevelt's inconsistency in vital matters of foreign policy occurred five years later, during the period of the 1940 presidential campaign. In September Roosevelt took two important steps that suggested to many contemporary observers that he was prepared to face the possibility of US involvement in the war against the Axis powers: he arranged, by means of an executive agreement, to let Britain have fifty American destroyers in return for British bases in the western hemisphere, and he announced an embargo on all sales of scrap iron and steel to Japan. But then, a month later, he told an audience in Boston: 'I have said this before, but I shall say it again and again and again: your boys are not going to be sent into any foreign wars.'

Roosevelt was not, of course, unaware of the inconsistencies in his foreign policy attitudes and pronouncements in the years preceding Pearl Harbor. To some extent the inconsistencies were the result of genuine doubts — doubts regarding the best way of ending or preventing international conflict, doubts regarding the best way of insulating the United States from the worst effects of such conflict, and doubts regarding the measures and policies that Congress (and 'the American people') would accept. To some extent, too, his inconsistencies reflected an attempt to compromise between the conflicting views of his principal advisers. On the question of sanctions against Japan, for example, there were those (like Hull) who felt that a tough approach might lead the Japanese warlords into even more desperate action in the Far East, and others (like Stimson and Morgenthau) who thought that sanctions — especially on oil — might so cripple the Japanese Empire as to prevent it from being able to perpetrate further aggression. Finally, of course Roosevelt was ever the pragmatist, always prepared to try a new approach if the old one had failed. His foreign policy of the late 1930s was no more the product of a careful plan than was his domestic policy of the earlier part of the decade. In many ways, both policies failed: the problem of unemployment had not really been solved by the end of the decade and was running, in 1940, at more than 8 million; and, as for the foreign policy, it culminated in the débâcle of Pearl Harbor. But in the longer term, the two policies were both successful, and in a curiously interconnected way. For it was the war against the Axis powers that really ended the Depression — and it was the ending of the Depression and the consequent full use of America's huge reserves of manpower and of her almost unlimited natural resources that enabled America to emerge victorious from the war.

In the months preceding Pearl Harbor, the United States and Japan had engaged in frequent attempts to solve their differences by negotiation. The expansionist Japanese Empire, deprived of vital supplies of iron and steel and airplane fuel by the American embargoes of 1940, was repeatedly asked by the United States in the early months of 1941 to withdraw from China and from the alliance with Hitler and Mussolini. In July 1941, Roosevelt announced a total embargo on US trade with Japan, who consequently found her oil supplies seriously jeopardized. The Japanese Prime Minister, Prince Fumimaro Konoye, and his ambassador in Washington, Kichisaburo Nomura, made brave attempts to avert crisis, and even went so far as to suggest that Roosevelt have a personal meeting with Konoye. But the Japanese Government was under strong pressure to continue both its expansionist policies in Asia and its defiance of the United States. This pressure resulted in the overthrow of Konoye in October 1941 and his replacement by the militant General Tojo. Both sides thought war to be inevitable by this stage and, as all the world knows, it was occasioned by the sneak attack by the Japanese (even while their representatives were 'negotiating' in Washington with Hull) on the American fleet at Pearl Harbor in Hawaii.

There ensued endless debate in the United States both during and after the war as to whether and how the Pearl Harbor disaster could have been averted. Who was at fault for leaving the Pacific fleet almost unguarded in so vulnerable a position? Why were the surreptitious movements of the Japanese not known to US intelligence? How far did Roosevelt, in his anxiety to rally public opinion to the necessity of war, engineer the Peal Harbor disaster (no doubt indirectly and unwittingly) by his own policies? These are interesting questions and none of them is susceptible to a straightforward and categorical answer. But an even more intriguing question concerns the strategy of the Japanese. Pearl Harbor crippled the American fleet; the Japanese thus began the war against the United States with the military cards stacked very much in their favour. But it was only a question of time before the immeasurably superior American resources of goods and manpower began to swing the Pacific into the American camp.

Would the Japanese have stood to gain more if they had used any other strategy in their dealings with the United States? Suppose, for instance, they had carefully avoided any sudden and dramatic deterioration in their relations and had quietly pushed on with their gradual infiltration into South-East Asia. Japan could probably in time have overrun Thailand, Malaya, and the Indies – particularly since the European powers interested in these areas had most of their troops desperately tied up fighting Hitler. Japan, by using this gradualist strategy, could have obtained abundant supplies of rubber, tin, and oil – and, at the same time, not taken any step that would have been quite so dramatic as to have united American opinion into a cry for war. In the post-war years, various countries – particularly the Soviet Union and North Vietnam – were to learn this lesson: that the way to embarrass an American government was to challenge its vital interests by slow degrees, for the only way in which an American government can produce a popular and strong response is when it can portray a given action of its opponents as having been a monstrous and blatant violation of the *status quo*. But in 1941 the Japanese did not know this lesson, or chose to reject it. The war was on.

1941–45

If we turn our attention now to the second of the three periods – the war – the figure of Roosevelt again looms very large. Once the Japanese attacked Pearl Harbor, many of the President's doubts were settled. All his advisers – indeed, virtually the entire American public – shouted one message with one voice: the United States must win the war. Not that the President did not have problems. But his problems were of a new and more manageable nature. In the agonizing months and years preceding Pearl Harbor Roosevelt's doubts and inconsistencies had revolved around a negative question: how best to stop hostilities abroad or, at least, to protect US interests and to prevent the United States from getting into war. But after 7 December 1941 Roosevelt's new problems concerned a far more positive and clearly defined objective: how to win the war. Roosevelt had already shown his abilities as a leader in one war, that against the Depression. Now, when the nation was involved in a global battle of arms, all those qualities of clear judgement and buoyant optimism returned.

Across the Atlantic, in London, there was an even more vigorous and determined leader, Winston Churchill, who had been Prime Minister since May 1940. Roosevelt and Churchill first met as President and Prime Minister in August 1941 when, on a warship in the Atlantic just off Newfoundland, the two men composed the set of principles that became known as the Atlantic Charter. There were many people, such as Roosevelt's close friend Harry Hopkins, who were fearful that the two leaders would dislike each other and that, in the words of Robert E. Sherwood, 'the formidable egos of Roosevelt and Churchill were bound to clash'.[1] It is an important matter of history, however, that they developed a deep liking and admiration for each other and that their mutual respect had a great deal to do with the harmonious relations that existed between the United States and the United Kingdom during the years when they were fighting the Axis together.

But the two men did have their differences, of both style and opinion. Roosevelt was temperamentally less inclined to take per-

sonal charge of tiny military details than was Churchill, whereas the
President was far more at liberty to make policy decisions on his own
authority than was the Prime Minister who was obliged to tell his
Cabinet and even Parliament of every important step that he intended
to take. In the realm of actual policy, the major disagreements came
as we have noted above over the question of the best place and time to
launch an invasion of Europe.

Roosevelt died on 12 April 1945, just before the war ended. He had
been one of the most loved and most hated of American presidents.
Those who loved him were convinced that his wise leadership had
been a prime factor in the Allied victory that lay just around the
corner when he died. But he also had his critics. We can ignore the
wild accusations of the hatemongers, but there are two important
criticisms of his wartime leadership that are worth considering, and
they are closely connected. It is often said, firstly, that Roosevelt was
so preoccupied with the military problems of the war that he gave
hardly a thought to the diplomatic and political problems that it involved. The second criticism is to the effect that, when he *did* think in
political terms, he was taken in by Soviet blandishments and, particularly, at the Yalta Conference of February 1945, he made major territorial concessions to Stalin that were contrary to American interests.

The voice of Cordell Hull provides the most plaintive testimony on
the first point. His *Memoirs* are full of complaints that he was not
consulted on many matters of great international significance during
the war and that Roosevelt (who loved the military side of events)
tended to ignore the political implications of military policies. Hull
writes:

> Prior to Pearl Harbor I had been a member of the War Council . . . and I took part
> in its meetings. After Pearl Harbor I did not sit in on meetings concerned with
> military matters. This was because the President did not invite me to such meetings.
> I raised the question with him a number of times. . . .
>
> I feel it is a serious mistake for a Secretary of State not to be present at important
> military meetings. I often had occasion to point out to the President that some
> development of a military character, which undoubtedly had been decided at one of
> these meetings, also had a strong foreign affairs angle of which I should have been
> informed at the time.[2]

Hull's complaints were partly no doubt motivated by a personal
resentment at being ignored — the more so since most of the diplomatic advice that the President did seek came not from Hull but
from unofficial advisers like Harry Hopkins or, in the early days of
the war, from Hull's Deputy at State, Sumner Welles. The fact
remains, however, that Hull's point was a valid one, and was later

made by a number of other authorities, including Henry L. Stimson and John J. McCloy.

The second criticism, that concerning Yalta, has aroused most bitter controversy. Opinions vary, from those that claim that at Yalta Roosevelt was deliberately selling out to the communists, to those (held by historians of the eminence of William A. Williams) that claim that he was holding out perversely against legitimate Soviet demands and thus precipitating the Cold War. Somewhere in. the middle is the view that Roosevelt was ill at Yalta and, while not intending to betray American interests, was too weak to make the effort to block — and, perhaps, too sick to understand — Stalin's devilishly clever demands.

There is no doubt that Roosevelt was far from being a healthy man at Yalta, and it is possible that the physical weakness that was evident to all who saw him at that period had something to do with the proceedings at the conference. But the effect of any physical weakness on the part of Roosevelt would most likely have been that more initiative than would otherwise have been the case would have been left in the hands of Churchill — hardly the man to give anything away to the Russians! It was, for instance, Churchill who insisted that the detailed questions concerning the dismemberment of Germany — something the Russians were anxious, for their own reasons, to finalize immediately — be postponed for further discussion in the future. Williams[3] and others have argued, indeed, that in those respects in which Roosevelt did seem to have the energy to assert himself, he showed himself to be more anti-communist than the British Prime Minister. On Eastern Europe, for example, it was only Roosevelt's intransigence — despite an earlier Churchill–Stalin agreement in which FDR had acquiesced — that prevented substantial and amicable progress from being made.

But there are two important subjects on which agreement was reached at Yalta: one concerning the voting procedure in the Security Council and General Assembly of the proposed United Nations Organization, and the other dealing with the Far East. Regarding the UN, it was agreed in principle that the permanent members of the Security Council (the Big Three at Yalta plus China and, it was eventually decided, France) would each have an absolute veto over any Council recommendation for UN action. The Soviets had wanted a veto that could be used to prevent even the discussion of any issue unpalatable to one of the permanent members, but they were persuaded to drop this demand. Stalin had also requested two extra seats in the General Assembly, one for the Ukraine and one for Byelorussia. Churchill supported Stalin on this, but it was only with the greatest difficulty that the two of them persuaded FDR. Roosevelt's mind was made up only when it was secretly agreed between the Big Three that, should Roosevelt find rigorous congressional opposition to the proposal, Britain and the Soviet Union would support any consequent American request for two extra seats. When news of these decisions reached the American public (and the secret agreement leaked out in a most unfortunate fashion), Roosevelt was immediately attacked. Why had he given way to the Soviet requests for extra Assembly seats? Why had he made secret bargains with Stalin? What other undisclosed agreements had the Big Three made? The criticisms, it should be noted, concerned the manner more than the substance of the agreements. Indeed, Roosevelt's fears that American public opinion would never accept the three-seat formula for the Soviet Union were never substantiated. Most thoughtful Americans realized that, if the voting-procedure agreements were important, they were so not because they represented American concessions to the Soviet Union but because they made more possible the eventual establishment of a viable United Nations.

This leaves the major and most controversial of all the Yalta agreements, those concerning the Far East. The Soviets agreed, in strictest secrecy, that 'in two or three months after Germany has surrendered . . . [they would] enter the war against Japan on the side of the Allies'. They also promised 'to conclude with the National Government of China a pact of friendship . . . in order to render assistance to China for the purpose of liberating China from the Japanese yoke' – a commitment which, it was understood, precluded the Soviets from giving aid to Mao Tse-tung's communists (unless they worked in harness with Chiang Kai-shek). In return for these promises the Soviets requested, and were granted, a number of important territorial concessions in the Far East: they were given, outright, the Kurile Islands and the southern half of Sakhalin (two areas that the Japanese had seized in the war of 1904–5), they were to be granted autonomy over Outer Mongolia, and were recognised as having 'pre-eminent interests' in Manchuria, an area technically under Chinese sovereignty. As a final gesture to the Soviets, the port of Darien was to be internationalized. All these agreements were kept secret, since there was clearly nothing to be gained from letting the

Japanese know that they would soon be at war with the Soviet Union or from letting anyone know what the Soviets were to gain for their efforts. Even Chiang Kai-shek, whose government was more affected by these agreements than was any other, was not told of the Yalta decisions, since the Big Three could not, in all honesty, be certain that secrets were safe if known in Chungking, Chiang's capital.

The Far East agreements at Yalta came under heavy fire when they became known, the more so when it became clear in the postwar years that the Soviet promise of friendship with Chiang Kai-shek (rather than the Chinese Communists) had been fulfilled only as long as the war lasted against Japan.[4] As in the case of the UN agreements, one constant criticism concerned the fact that the agreements had been kept secret. The American 'right to know' was sorely affronted by the fact that their President had come to agreements with Churchill and Stalin over which the American people had no control and about which they had no knowledge, but of course the actual substance of the agreements was also criticized as having been a sell-out to the communists. The conference became known in some circles as the Yalta give-away. And, in the Cold War atmosphere of a few years later, this pejorative description did acquire a certain retrospective justice with regard to some of the secret clauses, such as that opening the Manchurian door to Soviet advances.

But three points should be borne in mind if criticisms of this sort are made. First, Roosevelt was not really giving away much that he could choose not to give away; America was in no position to prevent the Russians influencing and even controlling Manchuria if Stalin was as anxious to gain that influence as we now know him to have been. Second, one of Roosevelt's prime concerns was to end the protracted and costly war against Japan. In February 1945, the atomic bomb was still far from completion and Roosevelt and his advisers were resigned to the unpalatable expectation that there were many months or even years of brutal man-to-man fighting ahead. The President was, therefore, extremely anxious to persuade the Soviet Union to share some of the burdens of the war in the Far East, and perhaps to help to bring the end of the war a little nearer. The territorial 'concessions' did not seem to him at the time to be too high a price to pay. Third, it was not clear at Yalta that an increase of Soviet influence in the Far East necessarily had to jeopardize American interests in that area of the world. In early 1945 it was far from obvious that Soviet–American relations would soon deteriorate rapidly. Assuming that the two countries would remain on even reasonable good terms, it might have been in America's interests to have the efficient Russians dominating parts of the Far East — particularly if the influence of the corrupt and inefficient government of Chiang Kai-shek was correspondingly reduced.

The war was brought to an end dramatically by the dropping of two atomic bombs on Japan. Hiroshima was bombed on 6 August 1945. Early on the morning of the 9th, the Soviet Union joined the war against Japan and, later on the same day, the Nagasaki bomb was dropped. After much vituperative debate lasting several days and culminating in an almost unprecedented intervention by the Emperor himself, the Japanese Cabinet agreed to surrender.

The mushroom cloud over Hiroshima has cast its shadow over the whole of subsequent history. Many of the questions that President Truman and his advisers tried to consider in the fateful weeks before Hiroshima have been asked again and again in the years since. Would the Japanese have surrendered had they been warned about the nature of the atomic bomb and perhaps of the places on which it was planned to be dropped? Should they have been given a demonstration (in Tokyo Bay, for instance) before it was dropped on people? Should the atomic bombardment have been delayed? Was Hiroshima thought of more as a means of embarrassing the Soviet Union than as a means of inducing the war-weary and impotent Japanese to surrender? The debates over these questions continue unabated. The quick answer to them all seems to be that almost all aspects of the Hiroshima decision were dictated by primarily military criteria. The chief concern of Truman and his advisers was to end the war as quickly as possible and to kill as few people as possible. It may be argued that they made tactical errors, that a demonstration or a delay (or even an invasion of Japan or the threat of one) would have ended the war more quickly or with less loss of life, though such arguments would be very hard to prove and, in most cases, implausible. As for the argument that the bomb was dropped for primarily political (i.e. anti-Soviet) reasons, this may have lain behind the motivation of some of Truman's advisers. But Truman himself, like his predecessor, seems to have let military considerations dominate his thinking to an excessive degree and he may not have been fully aware of the enormous political implications of his Hiroshima decision.[5] Indeed, Truman was not in any meaningful way really making a decision at all, but merely acquiescing in something that had acquired, by the time he became President, an almost irreversible momentum of its own.

1945–78

The third and final period — that stretching from mid 1945 to the
present day — has been dominated by the existence of nuclear
weapons. Sometimes (such as at the very outset of this period and in
October 1962) some of America's policy-makers have had to discuss
the real possibility of using atomic (or hydrogen) bombs; more often,
the discussions have revolved around ways of promoting America's
interests around the globe while at the same time avoiding having to
use these awesome weapons. In general, the attitude towards nuclear
weapons has been that America should own as efficient and varied an
arsenal as possible. This, it has been argued, would have two valuable
effects. First, military power — even in a nuclear age — would bring
political power in its wake; a nation with an overwhelmingly powerful
and well-nigh impregnable nuclear weapons system, therefore, would
be able to further its political aims around the globe with unprecedented ease. Second, the fact of American nuclear power would act
as a deterrent against the aggressive desires of other countries, nuclear and non-nuclear alike. These two positions, however, apply to
two different types of situation. It may be that a nation owning a
monopoly of nuclear power is given thereby increased political leverage around the world; but once there are two (or more) nations with
nuclear arsenals, the second argument — that nuclear power can act
as a deterrent — overrules the first.

As one would expect, therefore, American defence policy since the
Second World War has for the most part been the story of American
adjustment to the frustrating fact that, in a world of two nuclear
giants, the ownership of colossal military strength is more likely to
hamstring the policy-makers than to bestow upon them opportunities
for independent political action around the globe. In the past two or
three decades the real opportunities for independent political action
have usually been given to the non-nuclear or non-aligned nations
who could be reasonably certain that even their more questionable
foreign policies — and even their occasional nose-thumbing at one or
both of the two super-powers — would not endanger many other
nations and would almost certainly not involve the risk of nuclear
war. The Soviet Union and the United States, by contrast, have been

forced into constant caution. They have had to learn how to try to
fulfil their foreign policy aims by gradualism and to avoid specific
incidents that might challenge the other power or provoke it into
making a dangerous response. They have had to learn the lesson that
Japan had not yet learned at the time of Pearl Harbor, and it is a
lesson that in a nuclear age is infinitely more important than it would
have been in 1941.

In the months and, indeed, years following Hiroshima, the American leaders had not fully grasped the true nature of nuclear weapons
and the correspondingly new responsibilities that their ownership
placed on the United States. America's defence policies were based on
traditional concepts of power politics and the desirability of maintaining as free a hand as possible for world-wide American trade
and diplomacy. This desire for a free hand found its expression in such
policies as the Truman Doctrine and Point Four which together gave
the world notice that the United States was prepared to give aid of
various sorts to anti-communist nations in all parts of the globe.
When it suited America, she was quite prepared to give the impression of acting in equal harness with other nations — the most
remarkable and generous example of this approach being the European Recovery Program (or Marshall Plan), whereby money was
given to the ailing nations of Western Europe (the Soviet Union was
invited to join in but refused) in order to help them to build up their
economies. But, naturally enough, the United States always tried to
make sure that the decision as to how to act and with or against whom
lay, ultimately, in Washington.

Some of the more perceptive American thinkers began to realize,
soon after the war was over, that the United States would not inde-
finitely be in a position in which she could deal with the Soviet Union
just as she chose. Even if the Soviet Union did not have nuclear
weapons, she would certainly have them before very long, apart from
which she had a colossal conventional army. Furthermore, she
appeared to have the increasingly solid allegiance of several important East European states. In 1947, in a *Foreign Affairs* article which he
signed with the pseudonym 'X', George Kennan, an experienced
American diplomat with special knowledge of the Soviet Union,
argued that America should not imagine that she was in a position to
extirpate communism from Russia (or, for that matter, from her
satellites) simply by a show of force. America should be more realistic,
he argued: 'the main element of any United States policy towards the

Soviet Union must be that of a long-term patient but firm and vigilant containment of Russian expansive tendencies.'

This doctrine of 'containment' became the keynote of American policy towards the Soviet Union in the years ahead and provided the US policy-makers with the rationale that they needed for many of the alliances of the next few years — NATO (1949), the security treaties with Japan and the Philippines (1951), the ANZUS Pact (1951), and SEATO (1954) and CENTO (1958).

But for many people the containment doctrine alone was too passive — particularly after the dramatic communist successes (the Soviet atomic bomb and the success of the Communists in China) of 1949. After Truman left office the United States, guided above all by John Foster Dulles, tried to adopt a more active stance towards communism than that seemingly recommended by Kennan. Containment was not abandoned, but to it was added the concept of liberation. The United States would not only prevent communism from making any further territorial gains, but would also adopt policies (short of actual war) designed to help those people currently 'enslaved' by Moscow to liberate themselves from their Russian yoke. The two policies were linked by the alarming doctrine of 'massive retaliation' whereby, if the Soviets or their satellite governments sent one soldier one inch over their current boundaries — over what the Secretary of State, with his flair for the dramatic phrase, liked to think of as a trip-wire — the United States might possibly be prepared to retaliate with all-out war.

This 'containment-plus-liberation' policy was more impressive in theory than in fact. In the first place, the Soviet leaders, especially after the death of Stalin in 1953, showed little inclination to attempt anything so old-fashioned as a military conquest of new territory; their ways of spreading Soviet and communist influence were to sidestep the trip-wire problem and use economic and political rather than military tactics. Secondly, in the period between the Korean truce and the Geneva summit meeting, there was little of benefit to be obtained by the United States from militant threats and much to be gained from attempts to thaw the Cold War. Thirdly, on the very few occasions on which the 'enslaved' people of Eastern Europe appeared to want to be liberated — the 1953 rising in East Germany and East Berlin, and the 1956 Polish and Hungarian revolutions — the United States, quailing before the realities of Soviet nuclear power, conspicuously failed to help them even though her own bombastic promises had possibly been in part the inspiration for the revolts.

There was no major attempt to rethink the basis of America's defence and foreign policy until the beginning of the 1960s. After the missile crisis of October 1962, there was a notable relaxation of Soviet–American tensions, and each side showed signs of a new 'live-and-let-live' attitude. Both sides remained armed to the teeth but seemed genuinely predisposed to discuss with each other the appalling problems involved in bringing the nuclear arms race to a halt and achieving disarmament – this despite the ever-increasing American involvement in Vietnam.

Vietnam was one of the three states of French Indo-China that gained their independence in 1954. As a result of the Geneva agreements of that year, Vietnam was divided temporarily into two zones, the northern one of which was to be administered by the communist-led Vietminh. By the Geneva accords, general elections were to be held throughout Vietnam in July 1956. In the two years that followed Geneva, however, the American-supported Ngo Dinh Diem crushed most of the opposition to his dictatorial régime in the southern zone. With American connivance, he saw to it that the elections (which he and the Americans feared would have given Vietnam a communist-dominated government) never took place. By 1959 the North Vietnamese leaders, robbed of complete victory, began to encourage (and even to foment) rebellion in the South. The southern rebels, supported in due course by infiltrators from the North, set about trying to undermine the loyalty of the South Vietnamese people to the fanatically anti-communist régime of Diem. Their tactics were brilliant and ruthless, and induced repeated requests from Diem for American help. At first that help took the form of 'advisers' whose unequivocal advice was that Diem should fight back. Before long some of the fighting was actually being organized by the Americans.

In December 1960, the National Liberation Front of South Vietnam (NLF) was formed, and it had the full support of the communist leaders in North Vietnam. During the years of the Kennedy administration, American aid and *matériel* were stepped up considerably. When Kennedy became President the total US force in South Vietnam was about 600, a figure that had leaped to more than 20,000[6] by the time of his death less than three years later. Meanwhile, various elements in South Vietnam – notably a number of Buddhist and neo-Buddhist sects as well as the NLF – were increasingly resentful of the repressive régime of the Catholic Diem. Diem's unpopularity led

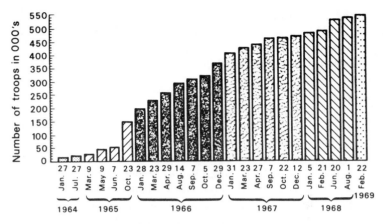

Fig. 3.1 American troops in Vietnam

the Americans to doubt his effectiveness as a leader, and they made no move to prevent his downfall and assassination in November 1963.

In the years following the deaths of Diem and Kennedy, the American commitment in Vietnam increased at a staggering rate (see Fig. 3.1). In the same period, infiltration from North to South by communist guerrillas was also stepped up. In August 1964, after an incident in which an American warship was allegedly shot at when sailing in the Gulf of Tonkin (North Vietnamese waters), Congress was inveigled by President Johnson into passing a vaguely worded joint resolution promising the President virtually unlimited support in his conduct of the Vietnam War. In February 1965, at the very moment at which Soviet Premier Kosygin was in Hanoi, the North Vietnamese capital, President Johnson retaliated against an attack on Pleiku by ordering the American forces to commence bombing North Vietnam. The American escalation of the war was based on the theory that the more the North Vietnamese were made to suffer, the more likely their government (and by implication the NLF and the militant Hanoi-led Viet Cong) was to surrender. The North Vietnamese, on the other hand, became all the more determined to discredit the Americans and to resist them if at all possible. At the diplomatic level an impasse was reached: the North Vietnamese refused to negotiate unless the Americans stopped the bombing of their country and agreed to the presence at the negotiations of representatives of the NLF, while the Americans demanded as a precondition to negotiations that the North Vietnamese end the guerrilla infiltration into the South. As the war dragged on there were several efforts, some overt and some secret, to bring about a negotiated peace; but, as a result of the stubbornness and pride of one side or the other, all these efforts failed.

The bombing of North Vietnam did not end the war in 1965; the bombing of fuel dumps just outside major North Vietnamese cities in 1966 did not end the war either. It was now becoming clear that, despite the superoptimistic statements of men who should have known better in the early days of the conflict, it was going to be a long time before the war in Vietnam would be over*. Not surprisingly, public feeling regarding the war became increasingly tense from 1965 to 1968. Polls were of course produced to show that, numerically, more and more people knew about the war and approved of the President's actions — a normal development in time of any foreign policy crisis. But what was probably unprecedented was that despite the urgency of the crisis and the attempts by Johnson to minimize dissent, those who opposed the President (including many distinguished academics and some of the country's leading journalists) did so with increasing clarity, authority, and confidence. Almost always in previous American history, any president in hot water abroad had merely to invoke the patriotism of the people and ask them to close ranks and they have tended to rally round him. But here was a case in which the more the President called for a patriotic consensus the bolder and more earnest his critics became.

In February 1968, the Viet Cong conducted an offensive (the 'Tet offensive') against American and South Vietnamese positions so devastating that it shook the American political leadership to its roots. Shortly afterwards, Lyndon B. Johnson announced that he had decided not to run again for the presidency later in the year. In May came the first talks, in Paris, between representatives of the American Government and those of the Democratic Republic of (North) Vietnam. In the USA itself, the volume and scale of anti-war protests built up to a crescendo as millions of students and their teachers joined

---

* At the end of September 1963, Secretary of Defense McNamara and the Chairman of the Joint Chiefs of Staff, General Maxwell Taylor, spent a week in South Vietnam. After their return to Washington they gave President Kennedy a thorough briefing. On 2 October an official White House statement said that 'the major part of the United States military task [could] be completed by the end of 1965' and that 'by the end of the year [i.e. 1963] the United States program for training Vietnamese should have progressed to the point where 1,000 United States military personnel assigned to South Vietnam can be withdrawn'. In October 1963, the US commander in South Vietnam, General Paul D. Harkins, said in Tokyo: 'I can safely say that the end of the war is in sight'.

hands with war widows, bereaved parents, injured veterans, outraged traditionalists like flinty old Dr. Spock, youthful black radicals like Bobby Seale, and disillusioned patriots to whom the only wars that America should fight were those that she could win. All were by now prepared to denounce a war that they variously saw as an error of strategic judgement, a failure of nerve, a crime, or a moral catastrophe.

It was against this background that eight years of Democratic rule in the White House came to an end as the electorate preferred by a slim majority that resurgent star of yesteryear, Richard M. Nixon, to Johnson's Vice-President Hubert H. Humphrey. Nixon, with no personal association with the Vietnam policies of the Kennedy and Johnson administrations, could pose as the outsider, the man who would end a war that others had started. After a year or two in the White House, this image became somewhat strained, particularly when, after consultation with his Assistant for National Security Affairs (later to be his Secretary of State) Henry A. Kissinger, Nixon extended the war in May 1970 and submitted Vietnam's neighbour Cambodia to intensive bombing. Nixon and Kissinger were shocked by the passion of the criticisms that this action heaped upon their heads. Nixon went out before dawn one morning and talked to demonstrators in Washington, while Kissinger was badly shaken by the abrasive strictures of a delegation of his former Harvard colleagues. A new wave of campus violence flared up in the wake of the Cambodia bombings and deaths occurred at Kent State University in Ohio and at Jackson State College in Mississippi. But Nixon and Kissinger continued to talk and act as though, somehow, the impossible war in South-East Asia could be won or at least fairly concluded. 'Peace With Honor' was Nixon's formula as he prepared for the 'Vietnamization' of the war (i.e. an eventual American pull-out). As late as Christmas 1972, after Kissinger's almost interminable negotiations with the North Vietnamese had led him to announce that peace was 'at hand', the Nixon administration saw fit to let another torrent of bombs rain upon North Vietnam.

Early in 1973, after the longest, costliest, bloodiest war in American history, peace was eventually signed. Virtually all the remaining American troops and advisers in Vietnam withdrew as quickly as possible and, within two years, the whole of Vietnam and Cambodia had come under communist rule. Thus, the war that had cost 45,000 Americans and perhaps half a million Vietnamese their lives had at last limped to its ignominious end.

It would be hard to overstate the passions aroused in the USA by the Vietnam War in the late 1960s. The war was on television screens in every home every night, presidential candidates were made and broken by their attitudes towards it, and its corrosive powers ate their way into all aspects of American life and thought. Yet it is arguable that, in a global context, the Vietnam War was not ultimately the most important political event of the period but that that accolade should go to the Sino–Soviet split.

The seeds of discontent between the leadership of the two biggest communist powers were sown many years earlier. Some would date the tension between Russia and China back to 1956 and their divergent reactions to Khrushchev's speech denouncing Stalin. Others would go back earlier and point to the mutual antagonism between Mao and Stalin as the latter gave aid and encouragement to Chiang Kai-shek in the mid 1940s. Fundamentally, the split probably reflected the rivalry for leadership of the communist world between representatives of two totally different concepts of communism.

By the mid 1960s, the split had become an indisputable fact and by 1969 the two were apparently almost at war — ostensibly over a question of border violations along the Ussuri River. As Moscow and Peking thundered abuse at each other, observers in Washington began to wonder whether there might not be some comfort to be gained by the USA. Even if you discounted the possibility, persuasively argued by Harrison E. Salisbury of the *New York Times* and other pundits, that the antagonism between the USSR and China might actually spill over into war, it seemed that their mutual animosities might successfully prevent them from taking aggressive initiatives with impunity in other parts of the world. Indeed, argued proponents of this view, it was precisely this Sino–Soviet confrontation that kept both the communist super-powers from being able to intervene more openly in the conflagration in Vietnam. Furthermore, if the Chinese and the Russians hated each other with sufficient venom, was there not a possibility that each might be tempted to relax somewhat its relationship with the presumed arch-enemy of the other, the United States of America?

In Washington, evidence for these and similar hypotheses was carefully sifted. Every sign of potential friendship towards America coming out of either Moscow or Peking was analysed and re-analysed. Could the time be ripe, perhaps, for discreet enquiries to be made of the People's Republic of China (possibly at the regular ambassadorial meetings in Warsaw) to see whether some sort of ties could not be established between the two countries for the first time since China became communist in 1949? Similarly, could the Russians be prevailed upon, despite their constant denunciations of American activities in Vietnam, to consider the possibility of a mutual reduction of nuclear arms? If the Americans could let both the Chinese and the Russians realize that the other side was proving amenable to American blandishments, it was not impossible that an important diplomatic log-jam could be shifted in such a way as to reduce the danger of world war and, incidentally, to bring considerable diplomatic benefits to the USA.

It was no doubt with something like this analysis in mind that Nixon's National Security Assistant Henry A. Kissinger visited China secretly in July 1971 in order to set the scene for President Nixon's official visit the following year. Before 1972 it would have been very difficult for any American president — least of all one with Nixon's early record of doctrinaire anti-communism — to visit China. The American sense of loss when China went 'red' in 1949 took a generation to wear off and, even by 1972, the differences between the two countries and their political and social systems were still fundamental. There was, for instance, no question at this time of the USA abandoning its official recognition of the 'exiled' Taiwan régime and establishing formal diplomatic links with Peking instead. The first, tentative signs of a new understanding between China and America came about not because of any philosophical *rapport* between Peking and Washington but largely as a result of the Sino–Soviet split — the fear in Peking that, as the Vietnam War eventually shuddered towards its end, the Americans and Russians might reach new understandings that could place the Chinese in the unenviable position of having both the world's major nuclear powers ranged against them.

Just as the Chinese were probably stimulated by their antagonism towards the Russians into entertaining the possibility of closer relations with the USA, so the Russians, too, felt the need for some degree of American friendship as their enmity with the Chinese continued unabated. Throughout the period of the Vietnam War American contacts with Russia were strained but this had not prevented Washington and Moscow from trying to get together over other aspects of their relationship. The Russians may have disapproved of American actions in Vietnam and the Americans expressed disgust at the War-

saw Pact occupation of Czechoslovakia in 1968. But these were matters over which the outsider could exert little pressure. What the
Americans and the Russians could discuss to their mutual benefit was
their relationship and relative status as the world's two most important nuclear powers. *Détente*, as it came to be known, probably began
in the wake of the Cuba missile crisis of October 1962 when the
confrontation between the two super-powers really seemed to have
brought the world to the brink of a possible holocaust. A few months
later, in June 1963, the Russians and the Americans signed a treaty
that effectively banned further atmospheric nuclear tests. In 1968 the
same signatories reached a pact over the non-proliferation of nuclear
arms. These two treaties came in time to be signed by a great majority
of the nations of the world (but, conspicuously, not by China) and
were viewed by the Americans and the Russians as two historic steps
along the way towards an eventual goal of world nuclear disarmament. In November 1969, against the background of President
Nixon's early withdrawals of American troops from Vietnam and his
newly-enunciated policy of the 'Vietnamization' of the war, delegations from the USA and the USSR met in Helsinki in Finland for the
first sessions of the Strategic Arms Limitation Treaty (SALT) talks.

By the end of the 1960s, therefore, there was a distinctly co-
operative atmosphere in Soviet–American relations. There were no
doubt many reasons for *détente*. It was no doubt stimulated in large
part by a genuine desire in both camps to do all in their power to
reduce the possibility of global nuclear catastrophe. But the impetus
towards *détente* was facilitated, too, by economic and political weaknesses in the Soviet Union and by growing Soviet–American business
and trading links as well as by the Nixon administration's de-
escalation of the American involvement in Vietnam. The relaxation of
West German–Russian relations at this time made possible by Willy
Brandt's *Ostpolitik* also played a part in reducing East–West tensions.
But above all, *détente* between the Russians and the Americans was a
by-product of the Sino–Soviet split and of the palpable desire of the
Soviet leaders to attempt to nip in the bud any Chinese diplomatic
initiatives that might take place in Washington.

These various diplomatic processes and manœuvrings became
increasingly visible in the 1970s. As American ping-pong players,
followed by Henry Kissinger and eventually by Richard Nixon himself, were invited by the Chinese leaders to visit Peking, similar
invitations started issuing from Moscow. Thus, a few weeks after his

historic trip to China, President Nixon undertook the first visit by an incumbent American president to Moscow. This was partly a way of reassuring the Russians that the United States had not been totally seduced by the blandishments of the Chinese. But Nixon's 1972 Moscow visit also took the form of a series of working sessions that produced an impressive array of agreements — culminating in a major breakthrough on the limitation of strategic arms. The impetus towards *détente* continued in the years to come. A Soviet delegation led by Mr. Brezhnev visited President Nixon in Washington and California in 1973 — right in the middle of the televised Senate Watergate hearings, which were suspended for the duration so as not to embarrass the summit talks. And in the summer of 1974, just a few weeks before his resignation, President Nixon again visited Moscow. Three months after Nixon's resignation, in November 1974, his successor Gerald Ford met Brezhnev at Vladivostok where agreement was reached in principle on measures that the two leaders hoped would lead to an eventual second treaty on the limitation of strategic arms.

Détente was not without its problems. At first, the Russian leaders had to tread warily because not only were they parleying with American leaders who were still prosecuting the Vietnam War, but they were also conscious that their own policy failures — bad grain harvests, enmity with the Chinese — lay behind their need to befriend their former sworn enemies, the Americans. On the American side, there were many, such as the Democrat Senator Henry Jackson or the Republican Ronald Reagan, who criticized the Nixon and Ford administrations and their principal foreign policy-maker, Henry Kissinger, for giving too much away to the Russians. They had a case. In strictly arithmetical terms and when viewed in the context of the ever-fluctuating ratio of American and Russian conventional forces, America's various SALT proposals could be interpreted as not ungenerous to the Russians. Furthermore, Jackson and his many supporters demanded that senatorial approval of SALT and similar treaty agreements should be tied to an insistence that the Soviet Union liberalize its intolerant policies towards domestic dissent and towards Russian Jews wishing to emigrate to Israel. Nixon, Ford and Kissinger stuck resolutely to the line that the impetus towards the limitation of strategic arms, and the co-operation with the Soviet leaders that this implied, were of such overriding importance to the world that they were worth obtaining even at the price of turning a blind eye towards Russian violations of the basic rights of many of its citizens. Their successors, President Jimmy Carter and his Secretary of State Cyrus Vance, attached far greater importance to the human rights issue (not only in the Soviet Union but throughout the world) even though this stance might appear to threaten to undermine the achievement of further *détente* and a second SALT agreement.

Whatever the eventual fate of *détente* and of the new American *rapport* with China, the man principally associated with these departures, Henry A. Kissinger, established for himself a place in the history books that few sub-presidential policy-makers ever achieve. Kissinger, a Jewish immigrant with a heavy German accent, had built up a distinguished career as a professor of international relations at Harvard. For years he had been on the peripheries of political power; a consultant to the Kennedy administration in the early 1960s, he later came into the orbit of New York's Republican Governor Nelson A. Rockefeller. In 1968, Kissinger was engaged by President-Elect Nixon to be his adviser on national security matters.

Kissinger's ebullience, stamina, and imaginative capacity to translate Nixon's ideas into practicable policies were such that the presidential adviser soon began to upstage the man officially entrusted with the conduct of America's foreign policy, Secretary of State William P. Rogers. Throughout Nixon's first term of office, Rogers was Secretary of State and Kissinger was the President's National Security Assistant. Occasionally, as in the December 1969 'Rogers Plan' on the Middle East, the Secretary of State took charge of an important policy departure himself, and he certainly dealt with the day-to-day affairs of the Department of State and the diplomatic obligations that fell to its senior official with dedication and dignity. But most of the more acclaimed foreign policy initiatives and negotiations – the Vietnam peace talks in Paris, the preparations for Nixon's China trip, *détente* with the Russians – were associated with the name of Henry Kissinger.

Rogers put up with this difficult situation with good grace and he and Kissinger did their best to observe all the diplomatic niceties in their relationship with each other. But by the summer of 1973, a few decent months after Nixon's second inauguration, Rogers left government service and the way was open for Henry Kissinger to become Secretary of State in name as well as in fact. Kissinger had never relished the thought of having to preside over a large government department and to concern himself with the minutiae of day-to-day affairs. Once Secretary of State, he still preferred to involve himself personally in the big issues and to leave other matters in the hands of subordinates. Thus, immediately following the Middle East War of October 1973, Kissinger took off on a round of visits to see the political leaders in, among other places, Rabat, Cairo, Amman, Jerusalem, Riyadh and Damascus; shortly thereafter he returned to the area to act as personal mediator between Egyptian President Sadat in Aswan and Israeli Prime Minister Meir.

Kissinger's 'shuttle diplomacy' at first aroused the breathless admiration of most observers and commentators, particularly when it achieved results – such as the Egyptian–Israeli disengagement agreement of January 1974. But the dangers of this kind of diplomacy, for Kissinger as for the USA, were at least as great as its potential benefits. Any form of diplomacy involves the risk of possible failure; but the failure of a Kissinger-style shuttle could prove especially serious. For one thing, some of the negotiations in which Kissinger involved himself concerned what were in the first instance other people's problems. Thus, America's prestige was to some extent being placed in the hands of other countries. If, as threatened to happen a number of times towards the end of his tenure of office in his dealings with the Middle East and southern Africa, Kissinger's shuttle diplomacy was to fail to produce fruit, American prestige might be seen to have suffered as a direct result of the whim of another government. Second, instead of insulating his nation's principal foreign policy officer from negotiations that ran the risk of failure, Kissinger was regularly putting his own reputation and that of the office he held directly and publicly on the line. Finally, by his personal involvement in this on-the-spot diplomacy, Kissinger was inevitably ignoring many other areas of policy to which a Secretary of State would normally be expected to devote some of his attention.

By 1976, with the Middle East apparently in deadlock again and with black Africa reinvigorated by the addition of the former Portuguese colonies of Angola and Mozambique and (aided by Russian equipment and Cuban soldiers) breathing ever more menacingly down the neck of Rhodesia and South Africa, Kissinger was coming in for a great deal of criticism. Nobody gets blamed so vehemently as the miracle man who fails to perform a miracle. A charitable view of Kissinger's situation by the time he left office in January 1977 would commend him for trying – as few other world statesmen would have been prepared or equipped to do – yet again to persuade the mutually antagonistic leaders in the Middle East and southern Africa to reach a settlement and avoid further bloodshed. To others he was a ruthless practitioner of naked *realpolitik* whose calculations had failed. Whatever the case, there is no doubt that Henry Kissinger, by his astute intelligence, his extraordinary capacity to persuade, and his indefatigable resolution backed up by a buoyant and competitive ego, dominated American foreign policy for eight years and left an indelible mark on world affairs.

It is a revealing comment on the nature of foreign affairs that possibly the most spectacular achievement of recent American foreign policy (one for which Kissinger had striven mightily and in vain) was accomplished by one of its least colourful personalities: Jimmy Carter. It was largely as a result of President Carter's painstaking personal diplomacy with Prime Minister Begin of Israel and President Sadat of Egypt that a peace treaty was signed between those two countries in 1979. Carter's achievement was considerable and he courageously invested a great deal of time and presidential prestige in a task many thought impossible. He had other successes, too. The Panama Canal was 'returned' to Panama, and it was under Carter that mutual recognition was finally negotiated between the USA and the People's Republic of China. But these successes were eclipsed in many minds by several almost equally dramatic failures. During the Carter years America's closest ally in the Persian Gulf, the Shah of Iran, was toppled from power and his place taken by the implacably anti-American (though almost equally anti-Russian) Islamic fundamentalist régime of the Ayatollah Khomeini. During the same period the Soviet Union, fearful of America's developing friendship with China and perhaps reading in Carter's disdain for war a disinclination to run risks for America's interests abroad, built up her conventional and nuclear arsenals in Eastern Europe and, half a world away, poured some 85,000 troops into Afghanistan. Thus, during the first half of his presidency, Carter talked optimistically of human rights, *détente* and of a second SALT Treaty with the Russians. Thereafter he found himself caught up in popular demands for strengthening Western defences and, in his final year, by the frustrating attempt to secure the release of US Embassy staff detained in Iran by followers of the Ayatollah.

Carter's successor, Ronald Reagan, brought back to the White House the simpler values of yesteryear. No less moralistic than Carter, Reagan was at once more assertive and less analytical, his rhetoric directed less at human rights abuses than at the evils of communism. Were the Communists (or Arabs or whoever) pushing us around? They had to be taught a lesson, said Reagan, in his gentle, avuncular way, as he dispatched US troops and *matériel* to the Caribbean, the Middle East or wherever. The rhetoric and the succeeding action went down well in a nation still irritated at recent examples of American impotence. But Reagan's deeds could never fully match his words. Troops might be sent to El Salvador, Grenada or the Lebanon, and Cruise and Pershing missiles to NATO allies in Europe, but there was no way Reagan could seriously take on the Soviets or their iron-fisted surrogates in places like Afghanistan or Poland. Nor did he try. The world was by now so dangerous a place, with global thermonuclear war a real possibility, that both Reagan and the shifting, elderly leadership in Moscow kept their mutual accusations within bounds and tried to ensure that they fought Syrians or Afghans rather than each other.

Themes

As we have seen, American foreign policy has changed in many ways since 1920, every few years adding a new and unexpected twist to the complex story. But there are certain general themes that recur throughout, and it is to these that we now turn.

If there is one such theme that almost all writers on the subject emphasize, it is that these years saw the eventual eclipse of the policy of isolationism. In the 1920s, according to this widely accepted version of the story, the United States retreated, after her brief foray into world affairs under Wilson, into her traditional isolationist shell, eschewing as far as she could all contacts with the rest of the world. Roosevelt, it is argued, tried to woo the nation away from this dangerous and selfish attitude, but his efforts were not totally successful until the Japanese attacked Pearl Harbor. Thereafter, so goes the legend, the United States has constantly tried, with varying success but unflagging earnestness, to play a full and constructive part in the affairs of the world, though the interventionism of the 1970s was perhaps more subdued in tone than that of the previous thirty years.

Like most legends, this one contains much that is true. But a close analysis of the facts suggests that the 'isolationism-to-interventionism' or 'isolationism-to-internationalism' interpretation of American foreign policy leaves a great deal unexplained. It is not so much an inaccurate interpretation as an inadequate one, one that purports to describe the overall strategic aims of American foreign policy but which at best describes one of the means used in the attempt to achieve these aims. One of the difficulties with the term 'isolationism' is that it has been used to cover opposite policies: selfish tariff barriers (such as Fordney—McCumber in 1922 and Hawley—Smoot in 1930) and generously intended treaties (the Naval Limitation Treaty of 1922 and the Kellogg—Briand Pact six years later). Similarly, if 'interventionism' or 'internationalism' began in 1941, it must include some policies (such as UNRRA or the Marshall Plan) that the United States pursued in close conjunction with its friends abroad, and many others (e.g. the Cuban policies of 1961 and 1962 and the invasion of the Dominican Republic in 1965 or Grenada in 1983) regarding which other countries were scarcely consulted until after the event.

Another problem with the term 'isolationism' is that in the twentieth century it could never really be an accurate description of the policy of a government which, willy-nilly, represented the richest and most powerful nation in history. Despite the distaste felt by many American policy-makers in the 1920s and 1930s for some of the events and personalities of Europe and the Far East, and despite the breadth of the Atlantic and Pacific Oceans, the United States simply could not avoid all involvements in a world in which, so recently, her President had played so conspicuous a role; for the fact was that even her negative responses to the outside world — the limitations, for instance, that she placed upon her international trade or the withdrawal in the Nixon era from much of South-East Asia — were certain to have a profound effect on international affairs. She had reached a position of such power and eminence that nothing that she could do, not even closing shop completely for a couple of decades, could leave the world unaffected. *Any* policy, even one of apparent 'isolationism', was, in effect, a policy of influencing, in one way or another, the trend of world affairs. Even if the US thought of herself as isolated from the world, therefore, the world was very far from being isolated from the US.

Thus, the United States was, despite superficial appearances, deeply involved in world affairs even in the 1920s. At the beginning of that decade America was trying to adjust to the new fact that she was the world's creditor and that New York was the world's financial capital. During the decade, private overseas investment soared. In 1919 private investments abroad amounted to $7 billion; by 1930 the total was $17·2 billion. In the field of international trade, too, American businessmen were not slow to take advantage of the opportunities provided by the disruption of traditional trade patterns and the availability of new markets occasioned by the war. Prior to the outbreak of the war the value of American exports had never reached $3 billion. In 1916, however, the total was $5·7 billion, and in 1920, $8·6 billion. The total was never again to fall below $3 billion except in the worst years of the Depression.

Some historians have been attracted to other concepts in their attempts to understand the patterns of US foreign policy. There are those who see it as having alternated between a Pacific orientation (which, with the exception of the height of the Vietnam war, had generally corresponded to the periods subsequently referred to as 'isolationist') and an Atlantic, or European, orientation. Others claim to see the wavering between 'idealistic' policies (a concept that conveniently embraces both the moral earnestness of a Woodrow Wilson, a Charles Evans Hughes or a Jimmy Carter and the more narrowly nationalistic delusions of a William Borah or a Charles A. Lindbergh) and 'realistic' ones (i.e. those of which the observer approves — which, in the first twenty years after the end of the Second World War, were likely to be the more 'interventionist' ones). But these dichotomies all suffer from the same weakness: they all assume that, at any given time, most influential Americans shared certain attitudes towards the world and translated those attitudes into more or less consistent policies.

In fact, however, there were probably no presuppositions that were shared by all American policy-makers at any given period — except, perhaps an obvious one: they have, throughout our period, been anxious to maintain for the United States as much freedom of action (a favourite phrase of Roosevelt) as is consistent with its security needs, to act not multilaterally but unilaterally. Put negatively, American foreign policy, like the foreign policy of any other militarily strong nation, has, virtually throughout the twentieth century and certainly since 1920, been designed to prevent the United States from having to commit herself in advance to any action or policy, unless that commitment were considered vitally necessary or unless it gave her further opportunities for independent initiatives than she would otherwise have had. This one central tenet of foreign policy, of course, is enormously broad and its constant adaptation to the particular circumstances that have arisen has occasioned much debate and not a little disagreement among those who made America's foreign policy. In the late 1930s for instance, there were senators (like Borah and Pittman) who thought that America's freedom of action would be best maintained by preventing her — by law — from involving herself in the tensions and animosities that were developing in Europe and the Far East; but there were members of the Roosevelt administration, like Hull, Stimson and Welles, who, with equal sincerity and with the same ultimate aim in mind, were convinced that America's best course would be to step in and try to bring her influence to bear upon these world-wide turmoils at the earliest opportunity.

The only difference between the pre-1941 period and the years that followed was this: after 1941, most of the men responsible for America's foreign policy felt that the best way to influence world affairs was by intention rather than by default and that, if the United States had to get involved in the affairs of other nations, she would do better to do so on her own terms rather than on theirs. This was not 'internationalism' or 'multilateralism' if by these terms is meant the partial surrender of national sovereignty as a result of altruism. The novelty of the years since Pearl Harbor is that the inactivity of the interwar years gave way to vigorous interventionism — in pursuit of exactly the same strategic goals that the inactivity of the 1920s and 1930s so conspicuously failed to achieve. As an illustration of this theme one can cite the alliances of the Dulles era. Secretary of State Dulles justified the series of Bismarckian alliances and agreements that he built in various parts of the world on the grounds that they would, as Kennan* had put it, contain communism. But another of their major purposes was that they would provide for the United States an official framework within which she would be able to put pressure on other nations over which she would not otherwise have any institutionalized leverage. The alliances could also give the United States far more scope for manœuvre in her dealings with the communist world (by enabling her to claim that she was speaking on behalf of many other nations as well as herself) than she would otherwise have had.

Nuclear and strategic policy, too, has displayed this desire on the part of those who are in charge of America's destiny to keep their own options as wide open as possible. Secretary Dulles expressed this as clearly as anyone when discussing in 1954 'the way to deter aggres-

*See p. 84.

sion'. What was needed, he said, was that 'the free community' should be 'willing and able to respond vigorously *at places and with means of its own choosing*'. (My italics.) The rocket-rattling of Dulles was not only designed to 'deter aggression'; it was also used as a means of maximizing American opportunities for exerting political influence abroad. America's occasional schemes for 'sharing' her nuclear power (such as the suggestion that NATO should support a series of nuclear-powered surface ships, each of which would be manned by a crew drawn from a number of member countries) were principally intended to reassure those elements within Western Germany that questioned America's enormous influence over German affairs. On the other hand, the Test Ban Treaty of 1963, the 1968 Non-Proliferation Treaty with the Soviet Union and the talks on the limitation of strategic arms (the SALT talks) were, to some extent, motivated by a desire to prevent any real bargaining power in international affairs from slipping out of American hands. This is not to say, of course, that American nuclear policy was not planned in such a way as to minimize the likelihood of plunging the world into a nuclear war. But given this obvious priority, American policy was in part an expression of the natural desire felt by the policy-makers in Washington to maximize America's opportunities for taking independent initiatives in international affairs.

This American desire for freedom of action has not been confined to the diplomatic and military fields. Indeed, it has been argued by William A. Williams[7] and other experts that America's main foreign-policy objective throughout this century was to maintain and indeed to expand her overseas markets. According to this analysis, any international commitment by the United States could represent a potential limitation on America's opportunities for economic expansion. Therefore, many US statesmen have, since America's vast and speedy industrial revolution in the late nineteenth century, been reluctant to sign any but the most carefully worded international agreements. Characteristically, those agreements that they have themselves initiated have tended to be negative ones in which the signatories have agreed *not* to interfere with each other's trading (or other) interests. On the rare occasions on which American statesmen have seemed to tie American hands in some particular area (Roosevelt's alleged 'concessions' at Yalta are a case in point), the commitment has tended, later on, to be regretted or even repudiated. Finally, of course, American statesmen have been happy to help draw up and sign treaties (like the Kellogg–Briand Pact) which have given them an apparently honourable substitute for any hard international commitments.

The attempt to keep America's hands free in her dealings with other countries has been an important theme throughout the years covered by this book. But there have been others. One of them is anti-communism. The United States, having sent troops to try to keep Russia in the First World War, kept them there in the years after the Bolshevik Revolution to help the White Russians. When it became clear that the Bolshevik régime was there to stay, however, the United States withdrew its soldiers and refused until 1933 to grant the Bolsheviks diplomatic recognition. With the sole exception of the alliance in the Second World War, there has been no sustained period when American policy towards the Soviet Union has been anything more congenial than correct. On occasions, such as during the late 1940s and early 1950s, it has been a very great deal cooler. The occasional troughs in Soviet–American relations have tended to coincide with American fear and intolerance of the putative threat posed by domestic communists and what the John Birch Society used to call 'comsymps'. The total and undisguised contempt for the new régime in Moscow with which the period covered by this book begins coincided with the cruel red-baiting of Palmer and others at home, while the period of the height of the Cold War saw the rise of McCarthyism.

Another recurrent theme is xenophobia. In the 1920s, America's legislators were keeping the country out of the League of Nations and keeping foreigners out of America. Just before America's entry into the Second World War, the political air was reverberating with references to 'foreign wars' and 'local squabbles' on which the United States would be well advised to turn her back. *The Congressional Record* is full of stirring phrases, such as these (from a radio broadcast by Senator Capper of Kansas, inserted in *The Congressional Record* on 21 January 1941):

> The American people should not be compelled to make ... sacrifices just to interfere in the quarrels of Europe and Asia ...
> I say no American troops on foreign soil; no foreign troops on American soil.

The international co-operation necessitated by the war made blanket xenophobia unfashionable, although of course there were plenty of Japanese and Germans to dislike. Within a few years of the end of the Second World War, however, xenophobia began to reappear, sometimes in the form of further immigration restrictions* (the McCarran Bill was introduced in 1950), most conspicuously in the guise of hysterical fear of the Soviet Union.

Many of the pronouncements that have been made at one time or another by members of the American political élite have been characterized by a certain moralism or self-righteousness. All governing élites, of course, tend to appeal to moral norms when expressing their policy preferences; one of the rules of the political game is that, publicly at least, you always claim that your actions and statements arise from what you consider not expedient but 'right'. But American policy-makers have been particularly prone to make frequent appeals to ethical norms, as though such appeals were a means of pre-empting criticism by making it immoral. A number of specific policies have been proposed and defended on purely moral grounds. One thinks, for instance, of the 'Stimson Doctrine' of non-recognition which was, according to McGeorge Bundy, Stimson's official biographer, 'a moral weapon, a moral sanction . . . designed . . . less as a method of bringing the Japanese to reason than a method of reasserting the American conviction that no good whatever could come from the breach of treaties.' Or take President Carter's condemnation of Soviet repression of dissidents. As for the more general assumption of American virtue, this was well illustrated by John Foster Dulles in a speech that he made in September 1952, just before he became Secretary of State. He said in part:

> Few would doubt that the past dynamism of our nation has genuinely stemmed from a profound popular faith in such concepts as justice and righteousness and from the sense that our nation had a mission to promote these ideals by every peaceful means.
> Soviet Communism reflects a view totally different from the United States' historic view. Its creed is materialistic and atheistic. It does not admit of any moral law.

One common characteristic of American foreign policy that should be mentioned is that the policy-makers have often seemed to eschew patience and to rely instead on the short, sharp, irrevocable, total solution, the cure-all, the wonder drug. In their analysis of problems, similarly, there is a tendency to oversimplify what are often complex issues and to interpret various shades of grey as though they were all black or white (see, for instance, the foregoing quotation from Dulles).

---

* Among xenophobes of the early 1950s, one of the more colourful was Representative John E. Rankin of Mississippi. In a speech on the floor of the House in October 1951, Rankin said: 'I am opposed to breaking down our immigration laws and flooding this country with the riff-raff of the Old World . . . It is time to wake up and put a stop to this undesirable infiltration, if we are going to save America for Americans.'

This predilection for the quick answer is no doubt partly derived from America's frontier experience, when a man had to clear the forest and be quick on the draw — to act first and then, if he had time, to think afterwards — if he were to survive.

Examples of impatient and oversimple policies are legion. One thinks, to take three modern instances, of the invasions of Cuba in April 1961 and of the Dominican Republic just over four years later and of the *Mayaguez* incident in 1975. As for the snappy and comfortably polarized analysis of world affairs, President Johnson defined the Vietnam War, in February 1966, as a 'conflict to decide if aggression and terror are the way of the future or whether free men are to decide their own course.'

Finally, American foreign policy has frequently been predicated on the assumption that other people are really embryonic Americans or at least that they should aspire to be. A corollary of this is the assumption that most foreigners should, under normal circumstances, like (or at least admire or respect) America and Americans. The first point is well illustrated by a remark made by Dean Acheson, who justified the new foreign aid programme shortly after the war on the grounds that 'we are willing to help people who believe the way we do, to continue to live the way they want to live'. And as for the second point, here is Dulles trying in July 1953 to persuade the Senate Appropriations Committee to accept increased aid to the Middle East:

> Our basic political problem in this vitally important region is to improve the attitude of the Moslem states toward the western democracies, including the United States, *because our prestige in the area has been steadily declining since the War.* (Italics mine.)

All of these various themes are, of course, closely interconnected. Foreign policy pronouncements by members of the American political élite often contain more than one of the characteristics that we have outlined. Look at some of the following examples:

Xenophobia plus anti-communism plus moralism

In a speech on the Senate floor on 13 December 1950, Senator Jenner of Indiana, whose powers as a phrasemaker would have been amusing had they not been so misguided, lambasted the foreign policies of the Roosevelt and Truman administrations. He said in part: 'For too many years we have been the pawns of alien forces — until, today, America, once the land of the free and the home of the brave, has been reduced to the role of a flunky to an international Frankenstein.' And who is that Frankenstein? Just in case his message had not come across, Jenner said later in his speech that 'the time has come to smash the Communist—Fair Deal internationalist conspiracy that is destroying us'.

National self-interest plus moralism

Lyndon B. Johnson, no doubt a little intoxicated by the election atmosphere in which he was revelling at the time, had this to say in October 1964 about his country's conduct of foreign affairs: 'Of course, we act out of enlightened self-interest . . . But the pages of history can be searched in vain for another power whose pursuit of self-interest was so infused with grandeur of spirit and morality of purpose.' In 1977, America's ambassador to the United Nations, Andrew Young, was more blunt and said in a *Newsweek* interview: 'I would define morality as enlightened self-interest.'

Mild xenophobia plus a powerful desire to be liked

Joseph P. Kennedy, in a speech in December 1950, talked of the enormous sacrifices involved in fighting the Korean War, and said: 'What have we in return for this effort? Friends? We have far fewer friends than we had in 1945.' He did not see why America should go out of its way to help other nations and station troops 'on the European or Asian continent', for this policy 'has made us no foul-weather friends'

Oversimplification plus anti-communism plus a touch of moralism

Dean Rusk justified the 1964 foreign aid programme on the grounds that it helps to determine 'whether peoples of newly emerging nations seeking stability and growth will be able to attain such goals within the community of free nations or whether the promises of totalitarianism will lure them towards Communist domination and loss of freedom'.

Moralism plus foreigners as aspirant Americans

Some years after his political career was over, one of the wisest of American foreign policy-makers, J. William Fulbright, described US attitudes like this: 'Americans like to think of themselves as a very superior, unique people. We hope other countries will move toward values that we approve.'

The statements that we have quoted in this section are taken from a wide variety of people. Some of the statements were made by responsible government officials and were meant primarily for an inter-

national and sophisticated audience; others, such as the speech by
Jenner, were made by irresponsible (in both senses) speakers and
were intended primarily, no doubt, for domestic consumption. A man
like Acheson would never have made a speech like Jenner's, and it
would be absurd to claim that *all* pronouncements on American
foreign policy and all actual policies have been derived from one set of
attitudes common to all members of the various élites in the United
States. Our claim, a more modest one, is that the various themes that
we have distinguished have all, in different guises, appeared time and
again in statements on foreign policy by American leaders from all
parts of the political spectrum. There are many good reasons in
American history and social psychology why these should be the
recurrent themes and attitudes; space and the nature of our task do
not permit a discussion of these factors here. But one distinction must
be made. The themes that have been discussed must be understood as
existing on at least two very important and distinct levels: on the one
hand, they represent attitudes, hopes, and fears with which American
society as a whole (and therefore, to some extent, her political élite) is
deeply imbued. As such, they act, to a limited extent, as pressures on
the policy-makers. But, on the other hand, they also provide the
policy-makers with a splendid framework within which to gain popular approval and legitimacy for policies that, while considered desirable, might not otherwise be popularly appreciated. When Secretary
Rusk resorted to the jargon of popular prejudice, for example, what he
was really trying to do was to justify the foreign aid programme in
terms that would activate in its favour the widest public support. A
good example of this technique is provided by President Truman
who, in his speech introducing the doctrine that became known by his
name, made shrewd use of a rhetorically impressive (but intellectually grossly oversimplified) analysis of world problems into a
conflict between the goodies ('us') and the baddies (who, although
unnamed, were, of course, the communists). There was also in his
speech a constant assumption that 'our' aims and values were those
that the peoples of the rest of the world would normally wish to
emulate. He said in part:

> We shall not realize our objectives ... unless we are willing to help free peoples to
> maintain their free institutions and their national integrity against aggressive
> movements that seek to impose upon them totalitarian régimes ...
>   If we falter in our leadership, we may endanger the peace of the world – and we
> shall surely endanger the welfare of our own nation.

To some extent, no doubt, President Truman himself was convinced by the literal meaning of his own argument. But he was also trying in this speech to persuade a conservative Congress and a sceptical public that American foreign policy should set forth on a totally new and untried direction. The best way of convincing people to try new and dangerous experiments is often to convince them that, in fact, the experiment is not really a new departure at all but merely an application to new conditions of old and tried principles. In his speech, Truman was clearly appealing to every traditional foreign policy prejudice in the book; he was couching his revolutionary appeal in the comfortable language of tradition. And his new policy was accepted.

A few words must be said finally about the role of public opinion in the story of American foreign policy. The most important thing to say is that the role is often exaggerated in the minds of the public themselves, in the minds of their leaders, and in the writings of subsequent historians. The great 'American public' has, of course, always been fiercely proud of its right to know what is going on and of the direct effect that it has (according to the best democratic theory) on the policies of its government. This interpretation of the role of public opinion is one that has been substantially accepted by many of America's leaders. Franklin D. Roosevelt, for instance, would not infrequently justifstify a proposed step (or, more often, proposed inaction) both in public and in private on the grounds that it was what 'the public' wanted. Otherwise excellent books are often full of references to 'the American public' (as though this were a definable historical entity) and are at pains to try and show that American foreign policy was an exact response to the state of 'public opinion' at any given time.

Despite the widely shared assumption that 'public opinion' has a direct effect on foreign policy, however, it has been persuasively shown that this is not normally so. The most that can be said for the influence of public opinion is that, in the words of V. O. Key[8], it acts rather like 'a system of dikes which channel public action or which fix a range of discretion within which government may act or within which debate at official levels may proceed'. In this negative role it can be influential and can help to prevent the political leadership from taking initiatives that might prove unpopular. President Ford, for instance, was not able to give increased military aid to the Thieu régime in early 1975 before the fall of South Vietnam or, indeed, substantial sums for Vietnamese rehabilitation after the war, because public opinion, clearly reflected in the polls and in Congress, wanted nothing to do with the fate of Vietnam by that stage.

'The public', of course, is a convenient fiction. There is no single American public, nor is there any single 'opinion' held by that mythical public. Each American is, rather, a member of many interlocking and overlapping groups — or publics — each of which tends to encourage its members to hold certain opinions about a limited range of subjects. In those few respects in which there is anything approaching a nationwide consensus, the national opinion almost invariably constitutes a pressure for conservatism rather than one for innovation. And of these nationally held opinions and attitudes, those that concern foreign policy are generally so vague as to be of no serious relevance to the policy-making élite — except, possibly, to suggest to them certain obvious bounds beyond which their decisions should not normally stray.

Far from being the prime determinant of foreign policy, therefore, public opinion tends to be ignorant, apathetic, and impotent. The reasons for this are not hard to find. Foreign policy usually deals with places that are geographically remote and with problems that are not perceived by the majority of Americans as having any direct effect on them. Furthermore, many Americans have, for complex reasons arising out of various factors in their history, tended to look with distaste upon the possibility of their government becoming inextricably involved in foreign affairs — a feeling that reappeared strongly in the aftermath of the Vietnam War. This widely accepted idea of American exclusiveness has had the by-product of making some Americans shrug their shoulders impatiently at news of their country's dealings abroad.

But even if 'public opinion' were more aware, more articulate, and better organized (as, on a few issues, it sometimes is), the likelihood of its becoming a major influence on the course of American foreign policy is minuscule. For one thing, the makers of foreign policy ensure that many of their actions are not publicly known at all or are, at the very least, not widely publicized. And, in any case, the options available to these policy-makers are largely set by external factors — factors over which they (and *a fortiori* domestic public opinion) can have little control or influence.

Four

THE WAR AND AFTER

The effect of the war years

Never do domestic and foreign policy intertwine as much as in time of war. And the Second World War − the most all-pervasive and truly 'total' war in history − had a profound and lasting effect on every aspect of American domestic life.

In the first place, of course, America's 15 million men and women under arms endured a series of experiences that were deeply to colour the rest of their lives. Some of them experienced physical and spiritual deprivation that they would not have considered themselves capable of withstanding; they saw hunger and disease and death on a scale that made the American Depression of the previous decade seem mild by comparison. And they lived a type of life and submitted to a degree of discipline that seemed to make a mockery of some of the very values − freedom and individualism − for which they thought they were striving.

There is a mass of impressionistic evidence concerning the effects of the war experience on the American forces. There are diaries, written memoirs, films, novels, and of course the memories of millions of Americans in their forties or older. Some of the most concentrated and carefully organized evidence is to be found in what was, in its day, a ground-breaking work of sociological research: *The American Soldier*, by Samuel Stouffer and others[1]. Stouffer and his colleagues examined the ways in which American soldiers adjusted to army life in general and to combat situations in particular. The army, unlike most American professions, openly demanded adherence to a set of undemocratic values − rigid obedience, strict social stratification, the impossibility of quitting, and so on. The authoritarian atmosphere of the army provoked considerable resentment which tended to increase as the war progressed. On the other hand, most soldiers (particularly those who had received a better education) felt that they were doing a necessary job and that it was their duty to try to rise within the army's rigid status system and not to rebel against it. Many, of course, did not rise very far in the army, and this was often frustrating. It was particularly so for soldiers who had enjoyed moderately high status in civilian life. Stouffer reports that the man whose rank was lower than he thought it should be often complained that promotions were based on favouritism and personal factors (a point which had some substance according to the Doolittle Committee, which reported in May 1946). Complaints of all sorts (especially from enlisted men) tended to increase as the war progressed: officers were respected less; job allocations were increasingly criticized; morale, initially high, began to tail off badly. Some of the men began to wonder, as one of them wrote, if the army didn't 'represent the very things that we are fighting against'. Particularly poignant was the attitude of the black who, not infrequently, found himself at home in the army only because he was already accustomed to the experience of being kept at the bottom of a rigidly stratified social system.

On the other hand, there was virtual unanimity in the army that the United States was fighting on the right side and that the war had to be won whatever the cost. The soldiers were not quite so sure as to why the United States was in the right and the Axis countries in the wrong: when asked, they would tend to resort to general slogans about America being on the side of 'freedom' or 'peace'. Similarly, there was great confusion as to why the war had started in the first place. The men knew all about Pearl Harbor, of course, but (and this is in sharp contrast to the certainty, twenty-five years earlier, that the war was 'the Kaiser's War' and that it was being fought 'to make the world safe for democracy') they were not sure whether they were fighting for Big Business, or for American values, or for British Imperialism, or against Japanese Imperialism, or against Hitler and fascism. There were not many soldiers who felt a sense of personal responsibility for the way the war went. Most of them were quite anxious, after doing what they assessed as being their own disagreeable but necessary stint, to get out of the army and let their place be taken by somebody else.

This rather gloomy picture of the American soldier is not quite the picture that the government tried to encourage, but this should not surprise us. In wartime the men were constantly deprived of most of the normal accoutrements of civilian life and, not infrequently, were exposed to serious physical danger and the real possibility of death; the authorities, on the other hand, had to strain every nerve in order to try to keep up the morale of all the unfortunates involved in the war effort and to persuade them to pull their weight. There was a constant tension between the natural inclination of all the participants to grumble and their reluctant conviction that they could not afford to do so. As we have seen, there were grumbles in plenty. But the military and political authorities — by encouraging the troops to 'hate' the Germans and Japanese, and by talking about 'our boys' as though they were uniquely virtuous and heroic — did a remarkably good job in maintaining army morale.

Army life did not concern the soldier only as a soldier; it made its demands on him too as a person. Many of the social developments of postwar America have at least some of their roots in the demands made by army life in the Second World War. In particular, the startling postwar rise in the rates of marriages, divorces, and births* and the rise in juvenile crime and delinquency, for instance, were all to some extent products of the disruptions created by the fact that millions of men had been whisked out of civilian life for an indefinite period and had then returned three-and-a-half years later. A taste for foreign travel, too, was acquired by many young people whose war service took them abroad for the first time. One of the more important postwar social changes, occasioned in part by the experience of army life, concerned race relations. As we shall see in Chapter 5, there were many reasons why the civil rights movement and the black revolution burst forth when they did. But there is abundant evidence to suggest that wartime experiences generally and army life in particular had a great deal to do with preparing the ground for the racial crisis of the later 1950s and the 1960s.

Blacks served in the US Army in the Second World War in almost the proportion — 8 or 9 per cent — that their numbers in American society warranted. Almost one-third of them were from the North (compared with only one-fifth of those who served in the First World War) and their educational level — overwhelmingly higher than that of the black soldiers twenty-five years earlier — was very nearly equal to that of southern white soldiers. Despite all this, however, blacks were clearly treated as different from and inferior to their white

* See Figs. 5.3, 5.4 and 5.5, pp. 166–7.

comrades. They found it harder to become officers, were kept for the most part in segregated units, and were discouraged from fraternizing with white soldiers. In countries where little significance was attached to racial differences, the white GIs brought their prejudices with them so that, for instance, word was soon spread among the English that 'nice' girls would not go out with 'coloured' American soldiers.

But the pressures of war made Jim Crow habits hard to maintain. Many prejudiced whites, serving alongside blacks, were forced to discover that blacks were not necessarily inferior fellows after all; blacks, by the same token, discovered that they had more in common with whites than they had perhaps previously realized. And, of course, they were all fighting a common enemy whose crimes included a blatant disregard for democracy and the liberty of the individual and, in the case of Germany, racism. The war, in other words, forced many whites and many blacks to realize as never before how close together were their most basic aims and interests. The hopes and aspirations of the black were raised; he really felt (despite the frequent reminders that, even in the US Army, he was considered as being only second class) that the war was being fought to end fascism and racism. Those blacks who were most sensitive and earnest regarding the aspirations of their race were also to prove among the most courageous soldiers of the war.

And then it was all over. Millions of soldiers came home in 1945 and 1946, the white soldiers hoping that life could be just the same as when it was interrupted by the call to arms, the black ones hoping, on the contrary, that life would be very different. They were both in for a shock. For all the troops, as we shall see later, the period of adjustment after demobilization presented a host of major social and psychological hurdles. But the black GI — particularly the Southerner — had added problems. He had perhaps risked his life on Guam or Wake Island or in Tripoli or Germany in defence of what he had been taught were the American values of freedom and democracy — and yet he could not buy a Coca Cola at the drugstore around the corner. Discrimination was not a new experience for him; but somehow it seemed after the war all the more degrading to its victim.

Back home, black leaders and liberal whites had in their own way been helping to set the scene for the civil rights movement that burst forth a decade later. It was in the dark days just before and during the war that the Gandhian tactic of non-violent non-co-operation was first used to a significant extent by the proponents of Negro rights.

The one really tangible achievement — Roosevelt's establishment of a Fair Employment Practices Committee in June 1941 — was extracted from the government after A. Philip Randolph had threatened to organize a march on Washington.

But demands produced counter-demands and for every advance made by black Americans there came a setback. The greatest setback was the hideous tragedy of the race riots in June 1943 in Detroit and elsewhere. Yet there is little doubt that the war experience, for whites and blacks, whether civilians or soldiers, did have the overall effect of bringing a little nearer to the surface the hitherto largely repressed aspirations of black Americans and also the guilt feelings of many of their white compatriots.

Blacks were not the only minority group whose fortunes were buffeted this way and that by the war. Some groups benefited from the war. Italo-Americans, for instance, many of them painfully uncertain of their status in America and even divided in their national allegiance during the difficult pre-war years, found that Pearl Harbor and the war against the Axis forced the issue for them. And, when it came to making a choice, scarcely one of them preferred Mussolini to Uncle Sam. For the overwhelming majority, the war proved both to them and to their non-Italian neighbours that an American of Italian origin could be just as patriotic as the next man. Jews, similarly, often a little suspect in earlier American history, found that their status in society became increasingly favourable, partly because of the conspicuous and brilliant part played by many recent Jewish immigrants in the war effort, and partly as a result of the sympathy engendered by the stories that leaked out about the atrocities in Germany.

Japanese Americans (including native-born Americans of Japanese descent) were less fortunate. Most of them lived on the West Coast, from which they were evacuated by federal decree. They were made to live in special government compounds and to suffer, in the name of 'security', all sorts of injustices and indignities. The whole episode seems to have been motivated by a combination of, at best, misdirected patriotism and, at worst, irrational hysteria. There was no evidence, throughout the war, of any serious subversion or disloyalty on the part of Americans of Japanese descent, and the evacuation order was one of the most blatant examples of government disregard for civil liberties in the whole of American history.

One of the overall effects of the war, however, was that it tended by and large to obscure racial and ethnic differences rather than to silhouette them. Indeed, it did more. It produced a degree of conformism and individual anonymity probably unique in the history of American society. Anonymity was, of course, to be expected in the army. But among civilians, too, individualism and eccentricity were at a premium. The factory worker submerged his personal plans and hopes and made his first priority the winning of the war. If, as occasionally happened, he was sent to another job or another plant on short notice, he was expected to comply. Women, too, joined the huge labour force and often gave the impression that they thought of themselves as workers first and as women only a very distant second. They wore slacks and tended not to wear make-up. And, like the men, they found that their working life was regulated from above to a degree that would have been intolerable in peacetime. If these men and women had any spare time, they might well have spent it listening to radio programmes or reading magazine articles that had possibly been vetted by the Office of War Information (OWI).

But these pressures towards conformism, compliance, and anonymity, unpleasant though they might have been, were several degrees removed from the war itself. The United States was not occupied; the continental United States was never bombed. To many Americans who never left the country, the war was little more than a nagging inconvenience. Sugar and gasoline were rationed. Housing was sometimes appallingly inadequate. But the war came at the end of a decade of gruelling depression and, by contrast, the war years were -- except for those who had to go to the combat areas — not unpleasant. So remote and irrelevant did the war seem to some Americans, in fact, that a remonstrative catch-phrase became popular: 'Don't cha know there's a war on?'

In some ways, indeed, the war was positively beneficial. In particular, it did what the New Deal had never succeeded in doing and ended unemployment. It also had the related effect of activating to the full America's productive capacity. A new series of alphabet agencies was set up just before and during the war. Some of the earlier of these were not very successful, but once the United States had entered the war and increased production had become a vital priority, agencies like the War Production Board (WPB) under Donald M. Nelson and, even more so, James F. Byrnes' Office of War Mobilization (OWM) achieved phenomenal results. A glimpse at Table 4.1 will give some idea of the enormous productivity stimulated by the war. On the question of productivity, Donald Nelson was to write later:

Between 1941 and the end of 1944 an almost magical transformation of American industry took place. Huge new plants dotted every section of the country. The agricultural South became heavily industrialized. Annual production of steel ingots rose 9 million tons. Aluminum production rose from 807 million pounds to 2,179 million ... Plane production, in dollar value, was multiplied by nearly ten, tanks by five, naval shipping by more than five, cargo shipping by more than ten. In 1938 our total output of fabricated metal had been 13 billion dollars' worth, and in 1944 it was 70 billions; while in the same period the machine tool industry alone expanded production by more than seven times[2].

Table 4.1. Index of manufacturing production (1947–9 = 100)

1920	39	1941	88
1921	30	1942	110
1922	39	1943	133
1923	45	1944	130
1924	43	1945	110
1925	48	1946	90
1926	50	1947	100
1927	50	1948	103
1928	52	1949	97
1929	58	1950	113
1930	48	1951	121
1931	39	1952	125
1932	30	1953	136
1933	36	1954	127
1934	39	1955	140
1935	46	1956	144
1936	55	1957	145
1937	60	1958	139
1938	46	1959	158
1939	57	1960	163
1940	66		

Nelson went on to mention one or two individual production wizards, such as Henry Kaiser who, by applying mass-production techniques to the building of cargo ships, was able to produce a ship that had taken 280 days to build during the First World War in a mere 80 days in 1942 – and, by 1944, in 22 days!

The battle for productivity posed new problems of its own. There was, for instance, the latent inconsistency between the traditional *laissez-faire* atmosphere of the American industrial scene and the extreme regimentation necessitated by the war. The 'excesses' of the New Deal at which some industrial leaders had baulked were nothing as compared with the strict and rigid controls under which they had to operate after Pearl Harbor. Organized labour, too, while sometimes pleased and sometimes upset at the innovations of the thirties, was a little shocked when told by the government that strikes − or even, under some circumstances, the normal processes of collective bargaining − were to be ruled out for the duration of the war. Despite these unprecedented infringements upon the normal economic processes, however, there was a remarkable level of compliance with the requests of the government on both sides of industry.

A second problem created by the need for massive and speedy production was of special concern to leaders of industry. Only a few years before, the sensational revelations of the Nye Committee had demonstrated that many industrialists had reaped enormous profits from the First World War. It was only a short step from this undoubted fact to the rather more questionable assumption that the war had been fought primarily in order to make profits for these men. This unfair and oversimplified interpretation of the conclusions of the Nye Committee had been eagerly lapped up by a public whose faith in the moral stature of big businessmen had already been undermined by the Great Crash and the revelations of the Pecora Committee. By 1940 many American industrialists were understandably sensitive about their popular reputations. While many of them were no doubt anxious to do all they could to help build up the nation's resources, they did not want to lay themselves open to new charges of war profiteering. The administration in Washington helped some of them out of this particular predicament by inviting them to sit on government-sponsored boards and, indeed, brought many distinguished businessmen more or less directly into government service. One famous example of this move from the world of business to that of public administration was Donald Nelson, who left Sears Roebuck to work for the government in 1942. Another was William S. Knudsen of General Motors, who was put in charge of the Advisory Commission of the Council of National Defense and who, in January 1941, became with Sidney Hillman the co-director of the new Office of Production Management (OPM). Between 1942 and 1945 Knudsen was production director for the US War Department. It was during the war, too, that James V. Forrestal, a distinguished investment banker, joined the US Government (as Under-Secretary of the Navy). Forrestal was later to become America's first Secretary of Defense. Another future Secretary of Defense, Robert A. Lovett, was also a leading banker until the war, when he was persuaded to accept the post of Assistant Secretary of War for Air. Edward Stettinius Jr, who was to become Secretary of State in the last months of the war, abandoned a phenomenally successful career in General Motors and US Steel just before the war in order to work for the government.

By bringing people of this quality into government service (and by refraining from bringing anti-trust suits against the most blatantly monopolistic combines so long as they were clearly trying to help the nation's war effort) the administration was in effect lending its own prestige to big business and thus pre-empting much of the ill-informed popular criticism that might otherwise have been levelled at the latter. It was thus creating for itself a valuable and constructive partnership with the industrial world that had never seemed really viable in the thirties. But it was doing even more than that. By tying so closely together the business and governmental — and military — worlds, Roosevelt and his colleagues were, without realizing it, pre-paring the ground for what was to become variously known in the 1950s and 1960s as the 'power élite', the 'military—industrial com-plex', and, more ominously, the 'warfare state'.

But the necessities of war, while creating some new problems, also forced Americans to try to solve many old ones. The dire conditions of the early forties engendered a resourcefulness and an inventiveness that were to be of benefit to America and the world in the years to follow. Any nation at war needs colossal supplies of rubber, but many of the most productive rubber-producing areas in the world were cut off by the Japanese conquests in South-East Asia. In 1942, accord-ingly, Roosevelt set up a special committee headed by Bernard Baruch to examine the problem. Baruch recommended severe cut-backs in the uses of rubber, but also, more significantly, he made shrewd suggestions that led to the establishment of a major synthetic-rubber industry in the United States.

Synthetic rubber was only one of several important scientific advances occasioned by the exigencies of the war. In the fields of biology and medicine, for instance, the special demands of war resulted in the greatly increased production and use of penicillin and dried blood plasma. It was during the war, too, that DDT powder was developed — a pesticide that, whatever the disadvantages that led to its eventual withdrawal, proved invaluable for troops in the Pacific who prior to its discovery had been frequently infected by various bugs with such diseases as typhus and malaria. The short-term effect of these medical advances was that a far higher proportion of troops injured in the Second World War survived than had been the case in the First World War. The longer-term effect was that the postwar average expectation of life was to be pushed noticeably higher than ever before. Such are the perverse side-effects of war.

The physicists and engineers, too, were stimulated by the demands of the war into some noteworthy achievements. There were, for instance, dramatic developments in aeronautics and electronics. By 1945 there were jet planes that were flying at more than three times the speed of their fastest pre-war predecessors. The war saw, too, the first extensive use of radar and of the high-frequency short-wave radio-telephones — two inventions that saved countless Allied lives. Important advances were also made in the use to which the combustion engine was put. The Second World War, like previous wars, was essentially a fight about territory, and the principal weapons used were, as in the First World War, tanks. But the tanks of the 1940s were faster, more efficient, and better protected than anything that the generals of a generation earlier could have imagined. In terms of weapons and tactics, therefore, the war was a traditional type of war; but the scientists made sure that it would at least be the most efficient war in history.

But by all odds the most spectacular scientific achievement of the war was the development of the atomic bomb. Between 1942 and 1945 more than 150,000 men and women — among them some of the world's most brilliant physicists — put in some of the hardest and most dedicated work of their lives. The 2 billion-dollar Manhattan Project was the best-kept secret of the war. Many of the people actually working on the project (and most of Roosevelt's Cabinet) did not realize that the misty and esoteric activities at various remote spots on the map were all part of a co-ordinated attempt to make an atomic bomb. The political and military implications of the successful development of the bomb were stupendous and have been touched upon in Chapter 3. But they are hardly more awesome than the sheer technological problems involved in the initial creation of the bomb.

The scientific advances of the war years were considerable and were in many cases the result of long and dedicated work by both American and non-American scientists. But these advances were, in their own way, limited. They were primarily new applications of old knowledge, new ways of producing or administering or exploiting things that had already been invented. There was little really original scientific research during those hectic days; there was neither the time nor the money for the kind of leisured and unstructured research that produces epoch-making inventions. But the scientists did not complain. For the most part, they were happy that their work could be of practical use in defeating the enemy. Indeed, like many of the leaders on both sides of industry, American scientists voluntarily accepted a degree of government regulation of their activities that would under normal circumstances have been totally at variance with their outlook. Under Vannevar Bush, himself a noted electrical engineer, the government set up the Office of Scientific Research and Development (OSRD), which was composed of subdivisions dealing with the various sciences. The OSRD played a vital part in the American war effort, and was a singularly successful example of the way in which a nation's brainpower can be harnessed to its vital needs in time of emergency.

Even America's writers and artists were in many cases induced to apply their special talents to the needs of war. A number of authors joined the Writers' War Board, through which the government channelled its requests for special literary pieces on war themes. The Office of War Information (which grew out of Archibald MacLeish's Office of Facts and Figures) would feed special messages to popular radio comedians such as Bob Hope. And the brave writers who sent back press reports from the combat areas, for example Ernie Pyle and Raymond Clapper, always bore in mind the official request that press stories should in no way lower public morale. There were, of course, plenty of artists of one sort or another who did not see why their talents should be enlisted — and, perhaps, stifled — by the immediate needs of war. These men were not unpatriotic, but they simply felt that the war was not something with which they could (yet, at any rate) concern themselves as artists. And perhaps they were right, for many of the most enduring artistic works of the war years had nothing to do with the war at all. On the stage, those years saw the first productions of *Oklahoma!*, *The Glass Menagerie*, and *The Skin of Our Teeth*, while the most widely read prose works included *Forever Amber* and *The Robe*. It was not until the late 1940s and early 1950s that important works inspired by the war began to appear — works such as *The Naked and the Dead*, *The Wall*, and *From Here to Eternity*.

If anything needed to be regimented during the war, it was the American economy. One of the constant and recurring problems of the years just before and during America's participation in the war was inflation. The sudden upsurge in productivity and employment occasioned by the war had, initially, some beneficial effects on an economy that had been flagging ever since the autumn of 1929. But the inevitable rapid rise in costs and prices was viewed by the administration with considerable alarm. The Office of Price Administration (headed at first by the distinguished New Deal economist Leon Henderson and later among others by Chester Bowles) tried to peg prices on some important consumer goods, and was responsible for the rationing of some foods and fuels. But, despite the authority vested in it by the Emergency Price Control Act of 1942, the OPA lacked real coercive power and, in particular, it let agricultural prices slip through its net.

For the first time since the first Agricultural Adjustment Act in 1933, America's farmers were officially encouraged to produce at full capacity and — for the first time in two decades — found themselves making handsome profits. But one result was that, in the months before and after Pearl Harbor, the consumer price index began to rise wildly — with food prices leading the way. The OPA might have held the price levels down a percentage point or two with its little rationing schemes, but it succumbed to the Farm Belt's demands that, if agricultural prices were to be frozen, then the level should be at 110 per cent of parity. By mid 1942, accordingly, the domestic economy was severely afflicted by rapid and dangerous inflation. And into the upward spiral that had been started by the needs of war and the demands of the agricultural community were drawn, inevitably, America's anxious business and labour interests.

Just after Labor Day, 1942, Roosevelt took the initiative. On 7 September he sent a powerful message to Congress asking it

> ... to pass legislation under which the President would be specifically authorized to stabilize the cost of living, including the prices of all farm commodities. The purpose should be to hold farm prices at parity, or at levels of a recent date, whichever is higher.
>
> I ask Congress to take this action by the first of October. Inaction on your part by that date will leave me with an inescapable responsibility to the people of this country to see to it that the war effort is no longer imperilled by threats of economic chaos.
>
> In the event that the Congress should fail to act, and act adequately, I shall accept the responsibility and I will act.
>
> At the same time that farm prices are stabilized, wages can and will be stabilized also. This I will do.
>
> The President has the powers, under the Constitution and under Congressional Acts, to take measures necessary to avert a disaster which would interfere with the winning of the war.

On 2 October, Roosevelt duly signed the Anti-Inflation Act that had been sent to him by a cowed and reluctant Congress. The

President took immediate advantage of the provisions in the new Act and froze a whole series of wages, salaries, prices, and rents.

Roosevelt's hectoring attitude towards Congress did not endear him to them. The electorate, too, was not quite as captivated by FDR as it had been in the middle 1930s. In the 1942 mid term elections, a month after the signing of the Anti-Inflation Act, the Republicans did better than at any other time since 1930 and came close to obtaining a majority in the House of Representatives. Relations between Congress and the White House, which had been so extraordinarily congenial in the early years of the New Deal, and had never been really bad even in the later 1930s, were now to deteriorate rapidly. A loose coalition of Republicans and southern Democrats found itself in a position to defeat, if it so desired, any major measures of domestic reform that the administration — and, subsequently, the Truman administration — cared to put forward. On occasion, this clash between the two ends of Pennsylvania Avenue (Congress and the White House) became quite dramatic. In early 1944, for instance, Roosevelt appealed to Congress for a drastic new tax Bill; Congress responded by passing a revenue Bill that would produce only the merest fraction of the sum for which the President was hoping. Roosevelt sent the Bill back with a stinging veto message, but the reaction on Capitol Hill shocked him. His Majority Leader in the Senate, Alben W. Barkley, resigned his position in protest — and was promptly re-elected by acclamation by his Senate colleagues. And Congress went on to pass its own revenue Bill over Roosevelt's head.

A year later the President was again in serious trouble with Congress. Henry A. Wallace, formerly Roosevelt's idealistic Secretary of Agriculture and his second Vice-President, had been nominated for the unlikely post of Secretary of Commerce in place of Jesse Jones. But the Senate, which normally gives its consent to Cabinet appointments almost as a matter of course, threatened to veto this particular nomination. It was only after the removal of the Reconstruction Finance Corporation from the Department of Commerce that Roosevelt was able to persuade the Senate to consent to the Wallace nomination.

Whenever the American Government had been involved in a war, some of its most conspicuous critics have usually been found in Congress. Lincoln's difficulties with the Radical Republicans are one famous illustration of this point; a later example is Senator Fulbright's Foreign Relations Committee and its Vietnam hearings. During the period of America's involvement in the Second World

War there were hardly any congressmen who thought that the United States should not be fighting the war, but there were many who were profoundly critical of the way the administration was conducting it. Roosevelt did not have to tolerate anything quite so irksome as the Committee on the Conduct of the War that had plagued Lincoln. But his administration's activities were closely scrutinized by Congress throughout the war — above all by the scrupulously efficient Senate Committee to Investigate the National Defense Program headed by the little-known senator from Missouri, Harry S Truman.

The overall effect of the Second World War was to unite American society to an unprecedented degree. Despite the obvious exceptions to this general trend (the growing suspicion with which Americans of Japanese descent and their white compatriots regarded each other, for instance, or the recurrent friction between the White House and the Congress), the early forties saw a nation united in a common purpose — winning the war — to which almost all else was subordinated. What is remarkable is not so much the extent to which the fact of war took hold of the lives of all Americans, but the extent to which so many Americans prided themselves on their ability to carry on their lives as though there were no war. The physical hardships imposed by the war on Americans who stayed in the United States were, as we have seen, minimal — and far less arduous than those imposed a decade earlier by the onset of the Depression. Regardless of the gloomy stories from the European and Pacific theatres of war, millions of young Americans seemed content to sit back and gossip about Errol Flynn's rape cases, to listen adoringly to Bing Crosby, to try to rip the shirt off the back of Frank Sinatra, and to follow the interminable cartoon adventures of Little Orphan Annie and Dick Tracy. The more profound domestic effects of the war were, in truth, not really apparent while the war was still in progress. But they became increasingly evident in the years after 1945.

After the war

One of the effects was that the size and scope of the federal government had undergone a dramatic increase. The number of its civilian employees rose between 1941 and 1945 from 1·4 million to more than 3.8 million (see Fig. 2.3, p.57); federal expenditure was greater in those five years than in the whole of previous American history.

During the war years, the White House had shouldered the responsibility for a host of vital and pressing matters concerning all aspects of the nation's life. As had happened during the only previous military crisis of similar gravity, the Civil War, the executive branch of the federal government had in effect appropriated to itself a series of 'emergency' powers which, despite the best intentions, it could not wholly discard once the war was over. But if the war had bestowed new powers and responsibilities upon the executive branch, it has also exposed many of that branch's weaknesses. In 1947, therefore – the same year as the National Security Act, which among other things combined the War and Navy Departments into a unified Department of Defense – a commission was set up under the chairmanship of former President Hoover to examine the organization of the executive. Hoover's major finding was that the number of federal agencies should be drastically reduced, a recommendation that was shortly put into effect. Congress like the executive branch, had found its role and its responsibilities greatly expanded by the demands of the war. As soon as the war was over, it too made a determined effort to rationalize its activities and to maximize its efficiency. The Legislative Reorganization Act of 1946 reduced the unwieldy number of congressional committees, regulated the activities of lobbyists, and placed much-needed restrictions upon the type of amendments that could be tacked on to appropriations Bills. Thus the war, while increasing the powers and responsibilities of the federal government, also had the effect of forcing the government to try to organize its own activities in a more rational and efficient manner.

On the industrial world the war years had both a liberating and a repressive effect. To the extent that they stimulated massive and unprecedented productivity, they clearly did wonders for the management side of industry. But insofar as labour was virtually forced to subordinate its interests to the exigencies of the prolonged national emergency, the war – as became clear immediately after its termination – had had an effect not dissimilar to that of temporarily plugging a volcano. Even during the war itself an undercurrent of dissatisfaction in the ranks of labour had occasionally made itself felt. In May 1943, for instance, John L. Lewis' United Mine Workers went on strike against the pay rise formula that had been decided by the National War Labor Board – a strike to which Congress responded with the anti-union Smith-Connally Act. But for the most part America's industrial workers spent the war years working hard and long and loyally refrained from making demands for better wages or working conditions that would embarrass their employers or the government.

As soon as the war was over, however, an avalanche of demands descended upon America's employers. Some of the labour leaders, it seemed, wanted all the accumulated frustrations of the war years to be satisfied immediately. Within less than a year of the cessation of hostilities, the United States had seen several very serious strikes in a number of major industries including automobiles, steel, and the railroads. For its part, management was ill inclined to make any concessions unless it could at the same time make compensatory price rises. The American economy, therefore, was faced in the years immediately after the war with the imminent threat of severe inflation. And into the economic cauldron were thrown other dangerous ingredients. For one thing, there was a strong feeling that the unpopular price controls imposed during the war years should now be dropped. For another, a large proportion of American industry had been converted to the needs of war, so that there was inevitably an acute shortage of many of the consumer goods that millions of Americans had assumed would somehow be available once the war was over. These factors (which were only marginally offset by the temporary retention of some price controls and by the unemployment created by demobilization) combined to make the second half of the 1940s one of the most inflationary in American history.

Reactions to the postwar inflation were varied and often confused. There were those who, after the traumatic experiences of the Depression and the war (fortified, in some cases, by an understanding of the ideas of Lord Keynes), were quite convinced that the American economy needed to be more carefully regulated than would previously have been acceptable. This view was shared by most thinking liberals and it received its apotheosis in the Employment Act of 1946. This Act established the President's Council of Economic Advisers and, in effect, took the remarkable step of laying the responsibility for full employment at the door of the federal government in general and the White House in particular.

But if the crises of the Roosevelt years had as one by-product elevated the status of the expert economist and the avowed planner in the eyes of liberals, the economic difficulties immediately following FDR's death and the end of the war greatly reduced that of the industrial worker in the eyes of conservatives. (The Republican victories in the 1946 congressional elections posed an interesting contrast to the Labour victory in Britain a year earlier. Perhaps the only lesson that can be drawn is that the war-weary British and American citizens wanted a change once hostilities were over.*) By 1947 the predominantly Republican Eightieth Congress was passing, over President Truman's veto, the Taft–Hartley Act, which outlawed the closed shop and secondary boycotts, empowered the president to postpone threatened strikes, and declared that unions could be sued in the courts.

While debate ensued in Washington as to the respective merits of the various liberal and conservative solutions to the nation's economic ills, the inflation went right on. It was a considerable shock to many Americans – and particularly to the demobilized troops – to discover that eggs had gone up between 1940 and 1945 from 33 cents a dozen to 58 cents (by 1948 a dozen eggs would cost more than 72 cents) and that, in the short period 1941–5, the cost of ten pounds of potatoes had shot up from 23·5 cents to 49·3 cents.

But high prices were not the only problem that nagged postwar America. There were severe social problems as well. Time and again a young man would travel home after demobilization full of rosy hopes and illusions about the tranquil and idyllic future that awaited him. If he had a girl friend or a wife, he had possibly built her up in his mind's eye into a romantic symbol that no woman could really be; or he might well, in response to the pressures and temptations of army life, have been unfaithful to her. And, of course, she could just as easily have built him up – or down – in the same way during their long period of separation. For millions of couples the bitter-sweet years just after the war were dominated by the poignant problem of trying to develop a warm but practical affection for each other. And, for millions of young unmarried men and women, these years saw the even more difficult problems of developing a normal attitude towards the opposite sex after several years of artificially imposed celibacy often interspersed with periods of wild and nervous promiscuity.

* The contrasts between British and American political and social behaviour in the 1930s and 1940s would make a fascinating study. In the thirties, the Americans, experiencing unprecedented privations, encouraged and accepted a major series of social reforms; the British, during the same period, had a series of bland Conservative governments. During the war the British suffered more acutely than the Americans but complained less – and they evidently built up a desire to create a socialist Utopia once the enemy was defeated. In the United States, by contrast, there was a colossal sigh of relief once the minor deprivations of the war were over, and practically no serious desire for major social reform.

Above all, perhaps, the returning soldier had to face the problem of getting a job. In addition to being constantly threatened by inflation, the national economy was also largely geared to the needs of war. During the huge and slow process of reconversion, it was not always easy for the ex-GI to obtain employment. If he were lucky, he might have been sent to college under the GI Bill of Rights (see Fig. 5.2). But if he did not qualify for this generous programme, his inability to find a job could seem all the more degrading — especially when he looked around him and saw a labour force that now contained millions of women. Could they, he might understandably have begun to wonder, be taking his job? Some of the men gave up trying to get a job at all; feeling that they had just spent the best years of their lives fighting for Uncle Sam, they considered that it was about time Uncle Sam looked after them for a change. Thus a combination of resentment, insecurity, and downright disillusionment took root in millions of homes in the late 1940s.

People looked for escapes of various kinds. Some of the escapes that they found were 'positive' ones — notably a remarkable religious revival. Between 1945 and 1955 registered church membership rose from just over 70 million to more than 100 million and the list of best-selling novels was topped year after year by works with religious or biblical themes and settings, such as *The Robe, The Big Fisherman, The Silver Chalice,* and *The Miracle of the Bells.* In 1953 no fewer than six of the eight bestselling works of non-fiction were on religious themes. Perhaps the increased interest in religion in the decade after the war was more a reflection of the social and psychological needs of millions of lonely and frustrated Americans than of any profound national return to spiritual values. But the religious renaissance of those years did have the effect of stimulating many thoughtful Americans to examine their consciences and to reassess their own system of values.

The need to escape from the disillusionments of the real world had its 'negative' manifestations as well. In particular, many Americans began to show serious symptoms of a return to the narrow intolerance that had characterized the years that immediately followed the First World War. The scapegoat in both cases was the domestic communist, the allegedly 'disloyal' American. The ground was prepared by a series of unconnected and relatively minor incidents which all took place against a background of increasingly tense Cold War. In March 1947 (the month of the Truman Doctrine), the President issued an executive order establishing a programme to investigate and assess the loyalty of employees in the executive branch of the federal government. In August 1948, a disreputable former communist, Whittaker Chambers, caused a stir by accusing a high-ranking government official of impeccable Harvard–New Deal lineage, Alger Hiss, of having transmitted classified material to the Soviet Union. In 1949 eleven leaders of the American Communist Party were tried and convicted for having violated the Smith Act of 1940, which had made it illegal to preach the overthrow of the American Government or even to be a member of any society that advocated that aim. Meanwhile, the Hiss case dragged on; although the statute of limitations made it impossible for him to be convicted of treason, he was eventually found guilty of perjury and given a heavy sentence. In September 1949 Truman announced that the Soviet Union had already detonated an atomic bomb. A month later the Chinese Communists took power in Peking.

By the beginning of 1950 American foreign policy was implacably at odds with the Soviet Union and official government pronouncements repeatedly emphasized the monstrous threat to the 'free world' posed by the malevolent international communist conspiracy. At home, popular fears and tensions, continually stimulated by ubiquitous rumours of disloyalty in high places, began to mount sharply. In January 1950, Hiss was eventually convicted. A few days later President Truman announced that work was to go ahead with the so-called 'hydrogen or super-bomb'. If this announcement was supposed to appease the red-baiters, it failed. They had had their appetites whetted by the Hiss case and were in no mood to stop now. Four days after the hydrogen bomb announcement the British released the news that Klaus Fuchs, one of her most brilliant wartime atomic scientists, had confessed that he had systematically betrayed atomic secrets to the Soviets. The red-baiters howled long and loud. Not only could America not trust her own leaders, but her allies, too, were tainted by communist subversion. The most notorious products of this vindictive and suspicious atmosphere were the ruthless investigations of the House Un-American Activities Committee (HUAC) and, above all, of Senator Joseph R. McCarthy.

Under normal circumstances the rantings of the Republican senator from Wisconsin against alleged (but generally unnamed) communists in high government posts would probably have gone largely unheeded. But McCarthy, in his desire to get national prominence, had hit upon the perfect issue at the perfect time. His first sally was to use a Lincoln Day rally in February 1950 as an opportunity to accuse the State Department of knowingly harbouring communists and fellow-travellers. When he was asked by a special senatorial sub-committee under Senator Tydings of Maryland to produce some names, McCarthy proved evasive. He would mention a name but deny that he was making a formal charge, he would ask for more time to collect evidence, or he would, under pretence of a more important engagement, simply not turn up to a scheduled hearing. In July the Tydings Committee issued a lengthy report which cast a very dim light on Senator McCarthy. In official Washington and among the nation's intellectuals McCarthy's wild and often unsubstantiated accusations tended to be belittled somewhat scornfully.

But in the far reaches of the nation McCarthy was becoming big news. Unsolicited funds poured into his office from admiring patriotic organizations throughout the country. 'McCarthy Clubs' sprang up in all sorts of places. And — a sure sign that the man had 'arrived' — McCarthy press conferences were always eagerly attended by hordes of scoop-hungry journalists. It was becoming clear, as the months lengthened into years, that he had become the focus of a small but vociferous Right-wing element in American politics and that, as a potentially influential figurehead, his antics could no longer be dismissed with a casual shrug. For all their dislike of him, many liberals and moderates began to fear him. The senator was riding high.

Alas for his ego, McCarthy found that the Korean War and the presidential election of 1952 were getting most of the big headlines. He did what he could to keep on the front page. He issued a stinging attack on a man regarded by President Truman as 'the greatest living American', General George Marshall. Marshall, the wartime Chief of Staff, later Truman's second Secretary of State, father of the European Recovery Program and, at the time of McCarthy's smear, Secretary of Defence, was deeply respected by most of his countrymen, and by none more so than his former comrade-in-arms, General Eisenhower. Yet such was the influence of McCarthy that presidential candidate Eisenhower, when whistle-stopping through Wisconsin in 1952, felt constrained to endorse the senator's candidature for re-election and to delete a flattering reference to Marshall from one of his own speeches.

'Ike', the popular hero, easily defeated the Democratic candidate, Governor Adlai E. Stevenson of Illinois, for the presidency. His speeches had bristled with indignation at the Truman record on what became known as K_1C_2 — the Korean War, administrative corruption, and above all, internal communism. The Republican Party won not only the White House but also both Houses of Congress. McCarthy's party was now dominant and he himself was assigned the chairmanship of the Senate Committee on Government Operations. Generally this chairmanship was not considered one of the most powerful jobs on Capitol Hill. Indeed, Senate Majority Leader Taft had engineered this particular appointment in order to try to bottle McCarthy up in a a Committee whose chief job was to scrutinize the intricacies of government spending.

But, in the words of Richard Rovere, 'Taft's bottle for McCarthy had never been corked; McCarthy simply poured himself out'.[3] He put himself at the head of his committee's permanent sub-committee on investigations and, ignoring the dull but important work of the parent committee, carried right on with the red-hunting that had brought him to national and indeed international attention in the previous three years. Although his party now controlled both the executive and legislative branches of government, McCarthy was relentless in his accusations of disloyalty against personnel in the Department of State and other governmental establishments. He hired a couple of henchmen, Roy Cohn and David Schine, and sent them galavanting around Europe investigating 'subversion' in American governmental institutions there. When Schine was drafted into the army, Cohn did all he could to try to obtain preferential treatment for him; when he failed, McCarthy's sub-committee proceeded to investigate the US Army on the grounds that some of its leaders (such, for example, as those who had refused to grant special favours to Schine) were playing into the hands of the communist conspiracy. Everybody from the Secretary of the Army down to the humblest mess orderly seemed to be called upon to testify at one stage or other in the proceedings. The Army–McCarthy hearings of May –June 1954 lasted for thirty-five days and were given nationwide television coverage. These were the early days of television and to those who had a set the new toy was often mesmeric. McCarthy knew that the eyes of the nation (more than 20 million pairs of eyes, to be precise) were upon him, and he revelled in his own importance. But if millions of people saw him bullying government officials and reprimanding army generals, they also saw him raising great numbers of ludicrously fastidious points of order and snarling cruelly at innocent victims. They saw him scowling and fidgeting with obvious boredom whenever it was somebody else's turn to speak. They saw him turn on members of his own committee and accuse them of trying to hinder his efforts. And they saw the army counsel, Joseph Welch, looking sadly but unflinchingly down upon McCarthy and saying: 'If it were in my power to forgive you for your reckless cruelty, I would do so. I like to think that I am a gentle man, but your forgiveness will have to come from someone other than me.'

The hearings gave Senator McCarthy more publicity than he had ever in his wildest dreams expected to obtain. The whole nation stopped what it was doing (or so he fancied) in order to look at him. But the hearings were also the beginning of the end. His most unattractive characteristics had been exposed for all to see. In December 1954, more than two-thirds of his colleagues voted for a resolution stating that he had ' ... acted contrary to Senatorial ethics and tended to bring the Senate into dishonor and disrepute, to obstruct the constitutional processes of the Senate, and to impair its dignity ... Such conduct [the resolution concluded] is hereby condemned.' Three years later McCarthy was dead.

McCarthyism was one of the more unpalatable episodes that Americans had to live through during the early fifties. But there were others. There were, for instance, the hearings conducted by Senator Kefauver, which uncovered a chain of corruption and gangsterism on a scale that most Americans in their innocence imagined had disappeared two decades earlier. Above all, there was the Korean War.

When President Truman was first told of the North Korean attack on the South on 24 June 1950 by his shocked and bewildered advisers, he came to the quick and firm decision that, whatever the risks involved, US troops should be sent to Korea immediately (under UN command if possible) to resist the communist assault. The following spring, in an even bolder display of personal decisiveness, Truman dismissed his commander-in-chief in Korea, General Douglas MacArthur, for repeatedly expressing the view, which was at variance with administration policy, that the war should be extended into an all-out attempt to overthrow the Chinese régime. MacArthur, who was one of the most revered generals in American history, returned to the United States with the air of a wronged hero, and was mobbed by sympathizers everywhere he went. He made a passionate speech justifying his own policy recommendations before a special joint session of Congress, and was seriously considered by many conservative Republicans as a possible presidential candidate. The whole episode certainly helped to make more acceptable in the popular mind the idea of a politician-soldier, and it is probable that the nomination and enormous electoral success of Eisenhower in 1952 was to some extent a product of the emotions aroused at the time of the MacArthur dismissal. On the other hand, the incident hardly endeared President Truman to the impulsive and dogmatically anti-communist elements in the American public, who were currently blaming him for just about everything that upset them.

But Truman had never been obsessed with popularity or the polls, and he even appeared to obtain a certain pleasure from pushing on, almost arrogantly, with policies that he knew to be unpopular but believed to be right. A case in point was the administration's firm attempt to deal with that dreary by-product of all wars, inflation. The Korean War was localized, not the sort of war for which the American people were really prepared to make great patriotic sacrifices. In particular, both management and labour — while admitting the general desirability of a wages and prices freeze — were much less inclined than they had been during the Second World War to acquiesce in the government's pleadings on this point. Truman's response was tough. The administration set up the Economic Stabilization Agency which, after a period of making vain requests, issued orders compulsorily freezing wages, salaries, and prices. Even more savage was the reaction of President Truman to what promised to be a very lengthy strike by the nation's steel workers in early 1952. Pleading national emergency, he ordered his Secretary of Commerce to take over and run the steel mills — a drastic step that was prevented only by a dramatic 6—3 decision by the Supreme Court.

Comfort and conformism

By 1953 Americans had been living with some sort of crisis for nearly a quarter of a century. There was nothing that most of them yearned for so much as national and international peace and quiet and the opportunity to get on with their own individual lives in as comfortable and uninterrupted a way as possible. This was precisely what the new Eisenhower régime seemed to offer. A few months after its accession to power a truce was signed in Korea. At home the government departments were put into the hands of sober and seemingly incorruptible businessmen. Every now and then noises from Washington would reverberate around certain sections of the community. Some con-

servatives were shocked when a Department of Health, Education
and Welfare (one of the recommendations of the Hoover Commission) was established, and when the government decided to go
ahead and take the initiative regarding the building of the St. Law-
rence Seaway project; some liberals heard with more dismay than
surprise that when the President attempted to obtain more electrical
power for the people of Memphis he refused to make use of the existing
Tennessee Valley Authority (which he had in an unguarded moment
denounced as 'creeping socialism') and, instead, tried to arrange new
contracts — which later fell through in any case — with two private
firms. But the biggest noises made in Washington in the early years of
the Eisenhower presidency were being made either by outsiders, such
as Senators McCarthy, Jenner and Bricker, or for foreign audiences
by John Foster Dulles. For the most part, therefore, the nation seemed
relaxed and happy with the prospect of four or even eight years of
uncreative, apolitical, but incontestably honest government. The
good citizens who put the Eisenhower régime in power could now sit
back comfortably and forget about politics.

These were the years of the great ascendancy of middle-class standards and values. America still had her few wealthy aristocrats and
her many invisible poor, but the accepted conventions of the day were
those of bourgeois comfort. In some ways the fifties were like the
twenties; there was the occasional dramatic rise or fall of some fabulous movie idol, the odd sensational murder, and the virtual refusal by
the government to acknowledge the existence on the domestic front of
any but administrative problems. But the Eisenhower era lacked the
panache of the Jazz Age; if neither the cruelties nor the absurdities of
the earlier period appeared in quite so extreme a form in the 1950s,
many Americans of the latter decade tended to be duller than their
parents had been thirty years before. They were less selfish and
aggressive than their parents, perhaps, but also a great deal less
imaginative. The Eisenhower era was one of keeping up with the
Joneses, a period that saw the sometimes obsessive subordination of
one's individuality to the perceived demands of society.

The reasons for this popular conformism were complex. Part of the
explanation lay in the economic statistics. Despite occasional recessions (notably in 1953–4 and 1957–8) and the alarming plight of the
farmers (who were battling against the old problem of surplus production), the nation as a whole was more prosperous during the 1950s
than any nation had ever been before. By 1960 the annual Gross

National Product was more than 500 billion dollars — getting on for double the figure for a decade earlier (see Table 4.2). The average gross income per family was $4,444 in 1950 and by 1960 had reached $6,819.

Table 4.2. Gross National Product (in current prices)

	Billions of dollars		Billions of dollars
1920	88·9	1966	753·0
1925	91·3	1967	796·3
1930	91·1	1968	868·5
1935	72·5	1969	935·5
1940	100·6	1970	982·4
1945	213·6	1971	1,063·4
1950	284·6	1972	1,171·1
1955	397·5	1973	1,306·6
1960	502·6	1974	1,413·2
1965	681·2	1975	1,516·3
		1976	1,691·6

These were years of great affluence, but during this time a number of subtle changes occurred in the ways in which people earned their money. In the Truman era there had still been more Americans in 'blue collar' jobs (as craftsmen, operatives, miners, etc.) than in 'white collar' (i.e. professional, managerial, technical, and clerical jobs). This was hardly surprising; most societies contain more doers than administrators, more earners by brawn than by brain. But by the end of the Eisenhower years, the USA had become the first nation to reverse this ratio. More and more people, instead of going straight into skilled and semi-skilled jobs in their mid teens, were going on from high school to further study. And while an increasing proportion of young Americans equipped themselves, through education, to enter 'white collar' jobs, machines were being invented and installed to do many of the more menial jobs that men had had to do before.

Related to this was a second development: the shift in emphasis from the manufacture of goods to the provision of services. At the end of the Second World War, roughly the same number of people were employed in both. But with the growth of such industries as air transportation, real estate, advertising, motels, restaurants, and financial, legal and insurance companies, employment in the service sector shot ahead.

A third important trend in employment patterns was the continued growth of the big corporation. In 1950, corporate assets in the USA totalled some $598 billion; by 1960 that figure had more than doubled to $1,207 billion. The annual revenues of General Motors were by now amounting to several times those of the state of New York. Among the most successful concerns were companies such as Lockheed or IBM that were involved in developing fields like aircraft manufacture and computers. Much corporate growth resulted from a wave of amalgamations and mergers so that by the mid 1950s a mere twenty-three corporations were providing 15 per cent of all employment in manufacturing. Thus, the number of Americans who were self-employed or employed in a family-size firm was small and dwindling; the apparently inexorable trend was for people to be employed by one or other of the corporate giants.

In an era of new, affluent, white-collar service industries and giant corporations, the newly-rich could easily be tempted to lose themselves in the sea of wealth that seemed to surround them and spend much time and energy monitoring and imitating the tastes of their affluent neighbours. This mindless conformism could be debilitating, but the only real casualties, because they were ignored, were the poor. In the 1950s the poor were in some instances very poor indeed. In the heart of many of the major cities were areas with decaying slums, overcrowded schools, and almost no facilities for the elderly. In rural America, small farmers would often put in an eighteen-hour day trying desperately to make ends meet — with the indispensable help of government subsidies and price supports. In the Appalachians, in parts of upstate Pennsylvania, West Virginia and Kentucky, there were mining families whose livelihood had eroded as the surface layers of coal had been stripped away and machinery introduced to mine the deeper seams. And there were 20 million people who were destined to experience most aspects of life as second-class citizens simply because they had not been born white.

Some reports of the hardship and poverty amidst the affluence of those days almost defied belief. There was the story of a mother in the Imperial Valley in California who was breast-feeding not only her infant but also, since there was no other food, her four-year-old as well; in Hazard, Kentucky, a child died of malnutrition during a miners' strike. Edward R. Murrow presented a gruesome picture of poverty among Florida fruit-pickers in his television documentary *Harvest of Shame*, while in Harlem or the Bowery in New York City it was not unusual to come across the semi-conscious body of somebody to whom chronic alcoholism was the chief form of escape from the relentless struggle for subsistence. Throughout the affluent 1950s, the bottom 20 per cent of American families earned less than 5 per cent of total income; as late as 1960 the average *per capita* farm income was still hovering around $1,250.

Severe deprivation, however, was something that most of the rest of post-war America found it could ignore. Material poverty was, after all, relegated for the first time in history to minority status and wealthier people liked to point out that the poor in America were usually better off than even the relatively affluent in some less favourably endowed societies. Apart from which there were so many other things to think about — things like bowling, 3-D movies, TV quiz shows, and newer and gaudier automobiles and home appliances. People were spending a smaller fraction of their incomes than ever before on the basic necessities of life, such as food and clothes, and rather more than they had ever done on luxuries. And those luxuries included many items — such as television sets, cars, vacations in distant but fashionable places, and subscriptions to glossy weekly magazines — that both extended and were partly promoted by the conformist tastes of the day.

In a society that is technologically primitive or materially deprived, people rarely get the chance to choose what job to do, where to live, what to wear; the person who is starving does not need to think about whether or what to eat. But for middle-class America in the 1950s, these were real issues. For the new suburbanites, choice — or at least the appearance of choice — was not a rare luxury but a new, omnipresent and often baffling reality. There were so many different types of toothpaste or flavours of ice-cream or models of automobile to choose from, so many apparent options even regarding the type of home you could live in or the career-pattern you could pursue. Gradually, people came to grips with the melancholy fact that a substantial amount of their time and energy had henceforth to be devoted to the problem of adjudicating between alternative — and often scarcely distinguishable — options.

How did Americans react when bewildered by choices such as these and on this scale? One common way was simply to opt out of decision-making altogether and to take one's cue from the decisions seemingly made by 'the Joneses'. This type of conformism was particularly common in white middle-class suburbia where, according to David Riesman[4], people tended to be 'other-directed', and it was in no small part a response to the almost paralysing range of choices imposed by the new affluence.

Conformism was related to the economy in another way, too. The new wealth, welcome as it was to people who had not experienced it before, seemed to many to be altering almost out of recognition the America with which they felt comfortable and in which they had been raised. Had you recently acquired some 78 r.p.m. records or a car with smart running boards? Were you brought up to believe that music should have a regular beat, that young people should respect their elders, that those who do wrong should be punished? Did you have a clear and fixed idea of the restrictions that time and distance imposed upon the speed and efficiency with which people could communicate and travel? All of these things were thrown into doubt and some of them into confusion in the Eisenhower years. Nothing seemed sacred and very little seemed immutable. Americans were by now prepared to move their home or change their job (or even their spouse) with an ease unknown to most people in earlier generations. If anything was to remain the same, from a style of clothing to a set of beliefs, people began to feel called upon to make out a case for *not* altering it. It can be stimulating to live in a rapidly changing society. But it can also be threatening, particularly to older people who are used to what things were like before. Change has its hazards for younger people, too; if nothing is definitely going to be permanent, what models can the child use while developing his or her fragile personality? When the kids accuse the parents of wearing old-fashioned clothes or using obsolete expressions, while the parents criticize their children's dating procedures as too forward, who can know which is right?

It was against this background that some people tried to shore up against the onrush of change all that they thought valuable in the America with which they were already familiar. The new age of the ubiquitous motor car and the television set was thus also an age that saw a powerful rearguard action in defence of the values treasured by traditional America. An age of technological change, the Eisenhower era was also an age of ideological conformism — of a return to God, to anti-communism, and to the time-honoured American Dream that virtue and hard work brought their own rewards.

It was also an age in which people's images of the world were increasingly likely to be moulded by the same standardizing media. For this was a period that saw a revolution in mass communications, in the means of transporting both people and ideas. In 1950 there were 5 million American families with television sets; in 1960 the figure was 45 million – or well over 95 per cent. Most programmes were shown on coast-to-coast networks which left little opportunity for local variety in programming. In 1950 motor vehicles travelled nearly 460 billion miles in the United States, a figure that had reached nearly 720 billion by the end of the decade; in the same period the number of registered automobiles had shot up from 40·3 million to 61·5 million (see Fig. 4.1). The federal and state governments undertook colossal road-building projects during this period, but gave hardly a thought to the great social, environmental, and aesthetic problems that they were helping to engender and magnify. This was pre-eminently the era of the motel, of the drive-in movie, a decade in which Jack Kerouac wrote *On The Road*[5] and Vladimir Nabokov *Lolita*[6]. One American family in five moved home every year in the Eisenhower era. It was a decade of huge new suburbs, particularly around the spacious cities of the south and west such as Houston, San Diego and Los Angeles – cities where young people went in search of well-paid jobs in expanding new fields such as electronics and

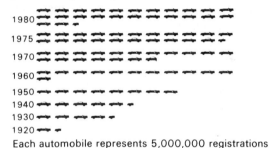

Each automobile represents 5,000,000 registrations

Fig. 4.1 Automobile registrations

aeronautics, and where the elderly went in search of a warm climate in which to retire. It was also a decade in which the centre of many of the older cities in the north and east began to show the first signs of the blight that was so to afflict them in the years to come. In general, the cities that flourished were those that could accommodate a life-style dependent upon the automobile; those that had been substantially established before the advent of the motor car became appreciably less comfortable in these years. The development of air travel during the fifties was even more staggering than that of road travel: in 1950, on domestic flights, a total of 8 billion passenger miles were flown, a number that had reached 30·5 billion by 1960.

By the end of the 1950s, more people could find out more, with
less effort, about the way in which other Americans were living than
had been conceivable a couple of decades back. Indeed, so persistent
were the new media of communication and transportation that it was
only a very impoverished American (or, just possibly, a very eccentric
one) who could avoid constant exposure to them and their effects.
And one of their principal effects was to help spread throughout the
nation a common perception of things, a common culture. Under
these circumstances individualism was at a premium. And it was this
very fact — the constant and almost unavoidable conformism of the
period — that produced the great characteristic of the last years of the
Eisenhower era: a critical preoccupation with the question of the role
of the individual in society.

Many of the most widely admired works of non-fiction during the
1950s were books in which the author had tried to analyse the role of
the individual in modern society. A number of thinkers, ranging from
brilliant originals like David Riesman *(The Lonely Crowd*[7]*)* to talented
popularizers like Willam H. Whyte *(The Organization Man*[8]*)* and
Vance Packard *(The Status Seekers*[9]*)* were disturbed by what they saw
as the evaporation of individualism in mid-century America. Much of
the most significant art of the period too — the abstract expressionism
of De Kooning and Pollock, the 'beat' poetry of Ginsberg — was above
all a plea for the individual to be able to express himself in his own
spontaneous way or, to put the same thing more negatively, a protest
against what was seen as the bourgeois conformism of contemporary
society. The individual, these thinkers and artists seemed to be saying, was increasingly obsessed with the need to impress his
neighbours and to follow the set of values dictated by the superficial
demands of society. Sociologists and psychologists had, of course, said
much of this before, and it was a message that no self-respecting
American brought up to believe in the traditional frontier virtues of
rugged individualism could receive with equanimity. But the theme of
Riesman and the others seemed to be peculiarly timely in the 1950s,
and it was eagerly lapped up by a society which was conformist in
nothing so much as its preoccupation with the putative evils of
conformism.

Despite these intellectual doubts, however, the surface of American
society remained remarkably unruffled during the mid 1950s. In 1956
Eisenhower — the reassuring father figure — was overwhelmingly
re-elected as President. Millions of Americans looked forward to four

more bland years during which, while weeping the occasional crocodile tear over the loss of individualism in America, they could all spend much of their time and money in the hectic communal pursuit of material comfort.

But life was not to be quite so simple as that. Eisenhower's second term saw one affront to America's dignity and calm after another. In September 1957 came the school integration crisis in Little Rock (see p. 146. The ugly scenes outside Central High School disturbed many Americans — not least because the depressing events were seized upon in many parts of the world as evidence that the United States was not quite the land of the free and the home of the brave that she had so often claimed to be. Then, a month later, came the first Sputnik. The effect of this Soviet scientific success on American self-confidence was devastating. The recurrent uncertainties and frustrations of postwar American society (which had been partly responsible in the earlier fifties for McCarthyism on the one hand and the religious revival on the other, and which had been increasingly submerged in a welter of single-minded materialism by the middle of the decade) were at last faced head-on. After the Sputnik, no serious-minded American could continue to shelter behind the delusion of his country's overwhelming superiority in all things. Perhaps, many people began to think, American society was too flippant, too materialistic, too easily impressed by the superficial glitter of popular success and insufficiently appreciative of its original thinkers. Perhaps there was, as the sociologists had been trying to say, a cult of the mediocre, the average — and perhaps the crafty and malevolent Soviets had quietly been developing a cult of excellence. In the last three years of Eisenhower's presidency many important elements within American society entered upon a vigorous debate on the role of America in the world and the role of the individual in American society. In particular, people were exercised as to how to keep open the channels of communication between the nation's most active thinkers and doers. Among the more specific and tangible products of this debate were the establishment of the post of the President's Special Assistant for Science and Technology and, in September 1958, the passage of a Bill to increase the grants given to students of such subjects as the natural and social sciences, mathematics, and modern languages — the National Defense Education Act. At a less institutional level the debate tended to take the form of a national soul-baring spree. Eminent political and social writers were now turning out books with titles like *America the Vincible* and *What Ivan Knows and Johnny Doesn't.*

Keeping apace with the apologias and the introspection came further body blows to American pride. In 1958 Vice-President Nixon was jeered, spat upon, and even stoned in various Latin American capitals, and in Caracas his car was almost overturned by an angry mob. A year later a young instructor from Columbia University who had won enormous amounts of money on a TV quiz show shocked his millions of trusting admirers to the core when he admitted that the show had been rigged. By 1960 — the year of the U—2 incident and of the cancellation of Eisenhower's trip to Japan — the American *penchant* for self-analysis and self-criticism verged on the morbid. Such bastions of American respectability as *Life* magazine and the *New York Times* ran articles on the question of the future role of America and Americans. President Eisenhower established the Commission on National Goals, which produced its thoughtful (but sometimes painfully earnest) report, *Goals for Americans*, just before he left office.

The Eisenhower era had seen a society, tired of crises, trying hard to look casual and relaxed. It was fundamentally a deeply conservative society, one that paid pious and frequent homage to what it liked to think of as the solid middle-class virtues of its traditional heroes. But it was also, at the more superficial level of day-to-day technological ephemera, a society obsessed by novelty and change. As in the 1920s, American society in the Eisenhower era revered the purveyors of scientific change but, at the same time, tended to be intolerant of those who advocated or even merely heralded any major social change. It was technologically adventurous but ideologically reactionary.

It was a society, too, that tended to be mesmerized by sheer 'bigness'. One had only to look, for illustrations of this point, at some of the monstrously impractical cars or the movie 'spectaculars' of the period — or at the world of 'big' business. Sheer size, like technological change, became a popular virtue. At the same time, the corporate giants were at pains to try to present a public image of personal friendliness. Many of the biggest corporations set up sports clubs and complex insurance schemes for their employees and even schools for their children. As for advertising, the bigger the corporation, the more it seemed to rely on the man-to-man (or woman-to-man!) approach. There was an increasing emphasis on the interests of the consumers and less and less on those of the owners; the uncle was getting ever more generous — and deliberately more faceless. The huge corporation and the dedicated but anonymous executive were among the most representative symbols of the 1950s.

By the late 1950s the latent contradictions within American society — so casually submerged in the early and middle years of the decade — began to show themselves. How could a society dominated by 'bigness' also be one that encouraged individualism? Why did the big corporations need to emphasize the 'personal' approach in their advertising if not because they were becoming conscious of their increasing impersonality? How could a society derive its values from middle-class bourgeois conformism and yet also make cultural and scientific progress? Why did the most affluent society in history also contain major pockets of poverty? Why was a society dedicated to equality also characterized by a degree of racial inequality unparalleled outside southern Africa? These were questions that, for thoughtful Americans, were posed by Little Rock, by Sputnik, by Caracas, by the TV quiz show scandals.

Furthermore, as time progressed it became increasingly evident that, the traditional American Dream notwithstanding, the nation's affluence did not happen to go just to those who deserved it. Many people became rich as a result of luck rather than judgement, or selfish calculation rather than moral virtue. Others remained poor because they happened to live in the wrong parts of the country. Even some people who were not badly off economically began to feel deprived as they regarded with envy the material welfare of the country's very rich. As the incidence of illiteracy even among the poorer and more isolated communities in America was minimized by the growing number of schools and colleges, and as the nation became wired up by television, many people who might not have considered themselves poor before gradually became increasingly aware of their relative deprivation. This nagging awareness was exacerbated by constant advertising — in the papers, on radio and television, on the roadside — which often had the effect of dangling before those who had been left out a constant reminder of the things of which they were still deprived. Poverty is never easy to bear. But when others are wealthy and you know that they are and can see that they are, even relative poverty can become intolerable.

As the 1950s moved towards their close, there were indications that the problems and conflicts and inconsistencies within American society might not be able to remain bubbling away under an apparently calm surface for much longer. The American Dream may have worked for some, but the creed of traditional America could not for much longer sustain those for whom it had palpably failed. While affluent and successful America continued to project its bourgeois fantasies onto such traditional and reassuring personages as Doris Day and Janet Leigh, Howard Keel and Rock Hudson, the shape of things to come was more accurately suggested by the continuing appeal to America's youngsters of James Dean in his automobile, Marlon Brando on his motor cycle, and Elvis Presley pounding his aggressive way through a number like 'Jailhouse Rock' or 'You ain't nothing but a hound dog!'

However, even the critics and the malcontents were rarely revolutionaries in the 1950s. Serious social unease was generally thought to be rare and those problems that were identified were usually presumed to be susceptible to rational solutions. The problems and their solutions did not greatly exercise the Eisenhower administration and those who felt comfortable with it, but they provided stimulus and hope in the later 1950s for the rising generation of active, intelligent, and politically alert young men and women who were about to take their stand behind John F. Kennedy.

Five

THE 1960s: GETTING THE
COUNTRY MOVING

Was John F. Kennedy a 'great' president? Was his contribution to history primarily in the realm of concrete achievement or in the more intangible realms of thought and style? Questions such as these will always be hard to answer as Kennedy's tenure of office was so suddenly cut short by his assassination.

If there is one thing about Kennedy's presidency that can be said with reasonable certainty, it is that the rivalries and tensions in American society that had tended to be submerged during the better part of the 1950s began to manifest themselves with increasing clarity in the early 1960s. Politically this meant, among other things, that the far ends of the spectrum began to attain a degree of relative respectability that would have been impossible in the mid 1950s; intellectually it took the form of a fierce debate on the subject of underprivilege in an allegedly egalitarian society. To some extent, these divisions were consciously widened by Kennedy and his friends and advisers, the 'New Frontiersmen', for they talked about getting the country moving again and they deliberately provoked discussion about a wide variety of issues which an inert public had previously been reluctant to face. On the other hand, the mere fact that Kennedy was elected — and that his candidature aroused such spirited and even bigoted opposition — was perhaps a symptom rather than a cause of the growing restlessness among many elements in American society. That restlessness was to take many forms as the decade unfolded and we will concentrate in the first half of this chapter on two of them: the movement for racial equality and the unrest on university and college campuses.

The Black Revolution

The story of the civil rights movement should really begin in the earliest colonial days, when black slaves were shipped from Africa in the most barbaric conditions to the new American colonies. More than 200 years and a civil war later, slavery was officially abolished in the United States and for the brief period of Reconstruction America's newly liberated blacks rubbed their eyes with bewildered disbelief and set about trying desperately to make up for the centuries of misery and degradation that they had been forced to suffer. It was not long, however, before white society (which, for the black, meant southern white society) began restricting the freedoms that the black men among them had just begun to grasp. With a cruelty and a vindictiveness that had usually been lacking — if only because they had been unnecessary — during the centuries of slavery, southern society imposed and enforced, in the late nineteenth century, discriminatory laws and social practices which between them ensured for the black citizen a hopelessly inferior social position. The black was prevented from voting (or even registering to vote) by a bunch of dubious subterfuges, such as the notorious 'literacy tests', the 'grandfather clause' (whereby anybody whose grandfather had been a slave was disfranchised), and the poll tax. Black children were sent to manifestly inferior schools as a result of gerrymandered school districts and rigged entrance requirements. In most of the South blacks were systematically excluded from jury service and, consequently, no black had any significant chance of legal redress if robbed or fired or evicted by a white man. In the early decades of this century literally thousands of southern blacks were lynched. Yet so subservient was the black man forced to be that he tended to view any organized demand for equality with the white man as not only dangerous but even, perhaps, somewhat presumptuous.

During the world wars, as we have seen, blacks fought and died with their fellow Americans. Presidents Roosevelt and Truman took steps to eliminate a few of the most glaring racial inequities from the armed forces, yet the demobilized black often came home to a community where, except for his coloured friends, he was scarcely more welcome than if he had been a craven deserter. The stark contrast between the role Negroes had played on the international stage and the one they were reduced to playing in the more benighted communities of their own nation produced among America's 20 million blacks an unprecedented degree of frustration. In their search for better wages and living conditions, many of them began to move from the rural South to the urban North; in their anxiety to obtain better education for their children, they were brazen enough to request that the latter be admitted to hitherto all-white schools. If the bigoted southern 'redneck' was happy enough to see thousands of blacks fleeing northwards, he was most disturbed by the determination of those who remained to enable their children to participate in his exclusive education system. The white southerner had one valuable card to play: he could quote the 1896 Supreme Court decision (*Plessy v. Ferguson*) that upheld the principle of 'separate but equal' facilities for blacks. In the face of this argument, the onus was on the black to prove to an all-white court (if he could so much as gain admission to one) that his separate schools were inferior to the white ones.

By the mid 1950s, however, the black was in no mood to wait any longer. Organized black movements began, for the first time, to spring up in large numbers all over the country. Some of these movements were predominantly religious, some were concerned with political rights. Some believed in non-violent social action, some in appealing to the courts. By far the oldest of these movements, the National Association for the Advancement of Colored People (NAACP) and its (now separate) Legal Defense and Education Fund, had been trying for many years to ameliorate the lot of the down-trodden American black through decisions in the federal courts. Against overwhelming odds the NAACP had achieved an odd truce here and a paltry victory there. But its finest hour came in May 1954, when the US Supreme Court issued its famous desegregation decision in *Brown* v. *Board of Education of Topeka*. In *Brown* the court (in a unanimous decision written by the new Chief Justice, Eisenhower-appointee Earl Warren) declared, in part:

> To separate them [children] from others of similar age and qualifications solely because of their race generates a feeling of inferiority as to their status in the community that may affect their hearts and minds in a way unlikely ever to be undone ... We conclude that in the field of public education the doctrine of 'separate but equal' has no place. Separate educational facilities are inherently unequal.

A year and a half later segregated seating in the buses of Montgomery, Alabama, was abolished as the result of a black bus boycott organized by the Reverend Martin Luther King. The black revolt was beginning to become organized and it was showing tangible signs of success.

But a court decision and a successful bus boycott, while they did wonders for black morale, did little to improve the harsh social conditions to which the southern black was subjected. The *Brown* decision was to be implemented not immediately but 'with all deliberate speed' — a phrase which gave a loophole to die-hard segregationists. Many of them clung on desperately to this vague phrase and succeeded in preventing the integration of educational facilities. No court decision is any use until it is successfully implemented. At the beginning of the 1957 school year, in September, the Little Rock, Arkansas, school board in compliance with the 1954 decision decided to admit seventeen specially chosen black students to the hitherto all-white Central High School. Governor Faubus, in defiance of federal law, stationed the Arkansas National Guard outside the school, ostensibly 'to prevent racial violence' but, in effect, keeping the black students from entering the school. After an inconclusive meeting with President Eisenhower and nearly two weeks of national prominence, the Governor removed the National Guard from Central High and the black students were at last admitted to the school. Three hours later they were sent home for their own safety for, as Faubus had predicted, a huge, angry, segregationist mob had collected outside the school building and was threatening to do violence to the black children. There was some evidence that no such mob would have materialized had Faubus quietly let the children enter Central High when they were originally supposed to have done so; the relatively liberal Mayor of Little Rock claimed (with no doubt a healthy combination of factual accuracy and civic dignity) that the unruly elements among the rioting crowds were 'professional agitators' imported for the occasion from elsewhere. Whatever the causes of the Little Rock riots, they placed Eisenhower in what was for him perhaps the cruellest dilemma of his presidency. A staunch believer in states' rights and a man adamantly opposed, for all his military training, to the use of force, the President was faced with a situation that cried out for strong action from the White House. Eventually he took a series of actions that, while he felt them to be necessary, were most repugnant to him. Not only did he federalize the Arkansas National Guard (i.e. he put it directly under his own command and out of Faubus's), but more important he sent a thousand paratroopers into Little Rock to enforce the law of the land for the duration of the school year.

By the end of the 1950s, thoughtful people in all parts of the world were deeply concerned about the latest developments in relations between the races in the American South. In retrospect, the question that needs answering is not why there was a civil rights movement but why it came when it did. Throughout American history blacks had been treated with what was at best condescension and at worst savagery. But revolts do not usually come when things are at their lowest ebb. However acutely the black felt his grievances, he was unlikely to be bold enough to demand their redress unless he thought he had some hope of success. Furthermore, most American blacks were so accustomed to the inferior social position accorded to them and their forebears that it required some outside stimulus to jolt them into a realization that the *status quo* was wrong and could be changed.

We have seen in Chapter 4 how the Second World War provided such a stimulus. The contacts between white and coloured men in the army made each group revise its stereotyped picture of the other; each man realized, perhaps, that the other was not such a bad − or even different − type of person after all. Furthermore, the experiences of the black soldier (who often fought abroad for freedom and democracy and then had to return to the rigidly stratified society of the Deep South) increased his sensitivity towards the discrimination to which he was subjected by his white neighbours.

The war may have created the circumstances within which the subsequent civil rights explosion was made possible, but there were other factors involved as well. There was, for instance, the revolution in the media of mass communication (and, in particular, the growth of television) that was mentioned on p. 137. By the mid fifties, it was no longer possible for a moderately wealthy white American to plead ignorance of the existence and plight of his black compatriots. Meanwhile, the black, too, was finding out more and more about how white America lived; he was more likely to be literate and to see a regular newspaper than had been the case with his father − and he might even have had access to a television set. White America was finding out how it treated black America, while black America was being sensitized to what it was missing.

Along with the phenomenal growth in the mass media came an equally spectacular transportation boom. One important by-product was the large migration of blacks from the southern states to other parts of the country. By about 1945 no state in the Union had a predominantly coloured population. But there were few states, either, that did not have an important black minority. When the black left the cotton fields of the old Confederacy, his most likely destination was the centre of a northern city. He had heard that these cities contained great new industries, produced by the necessities of the war, in which he would be able to work. Between 1940 and 1960 some 3 million blacks left the rural South for the great cities of the North and West. This migration — coupled with the very high black birth rate (pp.153, 167) — led to a non-white population in many American cities of unprecedented proportions (see Table 5.1 last two columns). Between 1940 and 1960 the black populations of New York City and Philadelphia had doubled, those of Chicago and Detroit tripled, and that of Los Angeles had gone up by five times.

Table 5.1. Population of the ten largest cities since 1930

Thousands

City	1930	1950	1960	Non-White population in 1960	
				Total	per cent
New York City, NY.	6,930	7,892	7,781	1,141	14·7
Chicago, Ill.	3,376	3,621	3,550	838	23·6
Los Angeles, Calif.	1,238	1,970	2,479	417	16·8
Philadelphia, Penn.	1,951	2,072	2,003	535	26·7
Detroit, Mich.	1,569	1,849	1,670	487	29·2
Baltimore, Md.	805	950	939	328	35·0
Houston, Tex.	292	596	938	218	23·2
Cleveland, Ohio.	900	915	876	253	28·9
Washington, DC.	487	802	764	419	54·8
St. Louis, Mo.	822	857	750	216	28·8

These cities happened to be of vital political importance, for most of them were situated in heavily populated and politically pivotal states — which any serious presidential candidate would have to make certain of winning. As for the cities themselves, the movement of the newly affluent white middle class into the burgeoning Republican suburbs had made many of the metropolitan areas — hitherto solidly Democratic — politically uncertain. It followed that any new social element within these politically hypersensitive states and cities would be vital in the calculations of anybody seeking public office. For this reason the northern black found himself at the centre of an extraordinary amount of political attention. Few people could seriously hope to become mayor of Detroit or Philadelphia or governor of Illinois or New York without making some effort to gain the approval of the newly arrived blacks within their constituency.

This constant public attention was not an unmixed blessing for the urban black. For one thing, it produced a negative reaction among some urban and suburban whites, especially after 1964 when the first serious summer riots took place. Some politicians, such as Barry Goldwater, George Wallace and Ronald Reagan, gained political capital from these resentments and benefited from what became known as the 'white backlash'. Furthermore, political attention is not the same thing as social reform. Many urban blacks were wooed assiduously and promised the earth by power-hungry politicians — who, once in office, did little or nothing for them. Nevertheless, the concentration of blacks in politically pivoted urban ghettos was one of the main reasons for the growing preoccupation of white Americans with their black neighbours in the decades following the Second World War.

Those same years saw the dramatic resurgence of black Africa. In the two decades following the Second World War, some thirty black African states achieved their independence. American blacks read about — and even saw on television — great African leaders who like Moses led their people to independence and threw off the yoke of oppression. Some black Americans, such as the Black Muslims, felt a close affinity to the African nationalist leaders; others felt that fundamentally they were more American than African. But all black leaders in the United States were impressed by the African struggles for independence that they heard so much about in the early 1950s and were inspired by the apparent success of so many of those struggles by the end of that decade. By about 1960 the movement for independence in Africa was well under way, and the civil rights movement in the United States was about to turn into a revolt of major proportions. In the 1960s each movement reinforced the other. Although there was little formal contact between the two, there is not much doubt that the existence of each movement helped in some measure to inspire confidence and hope in the other and that, in particular, the emergence of militant nationalism in Africa was one of the factors that determined the timing of the civil rights movement in the United States.

For all these reasons, the question of race relations was by about 1960 ready to erupt into America's foremost social problem. The civil rights developments of the 1950s, dramatic though they had been at the time, faded into relative insignificance with the arrival of the new decade.

Café 'sit-ins' were organized in 1960 – a number of café-owners were obliged either to serve blacks or to shut their doors entirely; a year later, the Congress of Racial Equality arranged a series of 'freedom rides' – and, after much hatred and some blood had been spent, all facilities connected with interstate buses were desegregated; in September 1962, after a series of incidents reminiscent of Little Rock, the University of Mississippi ('Ol' Miss') admitted a black student. The following summer the world was shocked and horrified by the electric cattle prods, the fire hoses, the bombings, and the mass arrest of children that came to be associated with the name of Birmingham, Alabama. In August 1963, a quarter of a million people, black and white, representing a great number of civil rights groups, met at a giant rally in Washington to register their eloquent and moving plea for the many rights that were still denied to American blacks. President Kennedy (whose concern for the black cause probably contained, by mid 1963, more genuine humanitarianism and less political calculation than had been the case during the first two years of his presidency) listened sympathetically. He recommended to Congress the strongest civil rights measure the country had ever seen. Within a year that Bill (which among other things, desegregated places of 'public accommodation' such as hotels and restaurants) had been passed in largely unaltered form by Congress.

As the civil rights movement went from strength to strength, many of its leaders became more ambitious on its behalf and many of its opponents became more bitter. By 1964 its leaders, both black and white, were beginning to believe – some of them quite militantly – that there was no reason why they should not seriously demand, as their slogan put it, 'Freedom Now'. Diehard segregationists, on the other hand, hitherto content to dismiss civil rights workers scornfully as a bunch of unwashed Yankee beatniks, now began to treat the movement as a deadly threat to their most basic values.

In the summer of 1964 about a thousand students, most of them northerners, took off for the Deep South. The migration was largely organized by the most successful of the numerous civil rights groups, the Student Non-Violent Co-ordinating Committee (SNCC) and was known, officially, as the Council of Federated Organizations (COFO). But the world came to know it as the Mississippi Summer Project. The members of the project went south for a variety of motives, varying no doubt from sheer escapism and a desire for kicks to the most earnest idealism. In Mississippi they stayed with black families, set up 'Freedom Schools', and helped black citizens to register to vote.

The year 1964 was a presidential election year. One of the aims of the members of the Mississippi Summer Project was to send to the Democratic Convention at Atlantic City, New Jersey, delegates who had been freely chosen by all the Democratic voters of Mississippi in the hope that they would publicly embarrass – and possibly even replace – the delegation sent by the official lily-white Mississippi Democratic Party. With this aim in mind, COFO built up the new Freedom Democratic Party (FDP) which like its entrenched counterpart went through all the appropriate stages necessary to appoint delegates to the forthcoming national convention. Ward meetings were held which elected delegates to county meetings, and at the county meetings delegates were appointed to attend the state convention. At the state conventions of the two parallel Democratic Parties' delegates were chosen to go to the national convention, one list all white, the other largely black. The time came for the Atlantic City convention to begin. Suddenly the debonair students and their black friends, who were used to the primitive and dangerous rural life of Mississippi, found themselves, along with Lyndon Johnson, the major focus of national attention.

This leap to public prominence imposed new problems on the civil rights leadership. What tactics should they employ now that, at long last, they were face to face with their white opponents and indeed with the whole national machinery of the President and his party? In particular, what line should they adopt when the inevitable question arose as to which of the two Mississippi delegations had the correct credentials? Lyndon Johnson would, of course, win the presidential nomination by acclamation, regardless of the composition of the delegation that happened to be sitting in the seats reserved for Mississippi. But a major step forward would have been taken if the all-white delegation – the delegation representing the power structure of the most segregated state in the nation – was successfully challenged.

In fact, word came to the leaders of the FDP that, although the regular delegation had to remain seated in the convention hall, the FDP could send two of its members to sit in the hall 'at large' but with full voting powers, and, above all, that in 1968, and at all conventions thereafter, no delegation could sit if there was evidence of discrimination on grounds of race or colour in the method whereby it had been chosen. Moderate civil rights leaders, men like Martin Luther King, James Farmer, Bayard Rustin, and Joseph Rauh, urged the FDP delegation to accept the offer on the grounds that any step once achieved could never be gainsaid in the future. Others like Robert Parris Moses resented the offer (which was for them the final indication that gradualism had failed as a tactic and that integration was an unachievable aim) — and they also resented the suggestion by their erstwhile allies that they accept it.

The dilemma of Atlantic City made it quite clear to the more militant and radical of the civil rights leaders that, although it was all very well to teach a few blacks about their civic responsibilities and help them to register to vote, it would take far more than the summer efforts of a few hundred well-intentioned college kids to bring about any change in the behaviour of white America towards its black citizens. To the moderate leaders, on the other hand, the very fact that two members of the FDP delegation had been admitted to the convention hall at all was proof of the effectiveness of their gradualist methods.

This split between the moderates and the militants was brought to a dramatic head at Atlantic City, but it had been brewing for some time. During the summer of 1964 there had been violent riots in Harlem and in the black quarters of Rochester, Philadelphia, and other cities. These riots took the form of race riots, but they were more than that. In each case they began as the result of a small incident, usually one in which a black was reprimanded or attacked by a white policeman. The resulting riots, taking their cue from these initial incidents, were really a revolt by the oppressed against the symbols of authority. The blacks in the great northern and western cities were the victims of a particularly cruel fate. Many of them had come to these cities from rural southern areas desperately hoping that the myths that they had heard — about equality of opportunity in employment, housing and education — would prove to be at least partly true. When they reached the big cities they were soon forced to face the stark and unexpected fact that discrimination, while legally barred, simply took subtler forms than it had done in the South. When the black moved into the city the whites tended to move out into the suburbs — the landlords among them returning on occasion to pick up the often inflated rent from their black tenants. It would not be true to say that the blacks in the urban ghettos were poor in absolute terms. Those who could find work were often earning far more than they would have been able to earn in the South, and by international standards some of them were positively wealthy. Most of those who could not find work were somehow provided for, by state assistance and by their friends and neighbours. But they were desperately poor, materially and spiritually, when seen in the context of the comfortable bourgeois luxury that they saw around them. They were often living five or six to a room in a squalid claustrophobic slum less than a stone's throw from one of the wealthiest communities the world had ever seen. Under these conditions, the frustrations of the urban black community were never far from breaking point. Those frustrations sometimes found momentary relief in a free and easy attitude towards sex — with the result that the urban birth rate among blacks was 40 per cent higher than that of whites*. The overall illegitimacy rate among American blacks was about one in five; in Harlem the rate was almost one in two. The frequently undisciplined attitude towards sex, therefore, acted as both a cause and an effect of the unmanageable population explosion to which the black ghetto was subjected in the 1950s and 1960s. But the urban black found other outlets for his frustrated emotions as well. The incidence of violent crime committed by urban blacks rose at a staggering rate. Between the beginning of 1958 and the end of 1962 the rate of murder went up by 15 per cent, robbery by 32 per cent, larceny by 43 per cent, and rape by 13 per cent.

Social frustration does not always make for widespread sexual licence and violent crime. The immigrant families who eked out a living in New York seventy years ago working from dawn to dusk in their overcrowded tenements had little time to get depressed about the miserable conditions in which they were expected to live; much the same was true, too, of the southern black sharecropper as late as the 1950s. But the urban black of the 1960s was not starving; far from having to work all his waking hours in order to eat, he often had time on his hands. His arrival in the North had coincided with a substantial increase in automation, and in the resulting unemployment it was often the unskilled, non-unionized, newly arrived black who was the first to go. Thus, in cases that could be seen on a thousand street corners in the United States in the sixties, the black man often had nothing to do and nowhere to go, no sense of direction or purpose. If he picked up a newspaper, glimpsed at a TV screen, or listened to a

*If the black death rate had been equally high, the black population explosion would have been no more alarming than that of the white community. But the black death rate was, by the 1950s and 1960s, not much higher than that of the white death rate.

transistor radio, he would be reminded again and again by the ubiquitous advertising that social status could best be derived from the ownership of luxury goods and this status was conspicuously lacking in anybody — such as indolent, unemployed, licentious blacks — who did not have a healthy chunk of the material pie. The gap between hope and achievement for the ambitious urban black was dangerously wide — the more so since he and his southern brothers had for years been led to believe that the way to solve his problem was to rely on peaceful, constitutional methods. His frustrations were correspondingly great, as was his consequent urge to find new means of expressing them. It needed only the added irritant of a cruelly hot sun plus an instance of 'police brutality' to ignite an explosion which had long been smouldering.

The riots of 1964 confirmed the gloomy prognostications of many black leaders. They all regretted the violence and the deaths, but their attitudes towards the urban riot as a weapon in the struggle for equal rights diverged sharply. Some of them did all in their power to end the riots and to condemn those who were involved in them. But there were also more militant leaders who accepted that riots were a necessary and even justifiable expression of powerful frustrations. They went even further and said, with what proved to be alarming accuracy, that unless the squalor and misery of ghetto life were eliminated, there would have to be worse riots — verging on localized civil war — in the years ahead.

The riots shook the hitherto firm alliance between the moderates and the militants; Atlantic City virtually tore the erstwhile allies apart. From then on there were at least two movements; there were the gradualists, the men who still hoped that integration might work and who preferred to negotiate with the white power structure; and there was the young generation of black leaders, suspicious of the motives of all white men, who reached the firm conclusion that there was henceforth no alternative but for black men to fight for what they were to christen 'Black Power'. These young militants grew in numbers and influence and quickly developed new slogans, new tactics, and a philosophy of their own. Their most articulate and charismatic leader, Stokely Carmichael, equally at home haranguing an angry and volatile crowd or discussing Sartre and Camus, gave Black Power its rationale. All the other ethnic minorities in the United States, he argued, had achieved a measure of political and economic power only after a period in which they faced the rest of society with a united —

and closed — front. Blacks, therefore, owed it to themselves to buy black, to sell black, to vote black — to *think* black. Carmichael also saw Black Power in a global context and told black Americans that they were part of a movement whereby non-whites all over the world were gradually coming to be aware of their collective interests and their latent collective power. The gradualists, of course, called the Black Power militants 'racists in reverse' and for their pains were dubbed by the militants as 'Uncle Toms'. By the later 1960s, what had been a predominantly southern, rural, Christian, optimistic, integrated civil rights movement had become a predominantly northern, urban, secular, militant Black Power movement.

Along with this shift of emphasis came a shift of aims, of slogans, of heroes, and of iconography. Instead of the saintly Martin Luther King, the militant Huey P. Newton; instead of 'Freedom Now', the call was for Black Power (or even 'Kill the Pigs'); instead of integration or assimilation black leaders called for racial separation. Even the vocabulary changed. If it was often an insult to refer to a Negro as a black man prior to about 1967 or 1968 it became unacceptable to refer to him as anything other than 'black' thereafter. By the end of the 1960s, the movement — in common with the campus protest over the Vietnam War and other issues and partly in response to the growing incomprehension and hostility displayed by much of the white community — had become far more radical in its aims and militant in its methods than anybody could have anticipated a decade earlier. Black leaders talked ominously of working to alter the fundamental structure of American society and of doing so 'by whatever means are necessary'. Eldridge Cleaver said that 'the bullet that killed Martin Luther King murdered non-violence.' And just how extreme would the methods be that the militant black leaders were prepared to adopt? 'The sky's the limit' was the glowering response.

Whites were by turns scared, uncomprehending, excited, shocked, and in some cases sentimentally imitative. As for official white reaction, despite some genuine attempts both at federal and local level to improve black living conditions, many local authorities concentrated more on arming their police in readiness for the next explosion than on eradicating its causes. The President's Commission on Civil Disorders, reporting in March 1968 (a month before the assassination of Martin Luther King and the riots that followed his death), stated categorically that 'white racism is essentially responsible for the explosive mixture which has been accumulating in our cities'.

The white racism did not go away nor did the causes of black discontent. But by the 1970s the tense and ugly confrontations of earlier years tended to be less frequent and less virulent for reasons that we will examine in Chapter 6. Black power rallies gave way to calls for 'affirmative action' in favour of black applicants for jobs, and the murderous riots of Watts and Detroit were almost forgotten as middle-class whites in Boston and elsewhere expressed their vehement opposition to, or support of, the busing of black children to schools in white neighbourhoods and vice versa. Thus, while the problems of race relations were not solved by the 1970s, most of the issues took rather more subdued forms than in the 1960s.

The Student Revolution

Back in early 1964, when it was still possible to be optimistic and even smug about problems such as race relations, many of America's most idealistic students were looking forward to a summer vacation devoted to civil rights work in the South. But the dramatic events of the summer of 1964 – the urban race riots and the Atlantic City showdown – were to have a demoralising effect upon white liberals in the USA. Rejected by some of the very people for whom they had recently been risking their lives, they began to realize that the problems that they thought they had been solving were no more than the surface manifestations of what now looked like a far more complex social malaise.

By the end of that summer many thoughtful young Americans were asking themselves questions to which, a few weeks earlier, they thought they had found adequate answers. In what directions should you try to move society? On whom do you try and put pressure? What programmes do you advocate? What tactics do you adopt to get those programmes implemented? How do you get the American power élite to *listen* to you?

When the new academic year began, there was a marked increase in the number of student political organizations, a great many of them of a reformist or protesting nature. It was at this moment that the University of California at Berkeley declared a small strip of land at the edge of the campus out of bounds for political fund-raising and recruitment activities. This proved to be the spark that led to the formation of the Free Speech Movement (FSM) and eventually to large-scale demonstrations at Berkeley. The university authorities dithered; first they capitulated to some of the demands of the FSM, and then — a monumental tactical blunder — decided to take disciplinary action against the movement and its leaders, thereby releasing a wave of hitherto dormant sympathy.

The reaction to the university's decision to discipline the FSM leaders was stunning. One afternoon in December 1964, nearly a thousand young people, most of them students, simply walked into Sproul Hall (the administration building on the Berkeley campus) armed with bedding, food, and the musical inspiration of Joan Baez, and refused to budge. In the early hours of the next morning the California state police, acting on the authority of Governor Brown, arrested about 800 young demonstrators. Much of the $82,000 bail money was provided by members of the university staff, and, undaunted by their encounters with the state police, members of the FSM next embarked upon a series of successful classroom boycotts. In January the chancellor of Berkeley was replaced by a younger and more liberal man. As the weeks passed, the Berkeley rebellion took on new forms, some of them a little absurd. But the long-term effects of the rebellion were considerable and Berkeley became a by-word for student protest throughout the world for the rest of the decade.

The significance of the Berkeley rebellion is twofold. In the first place, many of the personnel involved (including its principal leader, Mario Savio) had been involved in civil rights work in the South. Many of the techniques to which the FSM resorted — notably the massive sit-in and the invitation to mass arrest — were conscious adaptations of methods that had already proved successful in Mississippi and elsewhere. Furthermore, the experience of dealing with the ruthless white cops of Dixie had hardened many of the Berkeley rebels, so that they were unlikely to be deterred by the appearance of a bunch of California state troopers. Even the slogans and songs of the FSM ('We Shall Overcome') were taken directly from the civil rights movement. Both movements were, after all, demanding very much the same thing: the right of the individual to participate fully in the political process.

Secondly, Berkeley — like Harlem and Philadelphia — was ignited by a trivial incident in which those in authority were deemed to have used their position in a harsh, arbitrary, and unfair manner. The student body, like the blacks in the city slums, tended to feel frustrated, powerless, cut off from any meaningful communication with the powers that be.

Total enrolments

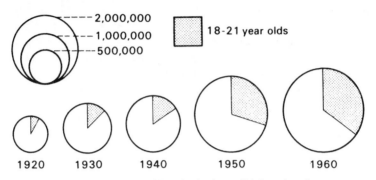

Fig. 5.1 18–21-year olds at institutions of higher education

There had been a huge increase – both numerical and proportional – in the size of America's college population since the mid-fifties (see Figs. 5.1 and 5.2). By 1968–9, the proportion of people between the ages of eighteen and twenty-one who were expected to enter full-time courses of higher education in the United States was close to 50 per cent. In Britain it was about 10 per cent and in the Soviet Union about 13 per cent. One by-product of this phenomenal growth of the college population was that some of the centres of higher education became unmanageably large. On the Berkeley campus, where there were nearly 30,000 people in the fall of 1964, many students felt that they had little more personal identity than the meat that goes into a sausage machine. They went through the inexorable four-year routine of classes, grades, term papers, and exams, and by the end of it all were expected, or so they felt, to be well-rounded, happily adjusted, bright, young, indistinguishable and undistinguished Berkeleyites. Not only did the Berkeley student often feel that he was too small a fish in too big a pond, but it was also widely felt that the various status levels – undergraduate, graduate, teaching staff, campus administration, University of California administration – were too sharply stratified, that they had too little opportunity of real contact with one another. This was a complaint to which some members from all of the strata probably subscribed, but about which they could, because of the very thing complained of, do very little. And it was a complaint that was particularly irksome to the most impotent of all the strata, the undergraduate body. The students felt increasingly alienated from those who appeared to hold the strings, and some of them reached the stage, by the autumn of 1964, of

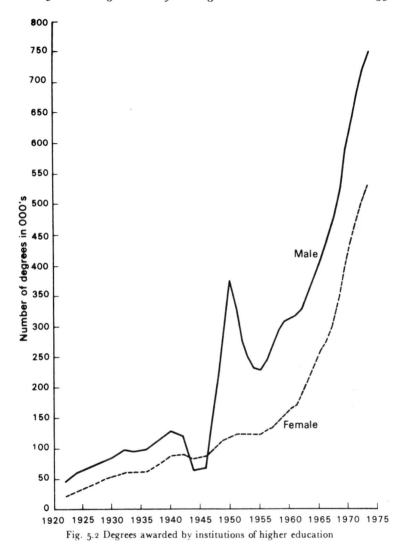

Fig. 5.2 Degrees awarded by institutions of higher education

resenting authority on principle, of assuming it to be guilty until
proved innocent. These feelings (like the similar feelings in the black
ghettos) had been lying just beneath the surface for some time.
Berkeley students, traditionally a more heterogeneous, adventurous,
and self-confident group than most, had already tasted blood when
they demonstrated against the House Committee on Un-American
Activities when it held hearings in San Francisco in 1960. But the

dramatic achievements of the civil rights movement during the summer of 1964 had helped to create a new sense of almost quixotic heroism among many American students, with the result that any incident — such as the tactical folly of the Berkeley authorities — could all too easily touch off a full-scale campus rebellion.

As the decade progressed, so did the nation-wide — and, indeed, world-wide — student rebellion. By the spring of 1968, stimulated partly by the sort of consideration that had first sparked off campus unrest in Berkeley and partly by issues related to the Vietnam War, a number of campuses in the USA, of which Columbia University in New York City was merely the most famous, were more or less in a state of siege. As news and pictures of the events at Columbia and elsewhere spread around the world, so did similar occurrences. In Japan, armed police used a degree of violence against rebellious students that was far in excess of anything experienced in the USA; in Berlin the student leader, Rudi Dutschke, was shot and seriously wounded; in Paris a student strike came close to causing a genuine popular revolution and was partly instrumental in bringing about the eventual end of the de Gaulle régime.

By this stage it was almost impossible to see the student rebellion in isolation from all the other factors with which it was intimately intertwined — the Vietnam War, the generational antagonisms derived in part from the postwar baby boom, race relations, and so on. These and other matters appeared to be converging during that fateful spring and early summer of 1968 — weeks that saw not only the Columbia revolt but also the end of Lyndon Johnson's hopes for re-election, and the assassinations of Martin Luther King and Robert F. Kennedy. That summer, all the forces of resentment and aggression in America gathered in Chicago as that city hosted the Democratic National Convention. For a few days, Chicago witnessed scenes that etched themselves indelibly upon the memories of all who experienced them — the vulgar political bossism of Mayor Daley and the insensitive brutality of his police, the often unmanageable yippies and hippies deliberately throwing the authorities off-balance with their bizarre antics, the aggressive radical activists whose often apocalyptic rhetoric scared those at whom it was aimed into irrational and panicky response.

As in 1964, a Democratic National Convention had provided the vortex into which had swirled many of the most powerful currents of American society. Unlike 1964, the Chicago Convention of 1968 had none of the carnival atmosphere by which most participants — non-Mississippians at any rate — would remember Atlantic City. And yet, somehow, Chicago came and went and America did not collapse and tear itself apart. Indeed, as the delegates and other visitors to Chicago lifted their heads up from their immediate preoccupations and read about the Warsaw Pact invasion of Czechoslovakia, some of them perhaps reflected upon the degree of relative tranquillity and stability that their own society and its political institutions could still muster. As that dramatic year continued on its eventful way and Americans prepared to cast their quadrennial presidential vote for one or other of those survivors of a former era, Hubert H. Humphrey and Richard M. Nixon, it was not impossible to see the beginning of the end of the most turbulent period in domestic American history since the Civil War a century before.

Age of Protest?

It is tempting to consider the two movements that we have been discussing — one concerned primarily with racial questions and the other centred on the campuses of America — as part of a single phenomenon. 'The Age of Protest' or 'The Era of Dissent' is the sort of sobriquet that historians already attach to the 1960s. And not without some justification. It can plausibly be argued that the social unrest and conflict of the period was its most distinguishing feature and that there was an underlying unity of motive between the protests of the blacks and the students. According to such a view, furthermore, the corner-stone of the arch of protest was something that indisputably cast its pall over every aspect of life in America from the early 1960s clear through until the mid 1970s: the war in Vietnam and the domestic disquiet that it increasingly aroused. How accurate is this portrayal of an age and of a society? How far were the various protests united in their personnel, their aims, their methods, their ideologies?

Chronologically, any attempt to equate these various movements is a little misleading. There was a civil rights movement before there was a movement for university reform, and both of these had achieved prominence before most people realized that there was serious and nation-wide opposition to the war in Vietnam. Furthermore, the various movements were concerned with apparently different aims. Many of the attempts to combine them into a single alliance failed. Indeed, unity — as is so often the case with reformist or protest groups

— was almost impossible to achieve within each movement let alone between them. But there were, nevertheless, fundamental respects in which civil rights, Black Power, Berkeley, Columbia, and the peace movement were all part of a bigger whole.

In terms of personnel, for instance, there was a considerable overlap. The leaders in the Berkeley rebellion such as Mario Savio had all received their baptism in radical politics in the civil rights movement; as the Vietnam War sank into an apparently endless slough of mud and dead bodies, more and more civil rights leaders joined the ranks of those who were protesting against the war. The nation's most famous civil rights leader, the Reverend Martin Luther King, hesitated to commit himself on Vietnam. He had no love of the war, to be sure, but he feared that his own effectiveness as a civil rights leader might be jeopardized if he were to become identified in the public mind as a habitual and undiscriminating protester. King weighed the philosophical arguments in favour of a public commitment on the anti-war side; but the argument that eventually tipped the scales was a practical one. The more money the country spent on Vietnam, the less it spent on schemes of domestic social reform. Vietnam, in King's mind, was directly responsible for the retrenchment on the Great Society programmes (see pp.174–7). Armed with this argument, he took the plunge and on 25 March 1967 took part in and addressed a peace parade in Chicago.

There is more than one possible explanation for this overlap of personnel between the membership lists of the various protest movements. Cynics have explained the overlap as arising from the fact that most of the protesters were alienated layabouts who could find an identity only by allying themselves with others who were as alienated as themselves. And there is no doubt that some of the people involved were protesting almost as a reflex action, joining in largely in order to submerge whatever individuality they might have had in the collective identity of a group. But many of the leaders of the various movements came to see at a deeper level a positive link between their respective aims. Each of the protest movements was in some sense an appeal on behalf of helpless individuals who were the unwilling or even unwitting puppets of a remote and apparently inaccessible decision-making élite. What the protesters wanted — for the black, the student, the Vietnamese peasant — was that he should have the opportunity (in the words of the Port Huron Statement, the manifesto of the Students for a Democratic Society) of sharing in 'those social decisions that determine the quality and direction of his life'.

There was also another explanation — a more ominous one — of the link between the movements that we have discussed and, in particular, between the more militant elements in the black and anti-Vietnam movements. After about the beginning of 1965, the American news media were dominated by violent and horrific stories from Vietnam. For millions of Americans, the daily newspaper and television diet consisted in large part of napalm raids, of 'lazy dog' attacks, of the accidental killing of innocent peasants and the deliberate killing of other innocent peasants, and of summary executions of untried opponents — and all these things were done by or at the behest of the American military command in Vietnam. The way to enable 'right' to triumph over 'wrong' (or so the powers-that-be seemed to be saying) was to use sheer brute force; and if force failed to achieve its objective, there was only one answer: more force. This message had its obvious applications to the domestic scene and was repeatedly reinforced by the frustrated aggressiveness of returning Vietnam veterans. It is not altogether surprising that some of America's underprivileged urban groups — notably the blacks — began to act as though brute force might be the way to bring to an end the wrongs that they were suffering in their own cities.

The collective significance of the racial and student movements and Vietnam lies not in any spasmodic organizational unity that these movements might have tried to achieve but in the fact that they arose in the midst of a mass impersonal society, one in which basic human values seemed to many to be severely threatened. They were a cry on behalf of the human dignity of the individual against the deadening hand of what was seen as being an increasingly conformist society, a bitter attempt by the almost impotent to assert themselves against (or at least to steady the hand of) those whom they perceived as being the omnipotent.

If the protest movements were all, in one way or another, methods of asserting the importance of the individual human being in society, in what way if any is it helpful to think of them as having had an ideology in common or of having all been 'Left-wing'? The concepts of 'Left' and 'Right', like the corresponding concepts of 'liberal' and 'conservative', have never reflected in any precise sense the realities of American politics. In the late eighteenth century, a conservative — a man of the Right — was usually somebody, like Alexander Hamilton, who believed in strong executive government and who thought that urban interests should predominate over rural ones. Such a person was thought to be a liberal in the 1960s and to lie to the left of the political spectrum. By the same token, Barry Goldwater was thought to be a conservative although his views were strikingly close in some ways to those of such early 'liberals' as Thomas Jefferson. In the past 200 years or so, in other words, the concepts of Left and Right, of liberal and conservative, have in some respects exchanged places.

But if American history does not help us to define these concepts very carefully, neither does American ideology. A conservative, in European terms at least, is normally somebody who wishes to conserve the main characteristics of the *status quo,* while anybody on the 'Left' is some sort of reformer. But in America this sort of definition would create some very strange bedfellows. For if anybody would have liked to alter the shape of American society even more than the most militant elements in the civil rights movement it was the John Birch Society. If there was something oddly reformist about the 'extreme Right', however, there was certainly an element of anti-quarianism about the so-called New Left of the 1960s. Their 'participatory democracy' and the emphasis on community action was a direct descendant of the local town hall democracy to which American romantics had so often looked back nostalgically, while the New Left's emphasis on the role of the individual contained more than a whiff of the Old Frontier.

Only in the most superficial sense, therefore, could the movements that have been discussed be labelled 'Left-wing'. Their importance is independent of whether they were at one and the same end of the political spectrum; indeed, there is no single spectrum in American political life. They were significant, rather, in that they were among the most spectacular manifestations of a new questioning spirit that pervaded many elements within American society in the 1960s.

The strains of suburbia

We have stressed the social disharmonies of the 1960s because they gave the decade its peculiar character. They were not powerful enough to destroy American society, nor were they, except for spectacular but brief periods, the direct and immediate concern of more than a minority. Many Americans during even the most turbulent periods of social upheaval carried on their daily lives with hardly more than a passing glance at the spectacular tensions that were exciting some of their compatriots

Americans were more affluent than they had ever been. By the beginning of the 1960s the average *per capita* income was $2,223 (it had been $595 in 1940 and $1,491 in 1950), and by 1965 32 million of the nation's 47 million families had cash incomes of $5,000 or more (see Table 5.2).

Table 5.2. Income distribution, 1966

No. of families (in millions)	percentage of families	incomes (in $)
12	25	10,000 plus
11	24	7,000—10,000
9	19	5,000— 7,000
7	16	3,000— 5,000
8	17	less than 3,000

The number of Americans gainfully employed continued to rise apace. By 1967 total non-farm payroll employment had risen to a record 65·6 million*. Sales of luxury items — cars, televisions, dishwashers, stereophonic records, record players, and tape recorders — continued to soar. The rates of both marriages and divorces began to rise again for the first time since the end of the Second World War, but the birth rate fell sharply, thus making the 'baby-booms' of the late 1940s seem, in retrospect, all the more conspicuous (see Figs, 5.3, 5.4 and 5.5, overleaf).

The babies of the late forties were the swinging teenagers of the mid sixties. They survived a major bout of Anglophilia, the girls in particular often shocking their parents by their uncritical adulation of the Beatles and their adoption of the British miniskirt. The culture heroes were young, the girls tried to look young, and their parents, after fighting something of a rearguard action in the early part of the decade, often capitulated and decided to try to behave like their children.

Women in particular tended to find it difficult in a culture that emphasized the virtues of youthful vigour and physical attractiveness to retire gracefully into gentle middle age, and this difficulty was compounded by the strains of living in suburbia. In the years

*Of these, 17 million were employed in manufacturing, 12 million in wholesale and retail trades, 8 million in service industries of various kinds, 4 million in transportation, 3 million in construction, another 3 million in finance and insurance, and at least 2³/4 million in the federal government.

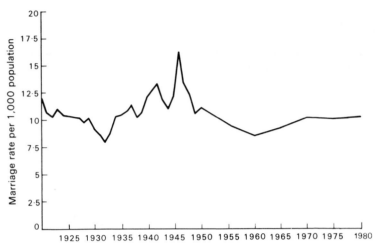

Fig. 5.3 Marriage rate

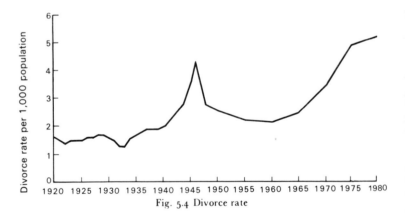

Fig. 5.4 Divorce rate

immediately after their political emancipation, American women —
particularly younger women — had tended to go on a self-indulgent
celebratory spree. They were not yet aware of the full implications of
emancipation and had no conception of the responsibilities that it
might eventually impose. In the 1950s and 1960s, however, America's
suburban housewives were caught in a painful psychic squeeze.
Emancipation had given them the vote, the opportunity for as good an
education as the men received, and the possibility of taking a job.

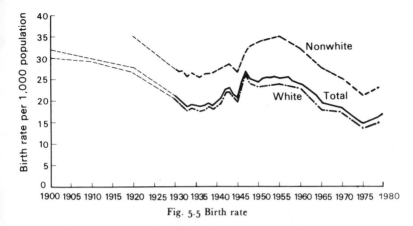

Fig. 5.5 Birth rate

They were, officially, permitted and even encouraged to play a full and equal part in society with men.

But the value system of suburbia had not caught up with the facts of emancipation. The suburban husband normally expected his wife to have the traditional feminine virtue of almost childlike submissiveness, and many a tough and sophisticated suburban woman found herself making herculean efforts to play this unnatural role. The woman was trapped. She had probably been told, as a girl, about female political emancipation, and had almost certainly been given encouragement to rise as far as she could up the educational ladder. Achievement, for her as for her brothers, was the criterion of success. But these appetites, once whetted, were not easily satisfied in suburbia, where a talented and energetic housewife could find little that was really creative to do. So she tended to fall back on the traditional female roles of mother, wife, cook, and hostess. If she had not been led to expect more, these roles would not necessarily have proved irksome. But they often did, and instances of female frustration were not hard to find. On the one hand, there was the obsession with youthfulness and femininity. Millions of middle-aged women, convinced that the way to be truly feminine was to try to look like a teenager, would live off a chalky low-calorie drink called Metrecal or spend many painful hours each week at a special slimming gymnasium. On the other hand, there was the aggressiveness, the assertiveness, the determination to succeed in a man's world. Some women entered the professions or the business world where, like blacks in a newly integrated college, they often felt compelled to try to outshine their colleagues in order to be fully accepted. There was also evidence that American women in the 1960s were becoming more determined than their mothers and grandmothers had been to obtain the same satisfaction from sex as their partners — a determination that was often so self-conscious as to be self-defeating.

But suburban living had its compensations; it was certainly very popular. By the 1960s more than a quarter of the entire American population was living in suburbs. Table 5.3 shows how, in the years 1950—60, the net flow of population in some of America's biggest cities was from the downtown area to the suburbs (and, for the really wealthy few who liked to live in splendid isolation but within reasonable driving time from urban sophistication, to the magnificent estates that became known as exurbia). This pattern (which would have been all the more striking were it not for the large flow of blacks into the downtown areas) was repeated in hundreds of smaller cities in all parts of the United States and had established suburban living as one of the major American social patterns by the 1960s.

Table 5.3. The movement of population from downtown to suburbia within the great metropolitan areas, 1950—60

Standard Metropolitan Statistical Area	1960 population	Percentage increase 1950—60
New York, NY	10,694,633	11·9
New York	7,781,984	−1·4
Outside central city	2,912,649	75·0
Chicago, Ill.	6,220,913	20·1
Chicago	3,550,404	−1·9
Outside central city	2,670,509	71·5
Philadelphia, Penn.	4,342,897	18·3
Philadelphia	2,002,512	−3·3
Outside central city	2,340,385	46·3
Detroit, Mich.	3,762,360	24·7
Detroit	1,670,144	−9·7
Outside central city	2,092,216	79·3

The move to suburbia was made possible by the continued increase in the sale of automobiles. By the mid 1960s almost 90 per cent of suburban families owned at least one car (the figure for families living within the official limits of America's biggest cities was just over 60 per cent). In the typical suburban family the husband would drive 10, 15, even 30 or more miles, along a fast, straight 'thruway' to his downtown place of work. His wife, of course, has a car too. She takes her children to school, visits her friends who are arranging the church bazaar, calls on the hairdresser, and perhaps goes on an expedition to one of the gigantic shopping centres that lie between her suburban home and the city limits. At the shopping centre, she will leave her car in the huge adjacent car park and within half an hour or so emerge wheeling towards the car a week's provisions. On the way home she might collect some money from a drive-in bank or have a cup of coffee at a drive-in café, or even note what movie is playing that night at the local drive-in cinema. Since she is on her way home and has a fast car, she will probably not spare a glance at the endless row of gaudy motels that line the thruway back into town or at the mountain of abandoned cars and blown-out tyres that litter parts of the countryside. If she keeps her eyes on the road as she should, she might manage to avoid being distracted by the ugly roadside hoardings. The automobile is essential to the suburban housewife, for neither the school (at which one of the subjects taught is how to drive a car) nor the church nor the hairdresser nor the shopping centre − nor, for that matter, the suburban home − is easily accessible by public transport.

This automotive suburban civilization of the 1960s was in many ways ruled by its females. Female tastes tended to predominate, not only in food, clothes, and domestic accoutrements, but also not infrequently in the social and political attitudes of suburbia. Children growing up in this environment would not see their fathers at work; but they did see their mothers making, apparently, most of the important household decisions. School, too, tended to be a world dominated by adult females. And at home, in the evening, the child would often see a weary father coaxed and cuddled and fed by a smart and decisive mother. It would be foolish to overstate this picture and to talk about a matriarchal society. But the fact remains that many qualities that have been thought of in the past sixty years as particularly characteristic of women (such as the tendency to vote Republican or to join social groups − and, of course, churches) were also increasingly characteristic of the new suburbs.

Suburban living sometimes left the men a little bewildered. They were not working in the area in which they lived and were therefore tending to live two separate lives, each of which imposed its own social demands. Many business corporations encouraged their employees to spend some of their leisure time together, but the suburban dweller was also likely to feel that he should make himself known in his home neighbourhood. The result would often be an endless round of feverish sociability in which a person considered himself a success in proportion to the number of people with whom he had had even the shortest and most superficial social contact. The logical extension of this compulsion was that a person should change his place of residence frequently so as to be always in a position to conquer new social worlds. (We have already had occasion to note that in the 1950s and 1960s one American family in five moved home every year.)

This frenetic socialization was, in some ways, the upper-middle-class equivalent of the ghetto riots. It was suburbia's way of trying to hold at bay the increasingly faceless nature of society, of keeping at arm's length the perceived dangers of alienation and loneliness. It was suburban man's way of trying to find an identity for himself in the face of a series of homogenizing pressures which, he imagined, threatened to obliterate his individuality.

The Kennedy Legacy

Although the volume and range of discussion about matters of major social importance was unusually large in the 1960s, there were moments of harmony — particularly in the stunned days and weeks after the assassination of President Kennedy. The social harmony of that painful period brought in its wake a major political bonus: a degree of co-operation between the two ends of Pennsylvania Avenue — the White House and Congress — that was almost unprecedented except at times of acute national crisis. It must be remembered, however, that many of the Bills passed at that time had been introduced in the first place when President Kennedy was alive. In particular, the two most publicized measures of all — the civil rights Bill and the tax cut — were programmes in which Kennedy had, towards the end of his life, decided to invest a great deal of his own prestige. Although these bills became law after his death, they were, in two important ways, essentially Kennedy Bills.

In the first place, Kennedy had tried to educate the country regarding the desirability of these new policies. He gave much time and attention in his last months to the question of civil rights, and his efforts were primarily directed towards creating a climate of opinion within which a liberal civil rights bill would be acceptable. He thought that he might be able to get such a Bill through Congress some time in 1964. The nation's economy occupied even more of

President Kennedy's time. Repeatedly during his presidency Kennedy had tried to impress upon public opinion that there was nothing sacrosanct about having an annually balanced national budget, that a short-term deficit could even act as a useful stimulus to greater productivity, and that a high rate of employment and a thriving economy were not necessarily incompatible. These ideas were not JFK's own; Keynes had put them forward three decades earlier. But Kennedy was the first major American politician to espouse them — and he did so despite the attendant risk of further alienating the large body of Americans who were deeply committed to what they liked to call fiscal integrity. During Kennedy's presidency the Gross National Product went up by 25 per cent and the national growth rate, meandering along at about $2^{1}/2$ per cent per annum in 1960, had reached 5 per cent in 1963. Nevertheless, Kennedy and his advisers became convinced that further productivity incentives were necessary if this sort of growth rate were to be maintained. The most powerful incentive, it was agreed, would be a major cut in taxes. A tax cut would have the added political advantage of appealing above all to the higher income brackets, and Kennedy assumed that he would need all the support he could get from the nation's businessmen in the election in 1964. Furthermore, a tax cut was clearly the best way of trying to silence those critics from the business world who disliked unbalanced budgets: if they wanted a tax cut they would have to accept the increased deficit that would inevitably accompany it.

But the civil rights and tax Bills were also Kennedy's Bills in a deeper sense. It is possible that they would have become law in 1964 if Kennedy had lived. But the most important factor in persuading a hitherto intransigent and even reactionary Congress to pass these liberal measures was the assassination of the President. Lyndon Johnson knew that Kennedy's death had left Washington with a feeling of embarrassed loyalty to the late President that had never been particularly strong when Kennedy was alive. In his first address to Congress, on 27 November 1963, President Johnson made shrewd political use of these emotions. He said, in part:

> ... No memorial oration or eulogy could more eloquently honour President Kennedy's memory than the earliest possible passage of the civil rights bill for which he fought ...
>
> And, second, no act of ours could more fittingly continue the work of President Kennedy than the earliest passage of the tax bill for which he fought ...

When one remembers how unpopular Kennedy was at various

times during his term of office, it becomes difficult to understand quite why his assassination caused such widespread and prolonged grief and why the events in Dallas became so deeply ingrained a part of the consciousness of so many people, Americans and non-Americans alike. There were certain obvious reasons. The assassination had many of the elements of classical tragedy: there was the hero himself, an attractive man and a brave leader who was struck down at the height of his powers; there was the lovely wife whose noble dignity in the days after Dallas it would be hard to forget; and there was, above all, the sense of waste, of futility. The whole thing was made to seem all the more pointless by the fact that the man who allegedly committed the murder was never brought to trial and that neither his guilt nor his motives were, for some people at least, subsequently proved. But there was more to it than that.

In the first place, the death of Kennedy was absolutely unexpected, isolated, out of context. One moment the President was a vibrant, handsome, vigorous, youthful leader; within half an hour he was dead. No illness, no lingering, no warning. And there was not even the satisfaction of being told that Kennedy died for a cause, that his assassination had at least exposed for all to see the evil machinations of extremists. Instead, it seemed that he had died for nothing, the victim of one lonely oddball.

Some people found this theory hard to take, even though it was the considered conclusion of the prestigious Warren Commission. Intelligent Americans on the so-called 'Right' of the political spectrum found it difficult to resist the temptation of assuming that Earl Warren (long since a favourite whipping-boy of theirs) had managed to suppress the fact that Oswald was part of a wider conspiracy.

And some thoughtful observers were suspicious of the extraordinary speed with which the commission did its job. Was the commission genuinely inquiring into the circumstances of the assassination or was it really acting as a prosecuting attorney, spending no time on any information that did not contribute to the hypothesis that Oswald, acting alone, had shot the President? Was the commission's speed also dictated by a desire on the part of Lyndon Johnson to have its superficially reassuring conclusions in the hands of the public well in time for the presidential election of November 1964? These nagging doubts were reinforced by the serious logical and factual flaws that were detected in the commission's findings by astute observers like Mark Lane.

The assassination itself was not, of course, seen on television. But it was the first great tragedy of the television age. Within minutes of the shots ringing out, millions of Americans knew what had happened. By the time Kennedy was pronounced dead, the great majority of Americans knew that he had been shot. For the next three days television did an extraordinary job. All advertised programmes were suspended and the networks broadcast nothing but news, interviews, and occasional film clippings of Kennedy's life. At a time of almost unprecedented nervousness and fear, television enabled American society to undergo a sort of communal catharsis. It helped to bind up the wounds of a stricken nation and played an important part in channelling the volatile emotions of the day toward the end of social unity rather than that of social discord. But it also ensured that the events of those few days would be stamped even more indelibly upon the minds and hearts of those who sat glued to their TV sets than might otherwise have been the case.

There are other reasons for the massive obsession with Dallas that are harder to explain because they are less tangible. Most people have, at one time or another, experienced the suppressed desire to yell blood-curdling obscenities in church, to humiliate or even destroy the symbols of authority and stability that surround them. And, in the deepest and most repressed confines of the American subconscious, the murder of a president represents the ultimate act of childlike defiance. Happily, the overwhelming majority of Americans succeed in keeping these dark desires repressed. But what happened when a president *was* killed? When they heard the news, Americans everywhere felt, among a host of painful emotions, a morbid thrill. But their thrill turned to a shiver as their feelings became clouded with only half-realized feelings of guilt. The guilt took many forms: a bout of national self-criticism, the secular beatification of the dead President, and the attempt to shove off the blame on to someone else — even (in, for instance, the satirical play *Macbird!*) on to the chief beneficiary of Dallas, Lyndon Baines Johnson.

There were political reasons, too, why Dallas remained such a volatile preoccupation of the American people, for the assassination turned Robert Kennedy overnight into a serious candidate for the presidency. Robert Kennedy was the third son in a family with a powerful sense of destiny. When brother Joe died in the Second World War the family ambitions became vested in the next brother, Jack. When Jack was killed, the mantle of leadership fell on Bob. He had inherited his brother's mission, and he was to die five years later while trying to inherit his brother's job.

Thus the implications of the presidency and assassination of John F. Kennedy on the future of American history were far greater than the simple facts about them would suggest. In 1960 the United States was an introspective nation suffering from a serious deficiency of heroes. The Kennedy presidency provided the nation with a strong tonic, one that gave many of those Americans who were interested in government a new vigour with which to discuss and argue and plan. Above all, it gave them a degree of enthusiasm that had not been seen since the early days of the New Deal.

Vigour and enthusiasm, of course, cut both ways. The more vociferously Kennedy's New Frontiersmen advocated their new policies, the more they aroused their conservative opponents. The range and intensity of political and social attitudes in the United States in the early 1960s were greatly increased by the efforts of the New Frontier. Getting the country moving also meant getting it divided. Kennedy's death, as we have seen, created a sense of social unity that was never in evidence during his occupancy of the White House. Lyndon Johnson, therefore, came to office at a moment when almost the whole nation was predisposed to close its ranks loyally behind its new leader — an advantage that Kennedy had never had. But this apparent social consensus did not represent real unity in American society. On the contrary, the social divisions and tensions that began to manifest themselves in the early 1960s were to shake the United States with increasing virulence as the decade wore on.

The Great Society

Lyndon Johnson's political honeymoon lasted for a year or two after he became president. In his first months in office he was regarded by many as a healer at a time of distress — a role he knew it was to his political advantage to play to the hilt. Accordingly, he adopted the stance of a man who would loyally and modestly continue to the best of his ability the policies of his fallen leader, the embodiment of his nation's grief about the past and determination about the future. But such a cloak could not sit comfortably for long upon a man who, in his days as Senate Majority Leader, had relished the exercise of real power and who, despite the appalling circumstances in which he had acceded to the presidency, was nevertheless determined to make the most of his occupancy of the nation's highest office. Thus, one of LBJ's principal initial political advantages — the hopes with which a bereaved nation invested him — gradually became, in his own calculations, a disadvantage. If he was to make his own mark on history, he would have to climb out from under the Kennedy legacy.

This meant winning the presidency in his own right. By election time in November 1964, Johnson had everything going for him. His party had nominated him by acclamation as its candidate (the Democratic Convention had turned into something of a coronation on nomination day) while the Republican opposition, in an apparent gesture of political suicide, had pinned its banner to a man certain to win no votes except from the extreme Right wing, Barry M. Goldwater. In the campaign Johnson had enjoyed ridiculing the wilder suggestions emanating from the Goldwater camp — such as that NATO commanders should perhaps be empowered to order the use of 'tactical' or 'conventional' nuclear warheads without specific presidential authorization, or even that such warheads might be used with profit to teach the North Vietnamese a lesson. 'In Your Heart You Know He's Right' said the Goldwater slogans. To which the Johnson supporters, playing up the image of their Republican opponent as an erratic sharp-shooter from the extreme Right, responded with such parodies as 'In Your Heart You Know He Might', 'In Your Head You Know He's Wrong', and even 'In Your Heart' (or, more cruelly, 'In His Head') 'You Know He's Nuts'.

In the November election, Johnson won the presidency with 61 per cent of the votes — the largest percentage in American presidential history. At last, a year after entering the White House, LBJ had been elected in his own right. And the honeymoon continued.

On 4 January 1965, still flushed with the warm glow of his stupendous victory two months before, President Johnson delivered the annual State of the Union address to a joint session of Congress. Most of his speech was devoted to what he called the 'Great Society' and was, in effect, a way of saying that the government and country should not be content with the Kennedy-inspired social reforms of the previous year but should expect a mass of new reformist legislation from the Johnson administration in the months and years to come. LBJ was initially as good as his word and a flood of social proposals flowed from the White House dealing with medical care for the aged, education, housing, immigration, urban and rural development, crime, black voting rights and much else besides. Nothing like it had been seen since the first hundred days of the New Deal back in 1933 and, although Johnson did not have a Depression to use as a political spur with which to goad the Congress as FDR had done, much of the 'Great Society' programme was successfully passed into law.

What lay behind this tidal wave of reformist energy? Was it simply that Lyndon Johnson was a master persuader, more adept at twisting congressional arms than his predecessor had been? Or did the real initiative come from Congress itself? Were the liberal measures of Johnson's first two years really an attempt by the American power élite to keep the real progressives at bay by making minimal gestures in their direction? Or had America really taken, in some sense, a tilt to the 'Left'? LBJ had never been the most radical social visionary. Indeed, for all his legendary skills as a political fixer, his views on domestic policy had in the past usually sounded rather conventional. There was a tense, frenetic quality to some of the 'Great Society' proposals and the language in which they were couched and advertised (cf. Johnson's 'war on poverty') suggesting that, alongside the hard work and good intentions that undoubtedly lay behind them, there was also anxiety. But anxiety about what?

Lyndon Johnson was a man riddled by anxieties. For one thing, he was resentfully conscious throughout his years as president that he could never replace John Kennedy in the affections of many of the nation's most powerful and attractive political figures. Perhaps he tried too hard to do so and perhaps the 'Great Society' was part of that effort. In addition, the very size of Johnson's electoral victory in 1964 seems to have given him a sense or urgency, as though his mandate for legislative reform would henceforth never be as great again. Further, LBJ knew that if you make a lot of promises, as he had done in the 1964 campaign, you have got to deliver the goods — and quickly. There is nobody so resentful as the person whose appetite has been whetted and who is then given a late and inadequate meal. But above all it was the looming, threatening cloud of Vietnam that pushed LBJ into hasty and often ill-conceived domestic measures. As he wrestled with the problems of whether and with what intensity to bomb North Vietnam or how high to raise American troop levels, Johnson felt that time and money for his beloved 'Great Society' were increasingly at a premium. For a while, the legislative programme was promoted with a flourish of unrealistically rosy rhetoric. But then, as Johnson built up the American involvement in Vietnam and had to devote more and more of his time and attention and his government's revenue to what proved to be a series of ever more severe mishaps, the 'Great Society' and the 'War on Poverty' inevitably took a back seat. Many individual domestic programmes worked well enough; some foundered. But the hyperbolic optimism with which they had all been launched gave out a rather sickly echo a few years later to those whose hopes and expectations had been so dramatically raised.

By the beginning of 1968, the liberal approach to domestic problems so optimistically invoked by the Kennedy men and then by LBJ himself was becoming discredited. Johnson looked and sounded tired, a broken man. At the end of March in concluding a television address about Vietnam he announced to a stunned nation that he did not intend to seek a further term as president the following November. The America whose presidency LBJ was so relieved to hand on to another was torn by severe social and political cleavages and by outbreaks of individual and communal violence unparalleled for a century. As the decade limped towards its end, the United States was certainly moving, as John F. Kennedy had wanted it to do. But in what direction — and indeed in how many inconsistent directions — nobody could say with confidence, least of all that great disillusioned lover of consensus and compromise, Lyndon B. Johnson, or the proud new man at the helm, Richard M. Nixon.

Six

THE 1970s:
TO WATERGATE AND BEYOND

'The squares are taking over'

There were times in 1968 when it looked as though the social tensions
and conflicts of the 1960s had reached a pitch of such intensity that the
very fabric of American society was threatened. Urban riots and
political assassinations were becoming more frequent, race relations
gave every appearance of deteriorating, student disaffection returned
every year with renewed vigour. Above all there was Vietnam. Early
in 1968 came the Tet offensive. Later that spring, public opinion polls
began to show for the first time a majority of Americans opposing the
war, and anti-war presidential candidates like Eugene McCarthy and
Robert Kennedy garnered much of the popularity that Lyndon
Johnson had enjoyed a few years earlier. Kennedy defeated McCarthy in most of the primary elections and immediately after his final
and most vital victory in California in June was shot dead. By the time
of the riots in Chicago at the time of the Democratic National Convention in August, an observer might have been forgiven for won-
dering whether American society was not engaged in some sort of
self-destructive spasm. Furthermore, as the repeated volleys of bitter
rhetoric and bursts of furious activity helped to alienate social and
political groups from one another, it was hard to see either a Humphrey or a Nixon administration really getting to grips with problems
of a scale and an intensity that were no longer susceptible to merely
political, administrative and economic solutions.

Nothing magic happened. Nixon was elected president and the
anti-war rallies and student protests continued. In 1969 armed black
militants took over the student union building at Cornell University,

Harvard was immobilized and, on 15 October, the largest anti-war rallies of all were held in Washington and elsewhere. The following summer saw a plethora of angry campus protests against Nixon's extension of the war to Cambodia; several lives were lost at Kent State University in Ohio and at Jackson State College in Mississippi when the forces of law and order fired upon protesters.

Nevertheless, it was becoming clear by about 1970 that the frequency, intensity and sheer volume of protests and riots were not quite as great as they had been. American society, a little the worse for wear, would survive. 'We are clearly, rapidly coming out of ... [a] period of sickness and malaise' said social prophet Herman Kahn[1] a few years later, 'and reverting to a basic squareness.' America, he went on 'is now a healthy country because the squares are taking over.' In public life at least. Why did this happen?

To some extent the squares no doubt took over because various demands of the radicals had been successful; 'the radicalism of the 1960s', declared former student leader Tom Hayden[2], 'is fast becoming the common sense of the 1970s.' And it was true that racial discrimination had been overcome in certain fields (most impressively in the South), students in some colleges had by the early 1970s achieved a measure of participation in campus decision-making, and the US Government (in the increasingly familiar figure of President Nixon's National Security Assistant Henry A. Kissinger) was in regular touch with both South and North Vietnam about ways of bringing to an end America's disastrous involvement in that part of the world. However, many of the issues that had so inflamed people in the later 1960s were still unresolved: the latest attempt to deal with *de facto* racial segregation in Northern cities – by busing black children to schools in white areas and vice versa – aroused storms of violent protest among white parents in Boston and elsewhere, while the American military presence in Vietnam, the most bitterly debated issue of them all, was not finally ended until 1973.

One reason for the apparent diminution of protest and social conflict was that, under the harsh régime of Nixon and his somewhat authoritarian Attorney-General John N. Mitchell, it simply became harder and more dangerous to take to the streets. Heads were broken, marchers arrested, newsreel pictures monitored, names filed. The Nixon administration, proud of its commitment to 'law and order', tended to equate legitimate protest with illegitimate crime and argued that by clamping down upon all those who disturbed the peace it was helping to make America's streets safe again for ordinary citizens — the 'silent majority' or 'Middle America' as the non-protesters were dubbed.

Perhaps a more profound explanation of the reduction of tensions in American society lay buried in the economic and demographic changes of the time. Coincidentally the later 1960s had seen the full flowering of the affluence that had bemused the new middle classes in the Eisenhower era and had also seen the swollen generation of postwar babies, moving through the age-profile like an orange down the neck of an ostrich, reach its adolescence and teenage. By the 1970s, these phenomena were already becoming things of the past.

Take, first, the affluence. It was calculated that the USA, with around 7 per cent of the world's population, had something in the region of 42 per cent of the world's income. The gross national product, $284 billion in 1950, had shot up to $982 billion by 1970. Despite continuing inequities and a number of appalling pockets of real poverty and deprivation, moreover, much of this wealth was widely distributed. In the 1950s *per capita* income in the USA, starting from a base of $1501, the highest in the world, went up in real terms by 14 per cent; in the 1960s real *per capita* income rose by no less than 38 per cent to reach a nominal sum of just under $4000. By the latter half of the 1960s, the American housewife was faced with an average of 6,500 grocery products when she visited the supermarket, while each week that passed saw American manufacturers trying to place a further 150 new products on the grocery shelves.

Not only was there a lot of everything; there was also the expectation, fanned by those who produced the goods that had to be sold for the economy to continue to expand, that there would and should be more. Shoppers were induced to buy in bulk. Two for the price of one, ten for the price of eight. Automobiles and detergents were 'new' and 'improved' and 'more for the same price'. Green, Pink and Blue Chip stamps were devised to induce shoppers to take greater advantage of the luxuries of modern shopping; you bought all the more (so went the trading stamp theory) in order to obtain more stamps — in order to obtain, in exchange for them, some further 'free' goods. More for more for more. The economy, the advertising pitch, and millions of individual psyches were all devoted, in a symbiotic embrace, to the idea that one was living in an age of unlimited adundance.

This affluence had coincided with a period in which an abnormally high percentage of the American population was in their teens or early twenties. The proportion between the ages of 15 and 24 had long been dropping steadily from 17·4 per cent at the end of the 1930s to 14·5 per cent at the end of the 1940s, down to 13·7 per cent at the end of the 1950s. By the end of the 1960s, however, it had leaped up again to a staggering 18 per cent. In absolute terms, the total American population had gone up between 1960 and 1970 by about 24 million — and the number of 15–24-year-olds had gone up in the same period by 12 million, an increase over the previous decade of over 40 per cent. In addition, the unprecedented drop in birth rates during the later 1960s and early 1970s ensured that the exceptional age-profile of the 1960s would probably never recur (see Fig. 5.5, p.167 and Fig. 7.2, p.220).

The only economic conditions familiar to the baby-boom generation of the 1960s were those of technological and economic expansion. This coincidence of, on the one hand, an apparently booming national economy and, on the other hand, so many youngsters just reaching maturity had led to the spawning of a whole range of consumer industries and advertising techniques designed especially for the huge new youthful market. It also enabled millions of youngsters to enjoy a unique sense of material security, a confidence — which their parents, with memories of depression and war could never quite share — that there were fool-proof economic back-up systems and safety nets that would ensure that all except the most unfortunate could more or less take for granted the availability of whatever food and shelter they needed. This helped to liberate them from many of the concerns that have preoccupied most people elsewhere and enabled them to devote their energies, if they were predisposed to do so, to other matters. If you cared about race relations or Vietnam, for example, or you resented the 'alienating and depersonalizing classroom situation', you could take time off from the regular institutions and procedures that supposedly gave structure to your life and make your protest, fairly safe in the knowledge that you would probably have no trouble in obtaining food and clothes and a roof over your head throughout the period that you 'opted out', and that you would also find reinforcement from any number of other young people who shared your approach to life and its problems and encouraged you in your expression of it. This combination of an affluent and expanding economy and an exceptionally large and visible peer group does not in itself explain the protests and the social and generational tensions of the middle and later 1960s, but it was one of its principal preconditions.

As time passed, however, the orange gradually slid further down the ostrich's neck as the proportion of adolescents and teenagers in the population reverted to something like its normal size. At the same time, Americans gradually began to adjust to the idea that their nation's economic resources were not unlimited, would have to be more carefully husbanded in future, and could not be expected to provide a comprehensive economic and welfare back-up system for all who needed it. Structural poverty and deprivation were in any case still widespread; white coal miners in the Appalachians, Mexican fruit-pickers in Florida and California, blacks in most urban centres, the unemployed, the sick, the elderly − all cried out for whatever fat could be pared from the national and state budgets. In addition, the new concern with the deterioration of the physical environment − the air, the water, the degree of safety at home and at work, the quality of food and drugs − re-inforced the economic stringencies of the 1970s. And so, most dramatically, did the increase in oil prices − and consequently in the prices of everything else − as the Arab world flexed its muscles in the years following the 1973 Middle East War; the consumer price index, which rose annually by 1 or 2 per cent in the 1960s and by between 3 and 6 per cent in the early 1970s, shot up by 11 per cent in 1974 and over 9 per cent in 1975.

Thus, a combination of economic and demographic factors helped to make the aggressive expression of social conflict less common in the America of the 1970s than in the 1960s. As one former radical leader put it in 1977, 'you can't make a revolution if you have to make a living.'

A further factor was the tired sigh of resignation that emanated by this time from many who would have been the leading radicals and protesters a few years earlier. Bayard Rustin, a leading black spokesman of earlier years, told this story in the 1970s. 'I once asked my mother: "Mama, how can you be so calm?" and she said: "It's too tiresome and annoying to be full of hate." ' Hitherto, America had always been the land of optimism, a society bewitched by the belief that (as they said during the war) 'the difficult we do immediately; the impossible takes longer.' Hitherto, foods and medicines, politicians and sportsmen, new weapons and rock stars, would be talked and written about in almost apocalyptic terms as the greatest that had ever existed. Why settle for less? was the message implicit in this type of cheerful hyperbole; why settle for the nursery slopes when you can have the whole mountain? Advertisers would tell you that this film or that whisky was the *ne plus ultra* of its kind; wartime slogans ('the war to save democracy') and policies (unconditional surrender, the A-bomb) would often seem to correspond to a streak of 'totalism' in American culture. There was an impatience to complete the job, and the certainty that the job could and would be achieved with total success. But in recent times American optimism had suffered some severe blows: the Russian launching of Sputnik in 1957 and the assassination of President Kennedy in 1963, the race riots of the mid 1960s, the Vietnam fiasco and Watergate. Already in the late sixties, Jack Newfield wrote that 'we are the first generation that learned from experience . . . that things were not getting better, that we shall *not* overcome.'[3]

Just as the optimism, the 'totalism' of the past had characterized conservative and radical America alike, so the new spirit gradually came to affect not only Nixon's 'silent majority' which had suffered such a series of assaults upon its dignity and its values in the 1960s, but also the radicals, the protesters, the erstwhile prophets of political confrontation and a 'counter culture'. In the early 1970s, as Bobby Seale ran for Mayor of Oakland wearing a shirt and tie, as Eldridge Cleaver found Christ and returned to the USA to permit the processes of law take their course, as Tom Hayden ran for a seat in the US Senate, their younger brothers and sisters all over the country were no longer attracted to the idea of setting up the barricades against institutional America. It had been done; it had achieved some objectives and failed in others; who had the energy to try and do it all again? Far better not to fritter away one's strength on fruitless causes but to place whatever reformist urges remained into upgrading the quality of one's own life − one's body, mind, and personal relationships. Some of the old rhetoric remained. People still talked of radical revolution and of the need to overhaul the fundamental infrastructure of society, made clenched fist salutes and wore jeans and long hair. But gradually these things tended to become the vestigial symbols of a revolt that had lost its head of steam, gestures of defiance that Herman Kahn's 'square' society increasingly found it could accommodate without much trouble. When phrases like 'power to the people' turned up in the advertising copy of the public utilities and black revolutionaries were invited onto the television chat shows, it was clear that much of the radicalism and the counter culture of the 1960s was no longer considered as a serious threat by those who upheld more traditional standards and values and that a practical *modus vivendi* was being worked out between them.

The Quality of Life

As the economic stringencies of the 1970s — shortages, unemployment, high inflation and the rest — cut their way into the national
consciousness, people became ever more concerned with the effect of
these things on their own bank balance, their own home, the quality of
their own life. The most frequently discussed issues of the 1960s had
been those of high politics, mass society, and international affairs;
those of the 1970s were more characteristically those that related to
the quality of life available to the individual and to the social circle of
which he or she was part.

The quality of life was often interpreted in terms of immediate,
physical, sensual and even sexual experience. Americans had a long
tradition of emphasizing the value of personal experience over that of
pure book learning and of celebrating physicality and physical prow-
ess; their heroes had usually been big, tough men of great strength and
health while their archetypal women were — well, as they used to say,
all woman. But something new seems to have entered the picture by
about the late 1960s.

For one thing, the traditional sexual stereotypes were no longer
universally accepted. Dr. Fred Brown of Mount Sinai Hospital was
reported (*Newsweek*, September 6 1971) as having discovered that the
reaction of young men and women to a gender identity Rorschach blot
had more or less reversed in just a few years. In the 1950s, the
aggressive and sharply-curved image had generally been identified —
by males and females alike — as masculine; by the late 1960s, according to Dr. Brown, young male and female patients tended to identify
the blot as feminine. By this time, big, strong, muscular men with
rock-like jaws and curvilinear ladies with hands on hips and scarlet
lips began to look dated, comic even. Many young men began to wear
their hair longer than their fathers had generally done and to wear
brightly coloured and sensitively textured clothes and to speak with
gentle voices. The American social psychologist Kenneth Keniston
observed that for many young men 'the old notions of masculinity are
not an attractive ideal any more, and . . . there is much more acceptance of what were traditionally considered — and this has to be put in
quotes — "feminine" qualities of . . . empathy, sympathy, com-
passion, love, tenderness, and so on.'[4] Young women on the other
hand were increasingly likely to adopt characteristics that traditionalists might have thought to be 'masculine' — to wear trousers, for
instance, and their men friends' sweaters, or to apply for jobs in the

hitherto all-male professions. In 1972, one of the vice-presidents of the Mattel toy company (the manufacturers of the popular 'Barbie doll') was quoted as saying that Barbie wearing blue jeans was now out-selling Barbie in a wedding dress.

As more and more women took advantage of contraceptive pills or other forms of female contraception, they could begin to take sexual initiatives and to show sexual appetites that in previous ages would have been widely considered both indelicate and dangerous. They were able to plan and to restrict as never before the amount of time put aside for child-rearing, with the result that more and more women found that their reproductive role went only a small way towards the achievement of any real fulfilment in life. Many women, particularly those with under-utilized educational and professional qualifications, began to feel an uneasy frustration if their lives were largely restricted to the performance of those roles traditionally thought to be 'feminine'.

This blurring of traditionally clear and separate sex roles was only partial of course and for many people was of sufficiently little con-sequence that it could cause more amusement than genuine confusion or disturbance. There were jokes about long-haired and gentle cou-ples, arm-in-arm, and how you couldn't tell which was which. The commercial interests weighed in with 'Unisex' clothes and sauna baths. There were also a number of semi-political manifestations as well. Members of the 'Gay Liberation' movement demanded the right of (primarily male) homosexuals to relate to each other with as much social freedom as did heterosexuals. And there was the much stronger (though in many ways fissiparous) Women's Liberation movement whose unifying theme was the insistence that women should be liberated from what they saw as their traditional role as, primarily, object rather than subject. In the women's movement there were, inevitably, the extremists whose chief aim sometimes seemed to be the total elimination of men from their lives. But millions of intelligent women, upset by the vacuous existence to which they felt society had condemned them, were beginning to make a determined effort to obtain the social and economic and sexual equality with men to which they considered themselves entitled.

The sheer physicality of sex was much discussed in the '70s. Figures were published to show that the incidence of sexual intercourse among teenagers was on the rise, that there was more adultery (even elevated in some sub-cultures to an organizedly 'swinging' life-style)

than had ever appeared to be the case before, and that all the traditional off-shoots of promiscuity — venereal disease, illegitimacies,
divorce — were also increasing.

Whatever the shaky reliability of any statistical report on so private a
topic, there can be little doubt that the members of the postwar generation who grew to adulthood in the late 1960s and the early 1970s had
a less inhibited attitude towards sex and towards sensual experience
in general than their parents and grandparents had done. These
youngsters, raised without personal memories of the depression and
the war and, for the most part, accustomed to a degree of affluence
and technological sophistication unknown to previous generations,
tended to find it relatively easy to develop considerable financial and
geographical independence from their parents. Furthermore, these
were the years in which the birth-control pill, the diaphragm and the
IUD were widely and cheaply accessible for the first time. Within
such a context it was only to be expected that there would be an
increase in sexual activity, particularly among young people. Accom-
panying this increase, there was a corresponding elevation of the
expression and satisfaction of sexual desire from its customary status
as something to be waited for and then rendered all due apprecia-
tion when its time came, to something approaching the apotheosis
of self-indulgence. Sex was no longer something that you had to yearn
for; by the later 1960s, there was a widespread impatience with the
'deferred gratification' of the old 'Puritan ethic'. Henceforth, said the
gurus of the new ethic, if you wanted to do something — particularly
an experience of a sexual or a sensual nature — why, then, you did it.

One of the ways in which a culture reveals itself is in the material
goods that it produces and in the ways in which these are marketed.
The sexual revolution of the later 1960s and the 1970s was clearly
reflected in the commercial advertising of the period. There was
nothing new about people trying to sell commodities by suggesting
that, along with the commodity, you might also get some sex. But the
use of sex in advertisements in earlier times had more often tended to
emphasize the legitimacy and normality of the sex that was on offer; it
was either happily marital sex or acceptable surrogate sex. What was
offered was never anything approaching real, physical sex but something far less definable such as warm and secure companionship. By
the last decade or so of our period things had become far more overtly
physical and the emphasis was on you, the individual sex-getter
rather than, as in days gone by, on you as part of a legitimate and

stable partnership. MILK DRINKERS MAKE BETTER LOVERS said the bumper stickers, while the California Pizza House asked if you had 'Had A Piece Lately?'

The sexual appeal was not always quite so wholeheartedly inviting or totally free of guilt associations. Indeed, one frequent theme in the advertising of the 1970s was the emphasis on slightly *outré* forms of sexual activity and the implication that sexual insecurity or irregularity were not as uncommon as you might think. 'While you're up here,' said the card in the airline seat pocket advertising an FM radio station, 'guess who's at home with your wife.' A television ad showed a man receiving luxuriously satisfying service at the barber: then a confidential woman's voice urged viewers to 'give him the Schick hot lather machine — because he shouldn't have to go to someone else for a little warmth . . .'

Someone somewhere was always having a new sexual or sensual experience and couldn't really be blamed for doing so. If anything was to be censured it was the avoidance of experience. In John Updike's novel *Bech: A Book*, the hero, Henry Bech, asks his mistress, Norma, when the opportunity of smoking marijuana presents itself for the first time, *'why* do you want to cop out with all these drugs?' and she answers:

> I want to have an *experience*. I've never had a baby, the only wedding ring I've ever worn is the one you loan me when we go to St. Croix in the winter. I've never been to Pakistan . . . My life is closing in and I hate it and I thought this way I could open it up a little.[5]

Or, in the words of the ad for a movie entitled *Sexual Secrets of Marijuana* (and this was the era *par excellence* of publicly available explicitly sexual movies), 'You must see this picture — OR YOU'LL NEVER KNOW!'

This emphasis on direct, personal experience of a sensual nature found further emphasis in these years in a resurgent stress on the stimuli of the five traditional senses — particularly the more undernourished of them.

There was, for instance, a thriving new 'smells' industry which manufactured and sold a vast new range of appropriately scented deodorants, after-shave lotions, mouthwashes, skin moisturisers, bath oils, and vaginal sprays. A 'tastes' industry, too, built up as exotic new 'ethnic' foods — Mexican, Italian, Chinese, Greek and 'Jewish' — went on sale in the most unlikely places and children insisted on being given sweet honey and cinammon cereals for breakfast garnished with frosted shredded wheat or bits of marshmallow. The tactile sense received attention as well. Clothes were made tight and textured, and places like the Esalen Institute in California would encourage you to be more sensitive towards body language, and to know how to touch and be touched and to feel from another person's nose or forehead or shoulders or back, and not just from their voice or eyes or hands, what he or she wished to communicate.

As an adjunct to this concern with the physical quality of one's personal life, many people developed a concern in the later 1960s and the 1970s for the wider environment in which they lived. These were years when America's appalling urban pollution, for so long a normal feature of life for the ghetto-dwellers, crept up appreciably upon the white middle and upper-middle classes. 'The urban environment' became a major preoccupation of reformers, and the desirability of crime-free streets, of fresh air and water, and of cleaner, quieter, safer automobiles and airplanes increasingly took up the energies of people who a few years earlier might have been involved in black voter registration campaigns or the anti-war movement. The seeds sown earlier by Rachel Carson's book *Silent Spring*[6] and by Ralph Nader's dogged pursuit of the big auto companies bore impressive fruit in these years. Consumer and environmental protection were ideas whose time had come as Americans became increasingly conscious of the vulnerability of their physical environment and of the interdependence between the physical quality of life in the USA and in other parts of the world. The world was like a spaceship and its resources were finite. This was most acutely true of those resources used for what used to be called 'fuel' or 'power' and was by the 1970s dubbed 'energy'. If, for instance, the Arabs cut down their supply of oil as happened in the months and years following the October 1973 Middle East War, Americans — the world's most prodigal consumers of oil — could be the ones to suffer most acutely.

In this new atmosphere, the hitherto almost unchallenged supremacy of the idea of growth, of bigness, began to come under attack. It was hard persuading people that (as E. F. Schumacher put it in the title of his bestseller) 'small is beautiful'[7], that more meant less, that heating had to be turned down even in the winter, that a large car was a poor investment, that lower wage settlements would bring more long-term benefits than higher, inflationary ones, that one should choose a small slice of the cake so that there was more to go around. Too often the response to this sort of proposition was that 'I'd do it —

but only if everyone else did.' But bit by bit the anti-growth lobby
began to make converts. Economic growth and population growth
were no longer accepted as unmitigated advantages. In addition to
Schumacher's *Small Is Beautiful*, other books, such as Paul Ehrlich's
The Population Bomb[8], the Club of Rome—M.I.T. study *The Limits To
Growth*[9], and Barry Commoner's *The Closing Circle*[10] stimulated an
awareness in the USA and other countries that the globe might be
hurtling towards disaster and that one of the principal causes lay in
the developed world's uncritical acceptance of the idea of growth. The
debate swung back and forth as the 'growth' lobby counterattacked
and the 'doomsters' fought among themselves and modified their
statements. Gradually, with the help of such palpable exhibits as the
shortages — and dramatic price increases — in such everyday commodities as oil, sugar, coffee and tea, people got the message. When in
late 1973 President Nixon talked gravely of a 50 m.p.h. speed limit for
government cars as a way of using up less gasoline, observers were
surprised to see how widely non-government people went along with
it too. For a while, car sales dropped and bicycle sales boomed. More
profoundly, these years also saw a spectacular drop in the size of
American families that took aback even that staunch advocate of Zero
Population Growth, Paul Ehrlich.

Alongside the debate about economic and demographic growth,
there also developed a new awareness of ecology, the interdependence
between people (and animals) and their natural environment. There
had been conservationists in America before; at the beginning of the
twentieth century, for example, President Theodore Roosevelt and
Gifford Pinchot had worked with great effect to preserve some of the
nation's most attractive and valuable forest land. But far more
characteristic of American history was the bulldozing, the mining and
the uprooting to which wave after wave of newcomers had subjected
their adopted patch. The great national parks, Yellowstone, Zion,
Yosemite and the rest, were a superb legacy of the foresight and
concern of such nineteenth-century nature lovers as Ferdinand V.
Hayden and John Wesley Powell. But many of the epic stories of
American folklore, the gold and silver rushes of California and
Nevada, the coal-mining in the hills of Kentucky and West Virginia,
the development of a coast-to-coast railroad and highway system,
were testimony to a widespread preparedness to consider the acquisi-
tion of material convenience as a priority over the natural amenities
that might have to be destroyed in the process. In a continent of

apparently limitless resources, such an attitude was understandable, defensible even. Why not 'tame' the forests, level the hills, dam the rivers, strip away the coal, and build sprawling cities which would dump their effluence in the sea or an adjacent lake? There was plenty more wood, more land, more water, more coal, more space. But as Americans came to perceive that their material resources could eventually be used up and that the physical quality of their own lives — particularly if they lived in or near one of the major urban agglomerations — was already being subjected to considerable strain, some attempt was made to slow down if not reverse this historical disregard for the environment. 'We have learned that "more" is not necessarily "better" [and] that even our great nation has its recognized limits,' said President Carter in his inaugural address in January 1977.

The 'environmental' or 'ecological' movement was oddly contentious. Nobody was *against* the environment, of course, anymore than anybody was *for* sin. But to many suspicious ears, particularly in the business and industrial worlds and even among union and welfare officers as well, any politician or pressure group that talked of conserving or improving the environment was apt to sound only one or two degrees removed from wanting to scrap plans for a factory or an atomic or electricity generator — i.e. to weaken the economic base and reduce the job opportunities of an area. At first, the leaders of environmentalism found themselves alternately ignored, criticized, and caricatured as 'ecofreaks'. In time, however, both the threat and the promise of the environmentalists seemed to become less apocalyptic and gave way to practical politicking.

By the mid seventies, there was less talk of 'spaceship earth' and 'the closing circle' as the former 'ecofreaks' turned their attention to such relatively modest aims as trying to persuade people to dispose of their beer cans in garbage bins rather than on the beach or to turn off the hose in dry parts of the country once the garden was adequately watered. The environmentalists also turned to the uses and abuses of technology. Just because something had been invented, they argued, that was not in itself a reason for building and marketing it. Suppose, for instance, it was noisy or dirty or harmed the atmospheric balance. Political circles were by this time not unresponsive to such arguments. Plans for a supersonic jet for instance, were defeated largely as a result of pressure from environmentalists who considered noise a serious form of atmospheric pollution, and a rare alliance between American environmentalists and industrial interests for long persuaded the political powers that be to deny landing rights at New York's John F. Kennedy airport to the Anglo–French Concorde. In the new climate of opinion, the federal government in 1970 set up an Environmental Protection Agency which, among its other activities, tightened up considerably the safety and exhaust regulations governing American automobiles. Similarly, there were moves to limit the use of chemicals (such as cyclamates) that might do consumers more harm than good, and of aerosol cans that could damage the ozone layer in the ionosphere that protects us from the more ferocious of the sun's rays. The individual states did their bit, too. In California and elsewhere you could help the environment as you applied for the right to pollute it. If you wanted to drive your car you had to apply annually for licence plates; but for the privilege of designing your own plates you could pay an additional sum which would go into a special environmental protection fund. Even industry showed willing. Coors' beer ran a 'Cash for Cans program' with the slogan 'We can all work together for a cleaner environment'. The public utilities, normally anxious to persuade consumers to make ever more use of the facilities offered, made occasional gestures in the 'less means more' direction. 'We have only one environment,' cooed the PR material for one big gas company. 'When you conserve energy, you help to protect that environment.'

Environmentalism and consumer protection never produced quite the passions, the aggressive thrust and counter-thrust of argument that race relations and Vietnam had done in the 1960s. But like them, these issues of the seventies concerned matters of the gravest importance and graduated from the slightly eccentric-sounding rhetoric of the early days to become common currency in the corridors of power. As the world did not, after all, seem doomed to plunge off into an ecological tail-spin by the end of the century, the protection of the consumer and of the physical environment began to take up their place alongside other issues of the moment among the considerations that most policy-makers would by the mid 1970s weigh as a normal part of their deliberations.

The mood of the seventies is harder to describe and analyze than that of the sixties, not only because we are closer to it but also because its very nature was to move away from the vogue for over-simple slogans so popular during the earlier period. In the 1960s Americans had often found it easy to define the big issues and to identify their goodies and baddies, their causes and solutions; in the 1970s people were more inclined to stress their doubts and their inability to see clearly how best to deal with the problems that faced them. 'Your strength,' said President Carter in his Inaugural Address in 1977, so far away in tone from Kennedy's 1961 Inaugural, 'can compensate for my weakness, and your wisdom can help to minimize my mistakes'. Doubt and bafflement were expressed as often as conviction. The old optimism was not entirely gone; but onto it was grafted a mature realization that not all problems could be easily solved and that some could hardly even be defined with confidence.

These uncertainties helped give the seventies a character all their own. After the palpably unsuccessful attempt in the 1960s to tackle broad social and international problems, many now turned inward toward a greater commitment to *self*-understanding. As outward certainties seemed shattered, the time seemed ripe for new pathways into inner certainty. One commentator, the historian Christopher Lasch, noted the move from politics to what he called narcissism, a fascination and an unease with self and role, a deep concern with personal and interpersonal performance in the theatre of everyday life. Who am I? And what is my relationship to the wider universe? The conundrum was as old as civilization itself and certainly no novelty to Americans with their penchant for self-definition and self-analysis. But whereas the question had often been set in a social setting in the sixties, it tended to take on a more individualistic (and/or cosmic) form in the seventies. No longer was the emphasis on 'my' relationship with — or desire to escape from — the black ghetto, the 'totalitarian' campus, the stifling world of bourgeois America; more typical were the new bodily preoccupations, a growing vogue for encounter groups and EST, a burgeoning of new religions, a strong emphasis on personal physical, spiritual and psychic health, on knowing your own mind and body, on trusting your own instincts in developing authentic personal relationships.

The new search for self-knowledge and for a finer quality of physical and spiritual life helped form an America that was less agitated than before, more concerned with traditional values, more conservative even. These, at least, were some of the qualities the Nixon administration of the early seventies professed to find in the America over which it presided, qualities which its leading spokesmen claimed to embody and to enhance.

Watergate

As American social conflict seemed to come off the boil by the early 1970s, the Nixon administration in Washington looked out and took some comfort and a great deal of credit. In October 1972, in the run-up to the election in which Nixon was to be triumphantly re-elected, the President said during a radio address:

> Four years ago, at the close of a turbulent decade which had seen our nation engulfed by a rising tide of disorder and permissiveness, I campaigned for President with a pledge to restore respect for law, order and justice in America. I am pleased to be able to report to you today that we have made significant progress in that effort . . .
>
> We have fought the frightening trend of crime and anarchy to a standstill. The campuses which erupted in riots . . . have become serious centers of learning once again. The cities which we saw in flames summer after summer a few years ago are now pursuing constructive change.

But there were continuing simmerings of unrest. Just as the final thunderclaps at the end of a storm can seem the most menacing, so the Nixon people were severely shaken by, for instance, the nation-wide Vietnam demonstrations on 15 October 1969 and by the outbreak of campus unrest following the Cambodia bombings the following May. The size and intensity of these and similar manifestations of discontent came as an affront to an administration that claimed to be able to suppress what it saw as unwarranted breaches of public order. As late as 1970, Nixon could refer publicly to anti-war student protesters as 'these bums . . . blowing up campuses . . . burning books' while his Vice-President, Spiro T. Agnew, was regularly castigating the nation's principal news organizations for feeding the appetites of the protesters. To the Nixon people political protest was usually likely to constitute a threat to public order regardless of who was protesting or why. And in its hyper-sensitive response to the occasional manifestations of public discontent that occurred in its first years in office, the administration began to sow the seeds of its own ignominious destruction.

For the leaders of any democracy, there is a potential conflict between the claims of civil liberty on the one hand and the desirability of civil order on the other. Any form of publicly expressed dissent constitutes, in however small a degree, a ripple on the surface of a calm society. A society that tolerates no such ripples is repressive (or is so perfect that none of its citizens has any complaints); one characterized by too many is unstable. Any sensitive democratic leader must wrestle with the problem of how much leeway to permit those citizens who take issue with him and his government's policies.

In normal times, American leaders have not found the balance too difficult to assess. A long tradition of practice has been built up based on the United States Constitution and its first ten Amendments (the Bill of Rights), the subsequent interpretations of the courts, and the common sense, goodwill and moderation of leaders and led. In abnormal times, particularly when national security has been deemed to be at stake, things have not been so easy. In 1941–2, in the immediate wake of Pearl Harbor, the otherwise liberally inclined administration of Franklin D. Roosevelt acquiesced in the forced evacuation of one hundred thousand Americans of Japanese descent living on the West Coast. In the aftermath of both world wars, similarly, government agencies were directly responsible for ruining, without an adequate hearing in many cases, the lives and careers of thousands of people purported to have had sympathies with un-American ideologies.

The period of the Vietnam War was not a normal period as these things go in American history. It is true that by no stretch of the imagination could the physical security of the USA ever be said to have been in jeopardy as a result of 'enemy' action in South-East Asia. But it is also true that domestic dissent had reached a pitch of such intensity by the late 1960s that America's policy-makers sometimes began to feel that their capacity to act in what they believed to be America's best interests was at risk. If, for example, American men were publicly burning their draft cards (and their president in effigy) and inviting arrest by openly trespassing upon highly sensitive government property and then being given star treatment by the mass media for doing so, how (Lyndon Johnson and Richard Nixon and their aides wondered) could the North Vietnamese be persuaded that the government of the USA was acting with genuine resolve?

Bit by bit, the men in power came to resent the dissenters and protesters and emphasize the exigencies of 'national' or 'domestic' security over the guarantees of the Bill of Rights. That liberal old sage Justice Oliver Wendell Holmes had once said that freedom of speech and action might be legitimately curtailed when the republic was in a state of 'clear and present danger'. As the Nixon people looked out of the White House after a year or two in office, as they regarded the unprecedented rejection by the Senate of two presidential nominees for the Supreme Court, the widespread hostility of the press, and the violence at Cornell and Harvard and the deaths at

Kent State and Jackson State, it required only a mild streak of paranoia for some of them to wonder whether Holmes' conditions might not be close at hand, at least as concerned the government itself. Was the US Government not, some of them wondered, in the clear and present danger of not being able effectively to ensure that its writ was obeyed? And since insecure governments tend to equate their own fortunes with those of their nation, it is perhaps not surprising to find Nixon and his White House staff regarding many of those who opposed them — in Congress, in the press, on the campuses, in the streets — as though they were traitors to America. An enemy of the government was an enemy of America.

What is more surprising is the various ways in which they set out to act upon this view. We all enjoy saying damning things about those who disagree with us and whom we dislike, and political leaders are not immune from this cathartic temptation. But they do not all build up policies — illegal, unconstitutional, secret policies — based on it. The Nixon White House did.

In one sense, the first inklings of what was to come can be traced back to the early career of Richard M. Nixon, to his gloves-off election campaigns in California against Jerry Voorhis for the House and Helen Gahagan Douglas for the Senate, to the 'secret fund' accusations that almost had Eisenhower ditch him as Vice-Presidential running mate in 1952, to Nixon's detestation of the press to whom he declared a notoriously undignified and irrevocable farewell after being trounced in a race for the Governorship of California in 1962. More broadly, it is important to bear in mind that Nixon and many of the men with whom he surrounded himself — John Ehrlichman, Bob Haldeman, Herbert Klein, Richard Kleindienst, Robert Finch, Murray Chotiner, Herbert Kalmbach, Dwight Chapin, Larry Higby — were men from 'out West' who, like Barry M. Goldwater from Arizona and Lyndon B. Johnson from Texas, probably had their share of resentful suspicion regarding the supposed clique of big power brokers 'back East'. America's fastest growing wealth was in the South and the West, the 'Sunbelt' states that housed the aerospace and allied industries and boasted booming cities like Houston, Phoenix and San Diego. Yet the image of a cool, superior, liberal Ivy League power élite in the North-East continued, and rankled. Nixon and his associates were not above a desire to teach these men a lesson and this too no doubt played a part in impelling the Nixon people to act as they did.

More immediately, however, one can trace the tidal wave that was eventually to sweep Nixon from office back to a day in July 1970 when the President gave his approval to a plan, drawn up by White House aide Tom Huston, which recommended that the investigative and intelligence branches of the United States Government be instructed to establish comprehensive procedures to spy on American citizens identified as enemies of the administration. The Huston plan advocated, among other things, the extensive monitoring of private mail and telephone calls, the planting of informers in radical groups, the burgling of private premises − all activities that, in special and carefully selected circumstances had no doubt been considered to be in the national interest by previous administrations but which had never before been contemplated, much less advocated and approved, on this scale. The plan did not last very long primarily because the venerable J. Edgar Hoover, head of the Federal Bureau of Investigation and no friend of radicals and dissenters, would not countenance it. Nixon therefore revoked the plan five days after agreeing to it. It is important in restrospect in that it was the first occasion on which Nixon gave the stamp of his presidential authority to a project in which the supposed requirements of domestic security took clear precedence over the laws and Constitution he was pledged to uphold and execute.

The next year, 1971, was not a happy one for the Nixon men. In the early months there were anti-war demonstrations, a lot of blood-curdling rhetoric, and several bombs deposited in buildings in New York and elsewhere. On May Day yet another massive anti-Vietnam rally built up in Washington. Two things distinguished it from the many that had preceded it. First, it included a large number of returned servicemen − 'Vietnam Veterans Against the War', as they dubbed themselves. And second, the administration's savage response − 13,400 arrests over a four-day period − constituted the most massive bust in American history.

But on 13 June 1971 came something altogether new, an event that pulled together all the strands of opposition with which the Nixon administration believed itself to be contending. The *New York Times* started to publish its serialization of parts of the 'Pentagon Papers', a series of top secret and top level documents leaked by a former administration official, Rand Corporation employee, and academic expert on South-East Asia named Daniel Ellsberg. Ellsberg had gradually become horrified by what he saw as the bungling and deception that had led successive American administrations into the atrocious morass of their Vietnam policies. Convinced that the details of this process should be known to the American public, if only to try to prevent things from getting even worse, he laboriously photocopied hundreds of secret documents and offered them to the press. The *New York Times* began to publish them, was restrained by an injunction from Nixon's Attorney-General John N. Mitchell, took its case to the Supreme Court, won and resumed publication. Thus the Nixon people, who might have rejoiced in the publicity given to the iniquities of the preceding Democratic administrations, found themselves at the losing end of a case in which the Supreme Court, the liberal press, the anti-war lobby and (as they saw it) an ex-government-official-turned-burglar-and-traitor were linking arms against them. The Ellsberg case set off paroxysms of anger in the White House.

The Pentagon Papers were damaging to former reputations but not to present-day security, and Ellsberg himself openly discussed his view of Vietnam and his motives for releasing the documents with considerable intelligence and conviction. Much of this was lost on the White House, however, where it was feared that leaks such as these might be damaging to sensitive areas of foreign policy (Kissinger's secret trip to China was days away). There had been a number of earlier leaks of classified information but this was the last straw. There were to be no more leaks. And to guarantee that all future leaks would be plugged, there was established what became known inside the White House as the 'plumbers' unit'.

At first, the only plumbers were David Young, on secondment from Henry Kissinger's staff; an ex-CIA man named E. Howard Hunt; and an obscure recruit from New York State politics and an ex-FBI agent G. Gordon Liddy. Their immediate boss was Egil Krogh. The plumbers worked in great secrecy, their activities known only to the senior members of the White House staff to whom they reported and to the nation's intelligence and internal security chiefs. Their principal assignment was to smear the name and credibility of Daniel Ellsberg and their most notorious effort in this direction was their fruitless break-in at the offices of his Beverly Hills psychiatrist on the night of 3–4 September 1971. By this time, Hunt and Liddy had recruited their own underlings and their 'plumbing' had gone off into all sorts of new directions — the task of blackening the name of Senator Edward Kennedy, for example, or of forging State Department cables purporting to show that President John F. Kennedy had been directly implicated in the assassination of President Diem of South Vietnam. The plumbers' unit was officially disbanded at the end of 1971 but, like the Huston plan of 1970, its spirit lived on.

As the all-important election year of 1972 approached, the White House was awash with activities of dubious propriety and legality, all arising ultimately out of the administration's no doubt genuine belief that its best efforts on behalf of the American people were being hampered by the unpatriotic and destructive criticisms of a handful of irresponsible liberals and radicals (or 'radiclibs' as the Nixon men dubbed them). Increasingly, the official agencies of the federal government were drawn into the web of partisan warfare. There were attempts to persuade the Internal Revenue Service to ease the tax burden on friends of the administration and to check up ruthlessly on the tax situation of various of its political enemies. The anti-trust division of the Justice Department was put on the trail of one or two powerful anti-Nixon newspaper and television moguls. Individual reporters, such as Daniel Schorr of CBS, became the object of special FBI investigations.

Most of these and similar activities were conducted at the instigation of members of the White House staff and were kept secret from Cabinet officers (except those directly concerned), Congressmen, and in some of their murkier details from the President himself. But as the scope of these undertakings broadened, various things happened. First, much of the original motivation got lost; the plumbers and others tended to forget that every activity was supposedly related to the need to neutralize genuinely damaging opposition to the administration. Illegality and *schadenfreude* became ends in their own right to the growing army of people involved. Second, as more people were drawn in, the problems of maintaining secrecy increased; every little crime and every little lie required its alibi so that by 1972 'covering up' had already become almost a way of life for a number of White House aides whose real activities were not known to the general public. Third, as the first stage of the presidential election campaign approached and various White House plumbers and their associates were transferred to the Committee to Re-Elect the President (officially abbreviated to CRP but universally known as CREEP), the atmosphere of surreptitious illegality, conceivably justifiable in the interests of national security, was consciously infiltrated into the realm of electoral politics in which it indisputably had no place.

Since December 1971, Gordon Liddy had been on the CREEP

payroll as general counsel in charge of intelligence. Early in 1972, the year of a presidential election that Nixon wanted to win by a huge majority as the final crown to a glorious career, Liddy produced a secret plan to annihilate the Democrats — a mind-boggling million-dollar effort that involved mugging squads, kidnapping, sabotage, the use of call-girls for political blackmail, break-ins, and various forms of electronic surveillance and wire-tapping. Attorney-General Mitchell, obviously shocked, told Liddy to go away and tone the whole thing down.

That spring was a relatively good period for the public image of President Nixon as, in the wake of his spectacular China trip, he walked away with the Republican primaries and completely outshone the forlorn attempts of one Democratic aspirant after another to qualify as the lamb for what began to look like the following November's electoral slaughter. Even the break-in at the Democratic headquarters in the Watergate building in Washington on the night of 17 June 1972, dismissed derisively by presidential press secretary Ron Ziegler as a 'third-rate burglary attempt', and regularly referred to thereafter by the Nixon men as some sort of 'caper' or 'prank', seemed at the time to provide little more than a momentary distraction from the onward march of King Richard. But that burglary was the direct outcome of the final — and approved — version of the Liddy plan.

George McGovern, the honest and honourable but hapless Democratic candidate for the presidency, did his best to point out the supposed links between this burglary and the Nixon camp. But he had no hard evidence of illegality by any except the men arrested in connection with the Watergate break-in and little more was thought of the incident until well after Nixon and Agnew had been safely re-elected in November by a popular margin approaching that of Lyndon Johnson's 1964 landslide and by even more electoral votes. On 20 January 1973, Nixon delivered his second inaugural address and talked of his hopes for America as it approached its two-hundredth birthday. A few weeks later, the five Watergate burglars, plus Hunt and Liddy who had been shown to be implicated, were found guilty on various charges of conspiracy, burglary and eaves-dropping. Judge John J. Sirica found the trial disturbing. 'I have not been satisfied,' he declared at the end of the court hearing, 'that all of the pertinent facts ... have been produced.' He let the defendants know that he was considering savage sentences that might be shortened if they had any additional information they wished to impart to the court. And there things might have stood had not one of them, James W. McCord, written a letter to the judge saying that there was indeed additional information that he would like to impart.

From then on, things tumbled out into public view in a dizzying welter of increasingly bizarre revelations. The United States Senate had already decided to set up its own investigations into the background of the Watergate burglary and in two months of riveting televised hearings beginning in mid May 1973 Senator Sam Ervin and his colleagues worked their way through witness after witness, beginning with the security man who had first given the alarm when he noticed that the Watergate building had been broken into. Gradually, all the earlier horrors, such as the Huston and Liddy plans, were now revealed to an incredulous public. The most sensational witness was undoubtedly the former presidential counsel John Dean who, in a cool and calm voice, recounted with apparently total recall the details of the White House cover-up. Dean's testimony was subsequently belittled by Nixon's former top aides John Erlichman and Bob Haldeman and by former Attorney-General John N. Mitchell, and the nation became obsessed with the question of who was telling the truth. If Nixon did not know about the Watergate burglary before it took place, when did he become aware of the extent to which his own underlings were involved? And how far was he involved in the cover-up? Substantially, as John Dean had said? Or inadvertently and by default, as Nixon and his remaining defenders were now suggesting?

The means of knowing for certain had appeared to present itself when, almost by accident, the Ervin Committee's staff discovered that Nixon had for some time been recording his Oval Office conversations. The Committee wanted to hear the resulting tapes but Nixon refused to make them available on the basis of a constantly re-defined theory of 'executive privilege'. The Committee completed its investigations without hearing the tapes; Bob Woodward and Carl Bernstein of the *Washington Post* and other investigative journalists who were following their own Watergate leads found plenty of evidence appearing to incriminate Nixon, but did not get to hear the tapes; the Justice Department's own Special Prosecutor Archibald Cox was fired by Nixon in November 1973 over the wishes of Attorney-General Elliott Richardson without having heard them. As pressure mounted, the White House proposed a compromise — that it issue summaries of what the tapes contained, thus preserving the principle of executive privilege and safeguarding the exigencies of national security. But this formula satisfied no one. Eventually as the legal and political net began to tighten around Richard Nixon, he released the tapes to the persistent Judge Sirica. But the public too wanted to know what was in them. In April 1974, in the face of almost intolerable pressure, the White House made public substantial — but edited — portions of the transcripts. In May the Judiciary Committee of the House of Representatives commenced impeachment proceedings against the President for only the second time in the history of the republic — impeachment being virtually the only way in which a president can be forced out of office. Meanwhile, the new Special Prosecutor, Leon Jaworski, went ahead with his inquiries and appealed through Judge Sirica to the US Supreme Court to force Nixon to release certain tapes that he had withheld. On 24 July, the Supreme Court, in a dramatic 8–0 decision, found for Jaworski; a few days later the House Judiciary Committee formally adopted three articles of impeachment against the President for debate by the whole House. And on 8 August 1974, following former Vice-President Spiro T. Agnew who had left office after corruption charges the previous October, Richard Nixon became the first president in American history to resign. He was succeeded by the man who had been brought in by a new nomination procedure to fill Agnew's shoes, former Republican House leader, Gerald R. Ford.

The Watergate President?

Richard M. Nixon will probably go down in history as the Watergate president, the man who was forced to resign as a result of a scandal. His name has sometimes been linked with those of Ulysses S. Grant and Warren G. Harding, among the least distinguished of his predecessors as president. Nixon's detractors range from those who deplore his misdeeds and those of his appointees as merely petty and distasteful, to those who consider him to have been at the helm of an attempt to undermine the very basis of two-party democracy. Nixon himself clearly wanted future historians to think of him as the man of peace, the imaginative statesman who engineered *détente* with Russia and created a new *rapport* with China, the leader who brought increased safety and security to the world and to the American people. These, and not his apology for any misdeeds he might have committed in office, were the constantly reiterated themes in his farewell talk to the American people. In his television interviews with David

Frost two-and-a-half years later Nixon said: 'I have done some stupid things, particularly in the handling of what was the pip-squeak Watergate thing; but I did the big things rather well.'

Which of these two pictures is the more accurate? Was Nixon primarily a devious political tactician anxious to win at all costs and to cover up his ways of doing so? Or was he a statesman of global stature whose vision of the post-Cold War world was designed to ensure international peace for a generation?

The indictment is tremendous. On the home front, long before Watergate, the Nixon administration was harassing anti-war demonstrators *en masse*, proposing palpably incompetent nominees for the US Supreme Court, and dismantling the residue of Lyndon B. Johnson's Great Society by impounding funds due to properly constituted federal agencies. Abroad, it was bombing Cambodia in an undeclared war. Nixon's most articulate and persuasive critics thus had a great deal of fuel for their fire before there was any suggestion of the surreptitious illegalities that collectively came to be known as Watergate. In Nixon's last couple of years in office, however, evidence accumulated that not only was he ignorant, as no competent leader dare be, of what was being done in his own name by his own appointees, but that he was also prepared to help to cover up the more questionable aspects of such activities once they were brought to his attention. The crimes of Nixon and his underlings were not, with exceptions, motivated primarily by a desire for personal financial gain; personal corruption (of the sort that ousted Vice-President Agnew) was a perennial temptation throughout the world of politics and was not at the heart of the damage done to the American republic by Nixon and his aides. What made Watergate different from the corruption of the Grant and Harding eras was that it constituted a conspiracy to strike at the roots of America's two-party democracy by illegally subverting the activities of the 'out' party. It was to this conspiracy and to the people directly responsible that Richard Nixon gave presidential cover. In this sense he will surely be remembered as 'the Watergate President'.

Even so, Watergate and its associated misdeeds may seem to have been small beer alongside the big international events with which the administration was associated. Nixon and his aides implied on many occasions that any domestic irritations that they suffered or incurred had to be comprehended in the context of the overriding needs of world peace and the administration's foreign policy. In June 1971, they condemned the publication of the Pentagon Papers on the grounds that this, like earlier leaks of classified material, would endanger national security; when Kissinger, at the hearings preceding his confirmation as Secretary of State in 1973, was accused of having been instrumental in authorizing wire taps, he acknowledged his part in this but cited national security as the excuse. And when US forces were put on a standby alert in October 1973 in response to Russian moves following the Middle East hostilities, reporters inquiring whether this was in part a gimmick to distract domestic bloodhounds from the scent of Watergate were given short shrift by the new Secretary of State: 'We are attempting,' said Kissinger disdainfully, 'to preserve the peace in very difficult circumstances. It is up to you ... to determine whether this is the moment to try to create a crisis of confidence in the field of foreign policy as well.'

Maybe so, but Watergate came so to preoccupy the administration and its principal policy-makers that in the closing months of Nixon's incumbency virtually no governmental initiative on foreign policy or any other subject was possible. It may be arguable, on some abstract scale of criminality, that Watergate was a trivial matter, that it was a distasteful episode in which, after all, nobody was killed and as a result of which the American Constitution was tested and found to work. To Nixon himself and the officers around him the original Watergate burglary was a foolish prank, a caper arranged by men whose zeal outweighed their judgement; let's get this thing behind us, Nixon would plead again and again, and concentrate again on the important task of governing the country. To critics on the radical Left, Watergate was just another example of power corrupting and was infinitely less heinous than the 'genocide' America had been committing in Vietnam. But the fact is that Watergate would not go away until Richard Nixon had gone away; people everywhere were obsessed by it. By 1974, the government of the most powerful nation on earth was in a state of almost total paralysis as Nixon and his remaining lieutenants agonized over ways of staving off the gradually approaching disaster that threatened to engulf them and of preserving what remained of their tattered reputations. Despite Nixon's whirlwind tours around the Middle East and to the Soviet Union in June and early July 1974, Watergate was unquestionably taking priority, in Nixon's mind and in the minds of millions of people in America and around the world who were mesmerized by it, over all

other political issues. In this sense, too, Nixon was surely 'the Watergate president'.

Back to 'normalcy'?

The daily instalments of the Watergate soap opera came to an abrupt
halt on 9 August 1974 when Nixon stepped down from the presidency.
But that was also the signal for all the other things that had long since
ground to a halt to start up again. Like domestic politics. Gerald Ford,
a nice, reassuring man, assumed the presidency and a month later
announced that he had pardoned former President Nixon for all his
presumed and as yet not fully substantiated misdeeds. Such a nice
man was Ford that his motives were probably the purest: that Nixon
had already suffered enough and that nothing would be gained if the
nation were to launch into a frenzy of vindictiveness against the
disgraced ex-president. But a political storm immediately broke over
Ford's head. His press secretary resigned. Critics lambasted Ford for
bypassing the normal judicial procedures and undercutting the
sanctity of the law. Others asked why the top crook should go free
while many of his underlings were — or were soon to be — in prison for
acting on his behalf. There was even dark talk of a political deal
between Ford and Nixon that the latter might have extracted as a
pre-condition to his resignation. The Nixon pardon was to haunt Ford
throughout his two-and-a-half years as president and was to re-
surface to his detriment in the election year of 1976.

The other thing that President Ford did on assuming office was to
pick up the threads of US foreign policy, left dangling a little uncer-
tainly after Nixon's trip to Moscow in late June—early July. In
November the new president met with General Secretary Brezhnev in
Vladivostok and came away having signed an agreement that looked
optimistically forward to a further extension of the SALT accords of
1972. By now, the long war in Indo-China was clearly approaching its
finale. Ford tried in vain to persuade the US Congress — which was
forever asserting an independence from the presidency that had
scarcely been perceptible in the pre-Watergate years — to provide the
wherewithal to stave off the final collapse of the Saigon régime of
President Thieu. In the spring of 1975 the war came to a spectacular
end as all of Cambodia and Vietnam finally fell to communist forces.
Throughout the world, people watched their television screens as
hundreds of thousands of bedraggled refugees fled down the Vietnamese coast in the path of the Viet Cong and there were searing shots

of people clinging to the undercarriages of departing aircraft in their pathetic desperation to escape from an unknown and unknowable fate.

The tragedy of Vietnam and the disgrace of Watergate were both over just in time for Americans to be able to celebrate wholeheartedly their country's two-hundredth birthday. One might have expected these two unprecedented traumas to have produced in their wake a sense of national humiliation and of introspective self-criticism — particularly as the ghosts of Washington, Franklin, Jefferson and the rest began to stir with the approach of the magic date: 4 July 1976. There was a certain amount of this; for example, some families generously adopted Vietnamese war orphans as their contribution to the alleviation of the suffering that they saw their own country as having helped to cause. But for the most part, far from being weighed down by a sense of communal guilt, Americans sighed with relief that their nation's worst trials seemed to be over and then cheerfully turned their attention to other things. Perhaps Vietnam and Watergate were simply too unpleasant to think about now that they were over. President Ford, forever trying to do the decent thing and not always getting the credit for it, made welcoming gestures to Vietnamese refugees admitted to the US in order to start a new life for themselves. The public response was predominantly one of ungenerous criticism; don't we have enough troubles of our own without this influx? Similarly, Congress (still jauntily displaying its power, but undoubtedly reflecting public opinion as well) turned down the President's request to appropriate money for the relief and rehabilitation of war-torn Vietnam. Vietnam had come and gone; the American people were tired of Vietnam.

They soon tired of Gerald Ford too. He had been the perfect anodyne after the Nixon nightmares and had gained nothing but the most profound respect for the way in which he had restored a sense of honour to his tarnished office. But Ford was essentially a simple man with small intellectual and imaginative horizons; the full grasp of national and international affairs eluded him. His one really adventurous foray into foreign affairs was the dispatching in May 1975 of US marines to 'rescue' the crew of an American merchant ship, the *Mayaguez*, who had been briefly detained by the new communist régime of Cambodia. In the event, the Cambodians had released the seamen before the marines went into action, and the overall result of Ford's operation was several American and Cambodian lives unnecessarily lost plus the souring of US relations with Thailand from whose territory the marine action had been launched. Ford tried to present this exercise in gun-boat diplomacy as proof of his determination not to let the USA be pushed around — particularly by the communist victors in the Indo-China war. Nevertheless, and in spite of occasional gestures of this kind, the President was in deep political trouble by the time the early stages of the 1976 election hove into view. He was challenged for the Republican nomination by a representative of its Right wing, ex-Governor Ronald Reagan of California, and only just managed to avoid the humiliation of becoming the first incumbent president in modern times to be denied renomination by his own party. His Democratic opponent, Jimmy Carter, a former Governor of Georgia, looked and sounded a little like an automaton as he flashed his unsmiling grin and came out with his flat and mechanical-sounding statements. But behind Carter's bland manner was a man of great intelligence, religious faith, and gritty determination backed by a superbly-honed political machine that against all the odds had cut a swathe through a host of other Democratic aspirants to make its man the front-runner in the November run-off. Carter also possessed the inestimable advantage of being personally quite untarred by the brushes of Vietnam and Watergate and of believing that the federal government in general and the president in particular should meddle in rather fewer matters than had recently been common. Carter, while wanting to be president, clearly abhorred what had become known as the 'imperial presidency'. Ford and Carter conducted a series of lack-lustre television debates — the first since the Kennedy–Nixon debates of 1960 — and an uninspiring campaign culminated in a victory for Carter as the voters turned an incumbent president out of office for the first time since 1932.

The relations between Ford and Carter in the two-and-a-half months between the election and the inauguration were civility itself and the handover of power was effected in a spirit of co-operation and goodwill rare in the annals of such matters. When Carter finally took his oath of office on 20 January 1977, his first utterance as president was a generous acknowledgement of all that Gerald R. Ford 'has done to heal our land'.

Carter in office proved better-intentioned but less effective than his candidature had suggested. As president he stuck courageously to his belief in human rights, even raising the issue with the Soviets or in Latin America when hard-headed observers felt no American interest could be gained. Carter tried, too, to impress upon the American public the urgency of the energy crisis, though even dubbing it the 'moral equivalent of war' failed for a long time to deflect Americans from their penchant for 'gas guzzling' automobiles. A new SALT treaty was negotiated with the Russians, though after the Soviet invasion of Afghanistan there was no way the president could persuade the US Senate to ratify his treaty. And the whole of Carter's final year was clouded by his patent incapacity, until literally the last minutes of the last day, to obtain release of the US Embassy staff held prisoner by the hostile new régime in Iran.

Carter was not without his successes, particularly in foreign affairs (see p. 96). But overall his was a lacklustre performance if measured by tangible results. In some ways his hands were tied by legislation limiting opportunities for presidential initiative passed in the aftermath of Vietnam and Watergate; Carter's could not have been an 'imperial presidency' even if he had wanted it to be. But the responsibility for many of his failures must be laid at his own door. Carter said the right things, showed vision, intelligence, humanity, integrity and tenacity. What he lacked was the capacity to make things happen, the personal magnetism to persuade people to do what he wanted. In 1980 the American electorate denied Carter a second term in office and replaced him with ex-film star, ex-Governor of California, Ronald Reagan.

Reagan at nearly seventy was the oldest man ever to assume the office of president and he epitomized all the virtues of a golden yesteryear. He would talk in language of appealing simplicity about 'getting government off your backs' and of giving it 'back to the people where it belongs'. He pleased his large and varied conservative constituency by promising he would 'stand up to the Russians' by means of huge increases in defence expenditure while, at the same time, making substantial cuts in levels of personal taxation and yet balancing the federal budget. The conjuring trick could not be done of course; 'Reaganomics' were more easily promised than effected. But where Carter's sophisticated intelligence had sometimes prevented him from espousing easy answers to complex questions and thus made him appear irresolute, Reagan's altogether simpler view of the world endowed him with a cheery sense of purpose and direction which many Americans found appealing.

Seven

THE UNITED STATES SINCE 1920

Historical periods are arbitrarily defined. Some forms of periodization, however, are a little more meaningful than others. If one were writing a military history one could reasonably begin at the outbreak or conclusion of an important war or battle; the political historian, similarly, can begin his narrative at the beginning of a new administration or a new form of government. But social history does not lend itself easily to this kind of precision, and the social historian is left to justify as best he can whatever terminal dates he chooses.

American society was not qualitatively different in 1920 from what it had been in 1919, and there is nothing magic about the turn of a decade. However, American history since about 1920 does fall, without too much intellectually dubious pushing, into a reasonably cogent pattern. Without claiming, therefore, that there was any major historical watershed in 1920, it is nevertheless worth looking at our period as a whole and examining some of the themes by which it is characterized.

Many of these themes are obvious. One has only to look at the figures in Fig. 2.3 (p.57) to get an idea of the immense increase in the sheer size of the federal government or at the statistics in Table 5.3 (p.168) to realize that America has become an urban − and, even more so, a motorized and suburban − society since 1920 rather than a rural and small-town one. As American society became increasingly urbanized and suburbanized it also tended to become (in terms at any rate of the ethnic identifications of its white majority) increasingly homogeneous − partly as a result of the immigration restrictions since the 1920s. It also became, in the eyes of some of its members at least, oppressively conformist. And increasingly violent (in 1965, for exam-

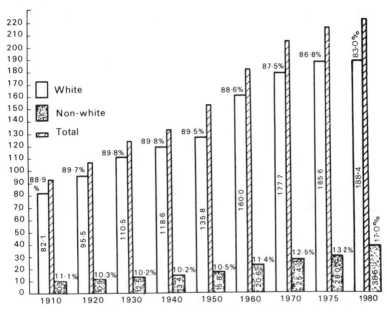

Fig. 7.1 Population of the United States (in millions)

ple, there were 216,500 crimes of violence — *excluding* rape and robbery — of which 9,850 were murders). A further obvious theme is the
widening scope and increasing assertiveness of the federal government and, above all, of the presidency. Another is the enormous
role that the United States has come to play in world affairs — and the
increasing acceptance over the past few decades that the role should
continue to be played.

But there are a host of other changes that have occurred during the
years since about 1920, and it is to a few of these that the rest of this
chapter will be devoted.

Affluence and attitudes

To anybody living in the USA throughout the past sixty years or so,
one of the most obvious and striking changes to have occurred is that,
for most people, life became appreciably more comfortable materially. Despite the occasional displays of ostentatious wealth in the
1920s and the appalling decay of the inner cities and the national

belt-tightening towards the end of our period, there is little doubt that most people were far better off by the 1980s than they would have been in the 1920s.

It is not only a question of more people having more money; indeed, it is arguable that the distribution of real income over our sixty-year period was generally rather poor and that the story was not a great deal more creditable in the 1980s than it had been in the 1920s. Of at least equal significance, however, was the sort of goods on which the money was spent and therefore the material quality of life that it helped to produce.

Americans had long been inclined to attach value to goods that embodied innovations in technology and this became pre-eminently so as the years covered in this book progressed. A lot of these technoligical innovations were small-scale stuff. For everything spectacularly new, like the motor car, there were any number of 'gimmicks' — frozen foods, non-stick frying pans, electric toothbrushes, automatic garage-door opening devices and the like. Even when it came to the big things — the automobiles, the refrigerators, the televisions, the computers, the photocopy machines — the principal American contribution was often the speed and efficiency with which these things were diffused through the population as a whole rather than the invention of them in the first place; Henry Ford is chiefly remembered for his assembly-line production methods, not for inventing the motor car. The American mind has always been distinguished above all for its technological resourcefulness rather than for its conceptual ingenuity and this was to have an influence upon the type of impact exerted by the material abundance that has been noted at various points in this narrative.

With the affluence of modern decades and the technology through which it was mediated there came a subtle shift in the values and attitudes of the people whose lives it was helping to alter. The more fundamental values were not substantially altered; the traditional American beliefs in liberty and equality, in hard work and deferred gratification, and in the US Constitution and the achievements of the Founding Fathers probably remained largely unshaken, as did beliefs about the sanctity of human life and of the social institutions upon which American civilization was based. But there also developed alongside these traditional values and in somewhat uneasy harness with them a set of attitudes which, while by no means totally 'new', had nonetheless not received quite the same widespread emphasis before. I have discussed them in detail elsewhere* but it may be useful to summarize them here.

First, there was a growing preoccupation with technique, with form, style, packaging, presentation, often at the relative expense of substance and content; an interest in gadgetry and short cuts, an interest, even, in appearance (or what came to be called, in a concept appropriate to the television age, 'image') as though it were part of reality. The practical means by which problems were solved tended to assume greater significance than the theoretical ends to which the solutions were supposedly leading. Advertisements offered you advice on how to improve your business acumen, your income, your tennis, your lovemaking; what was important was not so much what you did as that you did it well. Killing was a technique and the soldier in Vietnam prided himself if he did it competently. Loving was a technique and for every book on love there must have been a hundred on sexual technique. 'A gun,' said Shane in the movie, was 'as good or as bad as the man who uses it.' Much the same was said about radio and television and atomic research. The sheer availability of a new technique was generally enough to guarantee that it would be used and that any earlier technique would be superseded. The new technology, in other words, sometimes became an end rather than a means.

In addition, a boost was given in the later decades of our period to what one might call the value of 'participatoriness'. Participatoriness, like the infatuation with technique, was a social value; just as someone would gain approval if proficient in some technique, so approval also tended to be given to individuals, institutions or activities that induced people to participate in things together. The mass media, for instance, tried to foster the illusion (by the introduction of television audience shows and the radio 'phone-in') that the barriers between 'us' and 'them' had been breached. Politicians went out of their way to show what accessible people they were as the grandiose oratory of a William Jennings Bryan gradually gave way to the 'Fireside chat' or the informal television interview with Jack Paar or Dick Cavett. Leaders of industry would try to give their shareholders and workers a sense of participation in the business and union officials would make a point of consulting the men on the shop floor; government officials in Washington would pay careful attention to views expressed in Des Moines or New Orleans; legislation made it illegal to exclude people

Kissing Cousins (Temple Smith, 1977).

from places of public accommodation on grounds of race, and there were attempts to remove sexual discrimination also; some young people experimented with 'communal' living arrangements. Consultation, communication, access, participation, community — these were the vogue words.

There was also a strong emphasis in modern America on the value of 'transitoriness' — the belief that, since one was living in a world apparently beset by ever more pervasive change, particularly technological change, it was probably just as well to be adaptable to whatever unanticipated novelties were likely to come one's way. The American past was full of movers and changers, people who travelled vast distances and who altered whatever they touched out of all recognition. But what seems to have been new in recent times was the tendency to look upon change, like technology, more as an end than as a means. Stability to some people began to suggest obsolescence whereas that which was most valued was that which, not unlike the new disposable paper plates or towels or handkerchiefs, was essentially transitory. Not only did words and pictures and people travel much faster than would have been conceivable early in the century, but the rate at which technological innovations came and went was itself getting faster. Manufacturers proudly advertised products that were intended to become obsolete within an ever shorter time span; producers, like consumers, expected that whatever you might possess now, you would soon be likely to covet, and then to own, 'better' things. The objects of the past, like the past itself, came to be thought of as obsolete, discrete, disconnected, and of little relevance to the present. The 'latest' was often automatically thought to be the best, while words like 'old-fashioned' and 'out-of-date' were the new terms of abuse. By the same token the present was inevitably transitory and increasing attention was devoted to the speed at which the present was likely to merge with the future. Evocative new words and phrases were added to the vocabulary, such as *motel, astronaut, skylab, laundromat, thruway, re-cycle, heliport* — words redolent of an affluent and technology-filled existence in which everything worth while was on the move. There were 'drive-in' movies and banks and even your food could be 'to go'. Some argued that this attitude also affected people's relationships with each other, and even if people did not think of each other as 'disposable' in quite the same way as throw-way paper plates or handkerchiefs, there is no doubt about the transitory quality of many relationships in modern America. The growing divorce rate (see Fig. 5.4, p.166) was a striking indication of this. But in any case, as it became increasingly possible for you to travel around the country (and perhaps the world) and to work and live in a variety of places, you were bound to get to know far more people — and to know them far more superficially — than had ever been the case in small-town and rural America. Also, the 'service' nature of America's twentieth-century economy meant that you were likely to have more and more contacts of a depersonalized and transient nature with those who took your bus or train or plane fare or served your hamburgers or helped you with your insurance or tax forms. Hence the idea that psychological adaptability — the ability to anticipate and adjust to unexpected change — was a quality of especial value. Transitoriness was not only true of everything 'out there' but had to be cultivated, too, 'in the mind'.

There were other values, too, that competed for adherence in modern America. We have already had reason to notice the emphasis on direct personal experience — particularly of a sexual or sensual nature (see pp.184–8), the tendency to disregard the traditional optimistic American faith that everything will eventually work out all right (see pp.182–3), and the awareness that America's material assets were limited (see pp.188–91). These and many other attitudes jostled with those that we have mentioned — and no doubt many others that we have not — in the minds of Americans in the later twentieth century. By the 1970s, as the abundance of earlier years seemed to be not quite as expansive as before, there were signs of an accommodation between the 'traditional' values and those which had been given a boost in recent decades. Americans continued to venerate George Washington and Thomas Jefferson and the US Constitution, to hold dear such concepts (variously interpreted) as liberty and equality, and to admire individual achievement and hard work. But in addition many of them were perhaps more appreciative than in the past (and maybe more healthily cynical) of a politician's 'image', more likely to feel that they should take an active interest in community affairs, more tolerant of a person whose 'life-style' lacked stable geographical or social roots, and more prepared to enjoy without guilt the pleasures of the moment.

The United States and 'democracy'

Some have claimed that, along with the advent of great affluence and its ever-wider distribution, the USA has also become a more 'democratic' society in the past sixty years. Indeed, in the heyday of optimistic liberalism from the Marshall Plan in the late 1940s to the Alliance for Progress in the early 1960s, it was almost an article of faith for some figures in Washington that if you gave people money you thereby gave them food and, as a by-product, democracy. Leaving aside the faulty logic of this equation and the vexed question of just how evenly distributed America's wealth has been, has American society become more democratic in the years covered by this book? At a superficial and structural level the answer is probably yes. A higher proportion of its citizens than ever before is allowed to vote. Many of the democratic reforms recommended by the progressives have been adopted by various state and local administrations. Freedom of speech and the right of political dissent were advanced in a number of important Supreme Court decisions in the 1950s and 1960s, as was the right of an accused man to a fair trial. But democracy cannot be assessed by legal or structural criteria alone. The right to vote or to dissent is nothing if people do not choose to take advantage of it. A democratic society is one in which equal opportunities not only exist but are also used. The question that should really be asked about the United States, therefore, is whether it was really functioning, by the late 1970s, as a more 'open' society than it had been in 1920. Were the opportunities for social advance more equitably distributed by the end of our period than they had been when it opened? Was an individual more likely to rise – or fall – as a result of his or her own personal qualities and achievements than had been the case half a century earlier?

These questions are hard to answer definitively. It may be possible to demonstrate that personal income or educational opportunities were more evenly distributed in the 1980s than in the 1920s. But how does one investigate whether social mobility is greater now than it was then or whether it is more – or less – dependent upon personal achievement than it was sixty years ago? In the field of politics one can show conclusively that a higher proportion of adult citizens has the right and the opportunity to vote in federal and state elections than was the case in the 1920s. But how does one try to assess whether Americans were politically more concerned (or even aware) at the end than at the beginning of our period?

Some interesting research has been done into the question of social mobility. One common way of looking at the subject has been through biographical studies. The careers of men who were, say, business executives or Cabinet members or generals in the 1920s have been compared with those of their counterparts in the 1960s or 1970s. This kind of study can be most interesting, but it must be narrowly selective and can lead to conclusions that are hardly valid for society as a whole or even for the special élites under study. The biographical approach has an added disadvantage in that it usually defines a man's status by one of his social characteristics only. He is labelled as, primarily, a general or a business executive and his other social characteristics tend to be assessed in that context. In fact, in as diverse and as loosely stratified a society as the United States, mobility in one field does not necessarily mean overall mobility. A man can, by marrying his boss's daughter or by changing his job, gain one sort of prestige but lose another. Robert S. McNamara was head of Ford Motors when President Kennedy asked him to become his Secretary of Defense. McNamara, in accepting the offer, gave up the prestige of a huge salary and one of the key jobs in industry but gained, in return, the very different sort of prestige that accompanies a major Cabinet post. Did he rise or fall socially? And what was the effect on his social standing of his move from the Pentagon to the World Bank?

Another approach has been to look at the opportunities offered by society rather than at the people who take them. The scholar using this approach will examine the academic world or big business or the armed services and try to demonstrate that, for instance, more people enter these prestigious professions today (and, as a result of the extent to which manual jobs have been automated, fewer people enter lower-prestige jobs) than was the case sixty years ago. This approach is useful up to a point, but it assumes that certain jobs hold a constant position on the prestige ladder. It might nevertheless be true that a person graduating today from a very ordinary state college has about the same social prestige as was given to a smart and efficient janitor in 1920.

Mobility studies have tended to agree on one thing: that most Americans are inclined to believe, rightly or wrongly, that, in the past sixty years or so, it has become easier and more common for lower- and lower-middle-class men and women to acquire various middle-class characteristics (and, to some extent, for members of the upper-middle class to fall a little on the ladder of social prestige). The real Brahmins, of course, remain; so do the nation's most seriously underprivileged groups. But the class picture of the United States is probably more like an egg nowadays than it was in the 1920s and less like an hourglass*. The optimists interpret this as proving that the United States is an increasingly egalitarian society; the pessimists adduce it as evidence that American society is depressingly conformist and its value system stultifyingly bourgeois.

In sum, social mobility was commonly believed to be more widespread but less dramatic in the 1970s than in the 1920s. A higher proportion of Americans was likely to rise (or fall) in society in the seventies than in the twenties; but this movement tended to be only a rung or two up or down the ladder and was largely confined to those people who started life fairly near America's huge and burgeoning middle class.

Whatever the facts of the case, Americans have usually attached extreme importance to the *belief* that virtually uninhibited social mobility exists in the United States and that it has been one of the great American virtues. The American Dream has been based on the assumption that any lad can, if he is bright and resourceful enough, reach the heights. The major folk heroes have been the men who battled against great odds (often physical odds) and emerged triumphant. Perhaps the greatest of them all was the man who epitomized the 'log-cabin-to-White-House' myth, Abraham Lincoln. The belief that America is the one land where anybody can rise or fall in society largely as a result of his own qualities is still fairly widespread. It has taken some knocks in recent years, particularly with the publicity given to the appalling poverty and the undeserved discrimination that still blemish pockets of American society. But social mobility remains an important American value, one that, to this day, provides many men and women with an incentive to work harder and to try to improve their lot.

The belief in social mobility was also both a cause and an effect of the social tensions of the 1960s and early 1970s. The conservatives who threw up their hands in horror at such measures as the civil rights bills of the mid sixties or the 'War on Poverty' did so partly on the grounds that they would impose an artificial equality upon a society in which people should be able to improve themselves as a result of their own unaided efforts; the black rioters in Watts and Detroit justified themselves partly on the grounds that they were demanding

*This is true if class is measured objectively by such criteria as income, occupation, etc. But it is also the case if subjective criteria are used (i.e. when respondents are asked to which of the three classes they think they belong – upper, middle, or lower – they tend to opt for the middle class).

the right to compete for social prestige on equal terms with their white neighbours.

The belief in uninhibited social mobility took a back seat during the 1930s and early 1940s. The external challenges of the Depression and the war made it clear to most Americans that one's place in society was often conditioned to a considerable extent by factors other than personal abilities. Even in the 1960s and 1970s the Horatio Alger myth was tempered in most people's minds by a stern and unromantic realization that America's poor and deprived communities often had few means available by which to improve their lot while, at the other end of the scale, even the most headstrong and individualistic of men would often find some of the economic and social pressures of middle-class life almost impossible to escape. It was pleasant enough to look back to some of the great figures of earlier days (notably the heads of some of the great corporations, like Andrew Carnegie or Henry Ford) who had followed spectacular rags-to-riches careers. But by the 1960s and 1970s most of the big corporations seemed to be deliberately trying to avoid the impression that they were owned by colourful supermen and also to be playing down the extent to which they monopolized their particular market. Like the rebellious blacks in Detroit or the frustrated housewives in suburbia, the big corporations of these later years were groping for their own ways of adjusting to the demands of a vast and essentially middle-class society.

Labour and politics

How did America's working classes adjust to the emergence of that society? How, in particular, did those on the lower rungs of the prestige ladder adjust themselves to the idea of being 'failures' in a society that laid so much emphasis on status achievement?

To some extent, they may have been helped by religion. Several of the religious groups in the United States (particularly many of the more fundamentalist sects) put great store on the fact that the sign of salvation is not wealth but virtue. The impoverished and under-privileged Kentucky coal miner or the Californian fruit picker could, by investing his faith in one of these religious groups, obtain a sizeable yield. He could convince himself that he would go to heaven — and, better still, that the undeserving rich whom he resented so much might not.

Another way in which America's 'failures' adjusted to their ruthlessly competitive society was by seeing some of their own aspirations
fulfilled in the lives of their children. The garbage collector who
remained a garbage collector could always hope to be the father of a
college graduate.

One thing that could really alleviate the problem for the 'failures' —
to opt out or to denounce the rat race — was very rarely done except by
youngsters for whom the basic wherewithal of life was adequately
provided. Robert E. Lane, in *Political Ideology*, discovered that truck
drivers in 'Eastport' found it painful to admit that they were where
they deserved to be on the social scale, but that they would have found
it unbearable to concede that the American system of individual
self-help might not always enable the best people to get to the top.
America's lower class, in other words, tended to avoid fighting the
middle class because it was too anxious to join it.

This is one of the reasons why no major socialist or labour party
arose in the United States. But there are others. In the first place, it is
revealing to look at political history.

Until 1920 the American population was predominantly rural. In
the 1920s urbanization increased but there was no obvious increase in
working-class self-consciousness. Unionization remained almost
static. During the years of the Depression, as was seen in Chapter 2,
p.48, American labour became more efficiently organized than ever
before, but its political aspirations, such as they were, were largely
pre-empted by the New Deal. A few active radicals criticized the New
Deal throughout the thirties for what they saw as its excessive caution,
but for the most part Roosevelt obtained and maintained the constant
loyalty of America's working class throughout his occupancy of the
White House. The years following the Second World War — the years
of the Republican 80th Congress and the beginning of the Cold War
with the Soviet Union — were not encouraging ones for America's
aspiring socialists, nor was the McCarthy era that followed. By the
middle of the 1950s American industry had been extensively automated, with the by-product that there were more white-collar workers
than blue-collar workers. There was no longer, therefore, any obvious
class basis for a possible American labour party.

Even if there had been, however, American labour would have had
to exist as a large and growing third party before it could have taken
the place of one of the major national parties. But the American
political system does not smile upon third parties. The main *raison*

d'être of a national political party in the United States is to win the White House. In order to achieve this, a party must win a majority of the electoral votes — which means a majority of the popular votes in a wide range of states. Such a party must clearly have nation-wide and not sectional appeal and must, if it is to survive and grow, look like commanding the allegiance of a sizeable proportion of the nation's voters. Plenty of small parties have existed at various times in American history. On very rare occasions they have grown extremely fast and have obliterated one of the two major parties of the day. The Republicans in the late 1850s virtually took over the role in the political system that had been played by the Whigs. More often, one of the two major parties has, in the face of a serious third-party rivalry, simply extended its own appeal in such a way as to undercut its rival and thereby minimize its effectiveness. The Democrats did this, for instance, when they nominated Bryan, the Populist candidate, as their own presidential candidate in 1896. The Democratic Party has, less dramatically but with equally devastating effectivness, consistently undercut the American Socialist party by itself moving a little to the Left. But the Democrats have never had any reason to consider American labour as a serious rival, for no socialist or labour party has ever been sufficiently large to offer a real challenge to the existence of a major party.

There are also what might be termed ideological reasons why no serious labour party has ever emerged. Throughout American history there has been a strong tradition of political decentralization, a belief that each locality is the best judge of its own needs. This belief was an understandable product of the experience of a large and diverse nation which gained its independence as the result of a fight against what its leaders saw as excessive and even dictatorial executive power, and it reached its apotheosis in the writings of Thomas Jefferson. Its adherents have interpreted socialism (after giving more attention, sometimes, to the malpractices of its alleged followers than to the constructive writings of its thinkers) as advocating the political centralization that they abhor. Many Americans have also had a deep belief in God and have assumed that their faith has been rewarded by His favours; in their eyes, socialists (whom they have often equated uncritically with communists) are usually atheists. There have also been Americans, as we have seen, prejudiced against Eastern Europeans, blacks, Jews, Catholics, or indeed almost any social group that is not white, Anglo-Saxon, and Protestant (WASP). Historically, socialism has flourished in several WASP countries, but Americans have tended to look at Lenin or Trotsky or W.E.B. Du Bois rather than at the Webbs or Ramsay MacDonald as confirmation of their theory that socialism is alien to all that their America stands for. Thus, neither the political nor the ideological climate has been conducive to the development of a really large socialist or labour party in the United States.

Youth and age, leisure and work

What role has American youth played in this narrative? In Chapters 1 and 5 young people were much in prominence. In both the 1920s and the 1960s they were often rebelling against the new values of their parents and to some extent successfully establishing a new set of standards based on their own perceptions of the way society should be. In both periods the popular heroes were attractive partly because of their youthfulness (Lindbergh or the Prince of Wales in the twenties, the Kennedys in the sixties). In the world of the arts and entertainment, too, many of the popular successes tended to be young; Fitzgerald or Gershwin in the earlier period, Andy Warhol, Barbra Streisand, or the Beatles in the later.

There were plenty of differences between the two decades. In the 1960s the example of President Kennedy and his New Frontiersmen encouraged millions of bright young men and women to take an active interest in public affairs, something to which there was no real equivalent in the 'depoliticized' Jazz Age. Furthermore, the protest movements of the sixties displayed much more concern among the college generation about social inequities (but less, possibly, about cases of individual injustice) than had been the case with America's young intellectuals in the twenties.

But the similarities between the two periods were more remarkable than the differences. Both decades produced a rebellious and assertive younger generation. In both periods, too, America experienced a serious increase in social tensions and also an important burst of literary activity (the twenties saw some of the best works of Fitzgerald, Hemingway, and Faulkner, to name only the most famous; during the later fifties and the sixties, writers like Baldwin, Bellow, Malamud, and Mailer were producing important work). The 1920s and the 1960s were exciting decades, sometimes dangerous, often creative, never dull. They were, above all, years when American youth went

out on a limb and tried impatiently to change, or at least ignore, some
of the (to them) dated values of their parents.

One of the reasons for the ascendancy of America's youngsters in
the 1920s and 1960s was that there were so many of them. In the years
just after the turn of the century and, even more, in the decade
following 1945 (see pp.180–81), there were baby booms of major
proportions. But the high birth rate just before and after 1900 –
coupled with a series of dramatic medical advances that greatly
increased the average expectation of life* – also had the effect of
giving the United States a very large retirement-age population in the
1960s (see Fig. 7.2). America's constantly rising proportion of over
sixty-fives was, of course, largely unproductive economically. It also
created new social problems and exacerbated old ones. In particular,
American society was faced in the latter years of our period with a
major leisure problem.

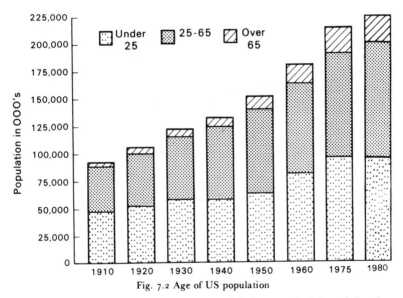

Fig. 7.2 Age of US population

The aged were not the only people with time on their hands by the
last years covered by this book, for these were also the years in which
millions of manual workers found their working week reduced as a
result of the invention of new and efficient machines. As a matter of
statistical fact, the number of leisure hours actually enjoyed per week

*Fifty-four years when our period opened and over seventy when it closed.

by members of the working population was not all that greater at the end of our period than at the beginning, while labour- and time-saving devices were sometimes capable of demanding almost as much time and labour as they saved. Nevertheless, the proportion of the population too old or too young to work increased and the growing strength of labour unions ensured that in many industries the official working week was reduced and the length and frequency of holidays increased. In addition, more and more people entered middle-class professions in which they were able to exercise some control over the details of their daily working schedule. For many people, leisure now began to be a major problem. This was not primarily because there was so much of it to dispose of but because there was only the flimsiest tradition of enjoying an activity from which no immediate and useful product emerged.

In the 1920s, as we have seen, many Americans liked to pass their leisure hours at movies or watching spectator sports. By the 1960s and 1970s, a healthier, better fed, better housed nation was not always more active in its leisure pursuits. There were, it is true, those who played more sport than they watched or took part in amateur drama-tics or did charitable work. But the great leisure activity was sitting at home watching television. In 1950 about 5 million American families had a television set; by 1960 the total was about 45 million and growing rapidly. By 1970 the average American was watching TV for about seventeen hours each week — roughly the equivalent of one-third of the entire leisure time of an industrial worker. What effects did this have?

The social effects of television are incalculable. It has clearly been a boon to the aged and the lonely and has helped to bring political and cultural education to those predisposed to be receptive to it. Tele-vision, with its regular diet of domestic comedy programmes was also a socializing agent, a means of maintaining an essentially middle-class value system. Politically television helped to win supporters for such telegenic candidates as John F. Kennedy and Ronald Reagan, but proved a liability for heavy-jowled scowlers like Joe McCarthy and Richard Nixon. It played its part, no doubt, in reducing social visiting among the more passive elements in the population and, according to some, almost killed the art of substantive conversation in the United States. And it played havoc with the fortunes of the giant movie industry, much of which was devoting a great chunk of its capital by the 1970s to the production of safe, tepid TV serials.

Some said that television was an important cause of the apparent rise in violence in America in the later years of our period. The argument went something like this. More people spent more of their time watching television than doing any other single thing other than working or sleeping. Consequently, if only by osmosis, the content of television programmes could hardly fail to have an influence upon the beliefs and actions of large numbers of people — particularly youngsters of an impressionable age. Since there was a great deal of violence on TV it was only to be expected that there would also be a great deal of violence in society as a whole, particularly by juveniles — an expectation sadly validated by the statistics. These views were fiercely debated during the post-war decades and figures were adduced to 'prove' or 'disprove' the alleged culpability of the little box. In fact, the role of television in all this was probably more complex. It could indeed bring to the surface or reinforce people's predispositions; if you had always had a hankering for a life of violence there were undoubtedly television programmes that would stimulate you further just as a television appearance by a political figure to whom you were already somewhat sympathetic could enlist your more active support. However, television was unlikely to create a wolf out of a sheep or an unswerving Goldwaterite out of a New Deal liberal. As for the argument that children were more likely than adults to pick up dangerously misleading messages from TV, some answered this by agreeing that certain programmes should perhaps be scheduled for late viewing but by adding that no nation's cultural standards should be entirely dictated by the psychological frailties of kids and psychopaths.

The debate went back and forth, reaching a periodic crescendo whenever dramatic incidents of violence — urban riots, a particularly gory murder, etc. — reached the attention of the general public. The anti-television phalanx widened the argument to include not just violence but sex too; the culpable media came to include, in addition to television, some of the more *outré* films and magazines as well. As with everything else in the 1960s and the 1970s, this debate became intertwined with the Vietnam War. Some people maintained that the nightly dose of horror footage from Vietnam on television was numbing American responses to violence and enabling people to commit it, or at least ignore it, to a degree that would have outraged their more sensitive selves a decade or two earlier; others argued, on the contrary, that the very fact that Vietnam took its place on TV alongside comedy shows and perfume ads gave it a sense of reduced stature and prevented Americans from inferring any messages — either good moral ones or bad violent ones — from what they saw.

The evidence one way or the other was inconclusive and, as Americans got used to the ubiquity of television by the later 1960s, discussion tended increasingly to focus on matters of detail (whether this or that particular show should be aired and, if so, at what time of day; at what age youngsters should be allowed into 'adult' movies; whether a specific scene or action should be cut out of a film). As in so many other matters, the more dramatic changes and the more painful adjustments to them occurred in the 1960s so that, by the end of our period, Americans were more and more prepared just to sit back in front of the TV set, beer can or *TV Times* or even remote control channel-changer in hand, and take in whatever came their way. You could while away your leisure hours watching television without having to make any exertions on your own part.

However, it would be misleading to suggest that 'leisure' was always sharply defined and something that people necessarily thought they had if they were not at 'work'. Indeed, there was something of a cross-fertilization of the traditional roles of each. At his place of work, for instance, a man would sometimes find himself expected to acquire and implement the skills of relaxed social intercourse; much of his time at the store, office, or places of call would be spent playing social games with other people, flattering them, persuading them, winning away their allies, giving them food or drink or cigarettes, introducing them to other people. Less and less time would be spent alone, simply and straightforwardly doing some sort of solitary work. And as our period progressed and the preponderant proportion of the work force shifted away from the manufacturing industries and the manual and 'blue collar' jobs towards the service industries and the clerical and professional and 'white collar' jobs, the injection of play elements into work situations correspondingly increased.

In the world of what were ostensibly leisure activities, on the other hand, there was a complementary injection of values associated with work. Sports, for instance, became more serious, organized, and co-ordinated affairs than they had once been. They became professionalized. Any nineteenth-century Rip Van Winkle would have been astonished to discover, on awakening in the later twentieth century, the extent to which every athlete, footballer, or tennis player

— even if his team was merely the local junior school — would feel obliged to make a great show of the exhaustive and abstemious period of training that he had undergone.

Thus, by the later years of our period, the worlds of 'work' and of 'leisure' had become somewhat interdependent and it was less and less easy to be sure of who was at which, or when. The old and the young, male and female alike, would often devote to their leisure-time activities the most strenuous application of the Puritan ethic while they would also all enjoy telling each other to 'relax' — even at 'work'. Perhaps there was only one form of leisure in latter-day America largely unalloyed by the work ethic, and that was television-watching.

Travel and space, town and country

At many points in this narrative we have had occasion to note important developments in transportation. The 'flivver' gave the 1920s much of their character and for many Americans one of the most poignant memories of the 1930s was that the Depression uprooted them from their homes and forced them to drive, like Steinbeck's Joad family[2], into remote and unknown parts. By the 1950s and 1960s the automobile had given America a new sort of civilization — suburbia.

The development of air travel did not affect the whole of society quite so profoundly. But the advances in this field in the past sixty years have been staggering. In 1927 Lindbergh crossed the Atlantic in thirty-three hours; today Concorde does it in three. In 1928 domestic airlines employed 1,496 people; by 1962 the number was more than 37,000. In 1930 85,000 passenger miles were flown; the figure in 1962 was nearly 34 billion and by 1970 it was over 100 billion.

By the 1960s, however, the most spectacular advances were being made not in passenger planes but in space research. In the early years of the decade the United States sent several astronauts separately into space as part of Project Mercury. Under Project Gemini, a space rendezvous was made by two astronauts in December 1965. The most ambitious of America's space programmes, Project Apollo, planned to put a man on the moon and to get him safely back to earth, a feat successfully achieved in July 1969. A number of less dramatic projects collected information about space and various heavenly bodies and gave an enormous boost to international telecommunications. The scientific advances represented by these projects were considerable but the mass public (and some of America's leaders) thought of them more as a series of prestige victories over the Soviets. The 'space race', like the 'arms race', had its hazards; in 1967 the American and Russian space programmes each sustained a major tragedy involving loss of life. Once the race had been won with the successful American manned mission to the moon, both sides gave increasing attention to less costly and potentially more fruitful research. Indeed, as a contribution to the new spirit of *détente*, the Americans and the Russians pooled some of their research into manned flights and, in July 1975, launched a successful Apollo-Soyuz mission which reached its climax when the American and Russian spacecrafts docked and a Soviet 'cosmonaut' and an American 'astronaut' met in space. Thereafter, the Americans discontinued manned flights for a while and concentrated on long-distance inter-planetary probes and the development of a 'skylab' serviced by a re-usable 'space shuttle'. For ten or fifteen years, American space research had been a major arm of foreign policy and had been the beneficiary of an expanding economy and a generous Congress. By the end of our period, however, the word 'space' was coming once again to assume the meaning for most Americans that it had held for their ancestors – the physical environment here on earth.

American history had always, in a phrase of David Adams[3], been characterized by 'the impact of man upon space'. In the nineteenth century this theme took the form of westward expansion, the saga of the prairie and the cowboy. In the twentieth (in addition to the extraterrestrial adventures recounted above) American civilization imposed itself upon space in a new way: the constant encroachment of the city and the suburb upon the adjacent countryside (and also, one might add, the growing influence of American cultural values upon America's friends, allies, and embarrassed beneficiaries around the globe). As the wide open spaces were conquered by the city, Americans tried to compensate for this rape by bringing the fruits of those spaces into the city itself. The interiors of hotels and motels and supermarkets – in the United States itself and, indeed, wherever there were American tourists and troops – would frequently be embellished with flowers, fountains, bucolic murals, and even the scents of the countryside. Many of the more obviously synthetic chemical products of urban sophistication – the creams and perfumes, the drinks and tobacco products – were advertised as being 'natural', 'fresh', and 'pure'. By the same token, the new suburbanites often lived in ranch-style houses, wore faded denims and enjoyed nothing so much as a rough barbecue in the open air. And even in the language in which they described essentially urban phenomena, the Americans of the later years of our period would look for metaphors derived from the untamed and unenclosed countryside: the wild city was the 'concrete jungle'; Kennedy's programme for predominantly urban reform was dubbed the 'New Frontier'.

The real open spaces, on the other hand, were all the time being made more convenient and accessible for the continuous stream of motorized emigrants from the big cities. Many of these travellers would get great pleasure from driving to one of the magnificent national parks — and would then pay a small fortune for the privilege of staying in a plush, antiseptic, air-conditioned, well-televisioned hotel.

What happened was that the distinction between the countryside and the city (like that between work and leisure) became somewhat blurred. The 'countryside' was tamer and the 'city' less so than sixty years previously. Americans, straining to achieve the best of both worlds, ran the risk of achieving only the second best of each. But their ambivalence towards both the town and the countryside was the expression of a deeper uncertainty. The first American colonies were founded by British immigrants, many of them Puritans. A strain of religious puritanism has run through the whole of American history and has played its part in the establishment of the values with which American society has become imbued over the decades and centuries. But American society has obtained many of its values, too, from the necessity of having to assimilate millions of immigrants. The 'Puritan' values have predominated in rural and small-town America and among white Anglo-Saxon Protestants (WASPs) and have found their expression in, for instance, the moral inflexibility of some forms of fundamentalist religion, widespread admiration for excessively hard work, and a scornful attitude towards the criminal, the drunkard, and those whose sexual behaviour did not conform to the strictest standards of chastity before marriage and fidelity thereafter. Those moral values that were more obviously derived from the waves of immigration were more characteristic of the big cities and their cosmopolitan populations. It was here (to take some of the less attractive examples of the urban ethic) that a businessman was likely to be admired if he could 'make a fast buck', that a student was envied if he could 'beat the system', and that a young man felt himself induced to tell his friends, with a surreptitious wink, about his sexual exploits*.

As the big urban centres grew, so the relatively permissive values of the city became more widely diffused. But this spread of urban values tended to lag a long way behind the sheer physical spread of the city†. The America of the 1950s, therefore, was a predominantly urban and suburban nation whose basic values were still in many respects derived from rural and small-town sources. America, the land of urban self-indulgence and the labour-saving device, still clung to a value system essentially derived from Calvin. The nation, in Andrew Sinclair's phrase[4], had 'an urban skin and a rural conscience', and this anomaly arose as the result of 'too rapid a change from village to megalopolis'. By the 1960s, when the post-war baby-boom came to maturity and when a booming economy made unprecedented affluence widely available, the clash between the old values and the new became even further intensified. Thus, the tensions and achievements of the 1960s might be understood in this context as America's attempt to catch up morally with the advances that had already been made physically.

This hurried changeover from a predominantly rural and small-town civilization to a largely urban and suburban one left in its wake much moral confusion. In the 1920s it was possible for America to elect to the presidency a genial small-town journalist from Ohio, Warren G. Harding — who then proceeded to gather around him some of the most crooked and ruthless city slickers ever seen in Washington. It was possible, too, for William Jennings Bryan, a man who had thrice led the Democratic forces in a presidential election and who had been America's Secretary of State, to assert with the sincerity of a bewildered child that the world had been created about 5,000 years previously and that Noah's Flood had probably occurred in the year 2348 BC. In the 1960s, similarly, it was possible for one of the nation's richest and brightest businessmen, Billie Sol Estes, to make millions of dollars out of a series of grossly fraudulent dealings that implicated even the US Department of Agriculture — and then,

*We are, of course, making too superficial a distinction between 'rural' and 'urban' ethics. It would, perhaps, be more accurate to say that the more puritanical moral system has tended to characterize small, static, and stratified communities, whereas the more permissive morals have been acceptable in more mobile and unstable communities — including not only big cities but also, until the end of the nineteenth century, the western frontier.

†Politically, too, the city was slow to take full advantage of the vast and rapid urbanization of the twentieth century. It was only in the middle and late 1960s that a series of Supreme Court decisions set in motion machinery that would enable the cities to be as dominant in the political system as the demographic map implied they should be.

as a lay preacher of the Church of Christ, to oppose mixed swimming in his small Texas town on the grounds that it was immoral. And Richard M. Nixon, who liked to talk of Whittier, California, as the sort of small town in which one learned to work hard and honestly and to respect one's parents, came to preside over the biggest political conspiracy in American history.

This ability to swing between the extremes of a fundamentalist Puritan morality and the outer edges of urbane sophistication is a characteristic feature of American society during the past sixty years. It is revealing to observe these apparently inconsistent characteristics blended together in some of America's most successful politicians. Few presidents have been as loved as Dwight D. Eisenhower, a man who could oversimplify complex issues and see them in straightforward moral terms — but a man who had also been a successful and powerful general. Few politicians have achieved so spectacular a rise to prominence as Huey P. Long, a man who combined the folksy chit-chat and the visible generosity of a farmhand with the ruthlessness of an unscrupulous and ambitious demagogue. Lyndon B. Johnson epitomized some of the virtues of WASP America: solid patriotism, for example, and an earnest belief that God was on America's side. But he was also known to be one of the wiliest wheeler-dealers in the slippery world of politics. This odd combination of qualities might not necessarily have made Johnson loved everywhere he went, but it certainly helps to explain some of the admiration that he aroused and, to that extent, some of his success as a politician. Above all, perhaps, there was Jimmy Carter, who clearly revelled in the small-town religion in which he had been raised and found no embarrassment in bringing it with him to the tough, unsentimental world of super-power politics.

If the value system of an ambitious politician is too solidly rural and WASP he may, like Bryan at the Scopes trial or Goldwater in 1964, arouse the distaste of the more sophisticated elements in American society. But if, on the other hand, he contravenes too conspicuously the value system of rural WASP America, then he can still be punished. Nelson Rockefeller, as sincere and conscientious a politician as the next man, possibly forfeited the 1964 Republican nomination for the presidency when he divorced a middle-aged wife who had borne him several children and then married a younger woman. Several men on Capitol Hill slipped, in recent years, too far on to the 'urban' side of America's moral tightrope and used political funds for purposes that were more obviously personal than is commonly the practice. One of them (Representative Adam C. Powell) was excluded from Congress; another (LBJ's former aide Bobby Baker) was imprisoned; a third (Senator Thomas Dodd) was formally censured by his colleagues.

To some extent Americans have faced these moral dilemmas at all times in their history. There has always been an ethical tightrope between puritanism and permissiveness, and many a figure in American history has tumbled off on one side or the other. Nevertheless, because of the urbanization of the twentieth century, this tightrope dilemma has been particularly characteristic of the years covered by this book.

Three further factors have helped it to become so. For one thing, the glare of modern publicity has meant that any prominent figure who seriously contravenes the national ethic is likely to see his misdeeds given vast and immediate press and television coverage throughout the nation. He cannot simply slip away incognito and start a new life.

Second, modern technology has made the practice of ethically dubious activities far easier than before. The computer, the duplicator, the telephone bug — these and similar inventions have put new temptations into the hands of men of power. The new technology can cut both ways, of course. Without photocopy machines Daniel Ellsberg would not have been so easily able to embarrass the American power élite by making available the Pentagon Papers; without the tape recorder, President Nixon would not have been able to make those ultimately damning recordings of his own conversations. But the ethically questionable temptations to a modern president are immense. He gives the orders to, for instance, an internal revenue service that keeps secret computer tabs on every taxpayer in the country, and to an intelligence network adept in the most sophisticated room-bugging and wire-tapping methods and capable of undetectable murder. When the inevitable frustrations of high office close in and seemingly sensible policies are frustrated by apparently ill-informed or merely intransigent enemies, the temptations to make untoward use of the modern technology available to the president must be very strong, and Nixon was probably exceptional more in the scale than in the methods to which he succumbed.

There is a third reason why these moral dilemmas have been particularly acute in the twentieth century, and that is because the American frontier was closed at the end of the nineteenth. The end of the frontier was widely taken to mean that, both physically and psychologically, America's dissenters would no longer feel able to go off to new territories and establish communities based on their own social and ethical theories. A sense of claustrophobia set in; Americans, like most other people, had to try to live together. And this meant coming to grips with existing social problems rather than moving away from them. The closing of the frontier did not, in itself, add any new variable to the complex formula of American public ethics. What it did was to force Americans to examine their ethical beliefs and to try to think through the implications of them. America in the twentieth century is probably neither more permissive nor more puritanical than in the nineteenth. But American society has tended in the past sixty years to be more concerned with problems of public and private morality and with the question of how much leeway the individual should be permitted by the wider community than was ever the case before. As society was felt to be oppressively conformist and as means of escaping from its pressures seemed to be ever harder to find, the moral integrity of the individual became a question of central concern.

E pluribus unum

Much space has been devoted above to some of the more dramatic expressions of this concern, but it also had a thousand less obvious manifestations. There were the millions of glum, identically uniformed garage hands or waitresses or supermarket cashiers working for nationwide chains, on whose breast would be pinned a printed card reading: 'Hi! My name is Bobby [or Joe or Sandy or Susie]. Can I help you?' There were the hundreds of millions of waxed-cardboard milk cartons produced each week on the folding spout of which were printed the extraordinary words: 'Your personal milk container'. And there were the clubs, the fraternities, the social groups of all sorts, many of them with their special handshakes or passwords, their secret songs and rituals, and, as likely as not, special badges for members ('Professor Elias J. Peterson. Call me PETE!').

One way in which the individual could try to maintain a personal identity in a vast modern society was to emphasize those respects in which his or her origins were different from those of other people. This was doubtless one of the factors behind the strong assertion of 'ethnicity' in the latter years of our period. Sophisticated urban Americans accustomed to jet planes and the bright lights would sentimentally affirm their 'ethnic' origins (in the food they ate, the names they gave their children and their streets and homes, and even the places which the wealthier of them visited on their holidays) as though they − or at least their parents or grandparents − had proudly brought a permanent sliver of old Palermo or Magdeburg or Omsk over with them. Record audiences watched Alex Haley's *Roots* on television and the genealogical industry promised that it could trace your ancestors, as Haley had done with his, back to their local origins.

Despite the apparently undifferentiated conformism which led some people to search for ethnic and other forms of personal identity, American society has in fact always been composed of − and has depended for its very character on − a large number of definable separate social groups. Just how diverse American society is, in terms of ethnic and national origin, at any rate, was illustrated by a report prepared by the Census Bureau in Washington in 1954.

Table 7.1. National origins of American population (in millions)

British	52
German	21
African	16
Irish	14
Italian	7
Scandinavian	6
Polish	5
Others	30
Total (1950 population)	151

The figures were reached by asking a cross-section of the population to list the countries from which their grandparents' families originated and then dividing the result by four. Table 7.1 gives no more than a general guide to the national origins of Americans, but it does demonstrate the important fact that the biggest single group comprised only slightly more than one-third of the total.

If one looks at the figures for religious affiliation in the 1950s, the extraordinary diversity again stands out. The figures in Table 7.2 are very rough; each church has its own methods of counting its alleged adherents. The salient fact is that no single group constitutes a majority; it would be quite wrong to consider all the Protestant churches as in any significant way united (see overleaf).

The United States is, too, a country of great geographical and economic diversity. Even if it had been peopled by a single ethnic and

Table 7.2. Religious affiliations of American (in millions: 1950s figures)

Roman Catholic	45
Baptist (nearly twenty different branches)	20
Methodist	10
Lutheran	7
Jewish	$5^{1/2}$
Episcopalian	4
Presbyterian	4
Mormon	2
Congregationalist	$1^{1/2}$

religious group, considerable variations in living patterns would of necessity have developed. In parts of Nevada there are about 8–10 inches of rain every year while in Mobile, Alabama, the average is about 68 inches. Temperatures vary from −44°F (recorded in Bismarck, North Dakota) to 118°F (Phoenix, Ariz.). In West Virginia and Kentucky there are destitute coal miners, in Texas fabulously wealthy oil and cattle tycoons. There are great automobile factories in Michigan and vast aeronautical works in the states of California and Washington. Nebraska lives off its wheat, Florida off its fruit and tourists. Thus the United States is still, despite strong popular fears to the contrary, a nation rich in diversity.

Too much diversity, however, like too much homogeneity, can have its disadvantages. It has not always been easy to maintain the unity and stability of American society. Indeed, throughout American history various national documents and institutions − such as the Constitution, the flag, Memorial Day, and the Founding Fathers themselves − have become sanctified and, as such, have helped to lessen the potentially disruptive effects of the diversity of American society. Throughout much of the past sixty years the history of American society has been a variation on this theme. It has been the story of an almost continuous mediation between strong centrifugal and centripetal forces. The centrifugal forces have included disruptive ones, such as the bootlegging gangs and the Ku Klux Klan, and more productive ones, such as the distinctive cultural contribution of American Jewry, or the abstract expressionist paintings and the 'beat' poetry of the 1950s. The centripetal ones have sometimes been the work of well-meaning ostriches (the National Origins Act of 1924, for instance); have occasionally resulted from circumstances largely beyond the control of the power élite (for example, the increased powers assumed by the federal government during the Second World War, or the development of the big television networks and the motel and supermarket chains); and have, on a few occasions been the product of the skill and vision of dedicated leaders (the 1935 Social Security Act or the 1965 Medicare Act are cases in point).

If the centrifugal forces, so strong in the 1920s and in new forms in the 1960s, were able to rule unchallenged, American society would disintegrate; if the centripetal ones were to become the exclusive influences upon social development, America would become unbearably dull. It is the constant battle between these two sets of forces, the recurrent grafting of some of the one on to some of the other, that characterizes the modern history of American society and explains much of its dynamism.

CHRONOLOGICAL TABLE

YEAR	DOMESTIC	FOREIGN
1920	18th Amendment (Prohibition) in force 19th Amendment (female vote) ratified Palmer Raids Sacco and Vanzetti arrested Election of Harding	
1921	Immigration Quota Act	Washington Arms Conference
1922	Fordney–McCumber Act	Mussolini comes to power
1923	Death of Harding; Coolidge President	
1924	National Origins Act Coolidge re-elected	
1925	Scopes trial	
1927	Lindbergh flies Atlantic Sacco and Vanzetti executed	
1928	Election of Hoover	Kellogg–Briand Pact
1929	Stock market crash	
1930	Hawley–Smoot Act	
1931		European countries go off gold standard Japan invades Manchuria
1932	Stimson Doctrine Reconstruction Finance Corporation Bonus Marchers Election of FDR	
1933	Agricultural Adjustment Act Tennessee Valley Authority Act Glass–Steagall Banking Act National Industrial Recovery Act Public Works Administration	Hitler comes to power London Economic Conference
1934	Securities and Exchange Commission	
1935	Works Progress Administration *Schechter* v. *the United States* National Labor Relations Act Social Security Act Public Utilities Holding Companies Act Revenue Act First (temporary) Neutrality Act	Italy attacks Ethiopia

YEAR	DOMESTIC	FOREIGN
1936	Second Neutrality Act *The United States* v. *Butler* FDR re-elected	Hitler takes Rhineland Ethiopia falls Spanish Civil War begins Rome–Berlin Axis Anti-Comintern Pact
1937	FDR's 'court-packing' plan *NLRB* v. *Jones and Laughlin* Third Neutrality Act FDR's 'quarantine' speech	Japan invades China Japan sinks the *Panay*
1938	New AAA Fair Labor Standards Act	Anschluss Munich Agreement
1939	Fourth Neutrality Act	Hitler–Stalin Pact The United States ends 1911 treaty with Japan Outbreak of the Second World War
1940	Smith Act FDR re-elected	Fall of Denmark, Norway, Holland, Belgium, and France Churchill Prime Minister Dunkirk Destroyer deal Increasingly stringent US embargoes on export of strategic materials to Japan
1941	Lend-Lease Act	Soviet–Japanese Non-Aggression Treaty Hitler attacks Soviet Union Atlantic Charter Pearl Harbor
1942		Battle of Midway Allies invade North Africa Battle of Guadalcanal
1943	Smith–Connally Act	Casablanca Conference Fall of Mussolini Allies invade Italy Teheran Conference
1944	FDR re-elected	D-Day Dumbarton Oaks Conference Quebec Conference Battle of the Bulge
1945	Death of FDR; Truman President	Yalta Conference Potsdam Conference Hiroshima War ends

YEAR	DOMESTIC	FOREIGN
1946	Employment Act Legislative Reorganization Act Republicans control Congress	
1947	National Security Act Truman Doctrine Taft–Hartley Act Marshall Plan	
1948	Truman re-elected	*Coup* in Czechoslovakia Berlin blockade begins
1949		NATO Berlin blockade ends German Federal Republic and People's Republic of China established
1950	H-bomb programme initiated McCarthy campaign begins	Korean War begins
1951	McCarran Act	General MacArthur dismissed
1952	Steel-seizure case Election of Eisenhower	
1953		Death of Stalin Truce in Korea
1954	*Brown* v. *Board of Education* Senate censures McCarthy	Geneva Conference on South-East Asia
1955	Salk vaccine Contraceptive pill AFL combines with CIO	Geneva Summit Conference
1956	*My Fair Lady* Eisenhower re-elected Montgomery bus boycott	Khrushchev denounces Stalin Hungarian uprising Suez
1957	Little Rock	Sputnik
1958		Nixon visits Latin America US Marines to Lebanon
1959	Khrushchev visits USA	Castro defeats Batista in Cuba
1960	Election of Kennedy	U-2 incident Paris Summit
1961	Bay of Pigs Peace Corps Act	Berlin Wall

YEAR	DOMESTIC	FOREIGN
1962	Trade Expansion Act Integration of 'Ol' Miss' Cuba missile crisis	
1963	Civil rights Washington march JFK killed; LBJ president	Test Ban Treaty
1964	Civil Rights Act Tax cut Harlem riots LBJ re-elected Berkeley FSM movement	Tonkin Gulf Khrushchev ousted
1965	Malcolm X assassinated Voting Rights Act Watts riots	US bombs North Vietnam and escalates troop presence in Vietnam
1966	'Black Power'	
1967	Nation wide urban riots	Middle East War
1968	Martin Luther King and Robert F. Kennedy assassinated Democratic Convention in Chicago Election of Nixon	Russians invade Czechoslovakia
1969	Manson murders Moon landing Chappaquiddick	
1970	Kent State	US bombs Cambodia
1971	Pentagon Papers	
1972	Watergate break-in Nixon re-elected	Nixon visits China
1973	Watergate hearings	US–Vietnam peace accords Middle East war
1974	Nixon resigns, Ford president	
1975		End of war in Vietnam
1976	US Bicentennial Election of Carter	Civil war in Lebanon Death of Mao Tse-tung
1977		Sadat visits Jerusalem
1978	Camp David	
1979		Israel–Egypt peace treaty 'Boat people' Iran revolution
1980	Election of Reagan	Afghanistan

REFERENCES

Chapter One   The 1920s: An Age of Rose-Coloured Nightmares

1. Bernard Baruch, *The Public Years* (Pocket Books, 1962) p. 203.
2. *Financial Chronicle*, March 9, 1929 (quoted in *American Heritage*, vol. XVI, no. 5 on The Twenties, p. 90).
3. William E. Leuchtenburg, *Perils of Prosperity, 1914–32* (Univ. of Chicago Press, 1964), p. 111.
4. Richard Wright, *Black Boy* (Gollancz, 1947) p. 19. More recent editions published by Cape and Longman, both 1970.
5. Sinclair Lewis, *Main Street* (Cape, 1966/Panther, 1970).
6. Leuchtenburg, op. cit., p. 272.
7. Robert S. Lynd and Helen Merrell Lynd, *Middletown: A Study in Contemporary American Culture* (Harcourt Brace, 1959/Constable).
8. F. L. Allen, *Only Yesterday: An Informal History of the Nineteen Twenties* (Harper and Row, 1957) p. 79.
9. ibid., pp. 209–10.
10. John B. Rae, *The American Automobile* (Univ. of Chicago Press, 1965) p. 88.
11. *The News and Times* of Downs, Kansas.

Chapter Two   The 1930s: The Depression, the New Deal and FDR

1. John Steinbeck, *The Grapes of Wrath* (Penguin, 1966) pp. 213–4. Later edition by Penguin, 1970.
2. Robert E. Sherwood, *The White House Papers of Harry L. Hopkins* (Eyre and Spottiswoode, 1948) vol. 1, p. 71.
3. Arthur M. Schlesinger, Jr., *The Coming of the New Deal* (Houghton Mifflin, 1959), p. 401.
4. Frances Perkins, *The Roosevelt I Knew* (Viking Press, 1946) p. 240. (Also published by Harper and Row, 1965, p. 301.)
5. ibid., p. 72.
6. Samuel Lubell, *The Future of American Politics* (Harper, 1965) pp. 60–61.
7. ibid., p. 61.
8. Benjamin Stolberg and Warren Jay Vinton, *The Economic Consequences of the New Deal* (Harcourt Brace, 1935), reprinted in Morton Keller (ed.), *The New Deal: What Was It?* (Holt, Rinehart and Winston, 1963).
9. Arthur M. Schlesinger, Jr., 'Sources of the New Deal: Reflections on the Temper of a Time', *Cambridge University Forum*, vol. 2, no. 4, Fall 1959, pp. 4–12. Reprinted in Morton Keller (ed.), op. cit.
10. Richard Hofstadter, *The Age of Reason* (Vintage Books, 1955) p. 306.

Chapter Three   Foreign Policy

1. Robert E. Sherwood, *Roosevelt and Hopkins: An Intimate History* (Harper and Row, 1948) p. 236. Revised edition 1950.
2. Cordell Hull, *The Memoirs of Cordell Hull* (Hodder and Stoughton, 1948) vol. 2, pp. 1109–10.
3. William A. Williams, *The Tragedy of American Diplomacy* (Dell, 1972).

4. See also Hugh Higgins, *The Cold War* (Heinemann Educational Books, 1974) p. 110.
5. For a differing view, see Higgins, op. cit., pp. 30–32.
6. According to Pierre Salinger in *With Kennedy* (Cape, 1966).
7. Williams, op. cit.
8. V. O. Key, *Public Opinion and American Democracy* (Knopf, 1961) p. 552.

Chapter Four   The War and After

1. S. A. Stouffer *et al.*, *The American Soldier*, 2 vols. (Princeton Univ. Press, 1949).
2. Jack Goodman (ed.), *While You Were Gone* (Da Capo Press, 1974) p. 224.
3. Richard Rovere, *Senator Joe McCarthy* (Harper and Row, 1973).
4. David Riesman, *The Lonely Crowd* (Yale Univ. Press, 1950).
5. Jack Kerouac, *On the Road* (Deutsch, 1958).
6. Vladimir Nabokov, *Lolita* (Weidenfeld and Nicolson, 1959/Corgi).
7. Riesman, op. cit.
8. William H. Whyte, *The Organization Man* (Cape, 1957 Penguin, 1964).
9. Vance Packard, *The Status Seekers* (Longman, 1960 Penguin, 1971).

Chapter Six   The 1970s: To Watergate and Beyond

1. Herman Kahn in *Newsweek,* July 4, 1976.
2. Tom Hayden in June 1975, in a statement announcing that he would seek the 1976 Democratic nomination for US Senator from California.
3. Jack Newfield, *Robert Kennedy: A Memoir* (Cape, 1970), p. 304.
4. Quoted in William Braden, *The Age of Aquarius* (Eyre and Spottiswoode, 1971), p. 167.
5. John Updike, *Bech: A Book* (Deutsch, 1970).
6. Rachel Carson, *Silent Spring* (Penguin, 1970).
7. E. F. Schumacher, *Small is Beautiful: A Study of Economics as if People Mattered* (Harper and Row/Sphere, 1973).
8. Paul R. Ehrlich, *The Population Bomb* (Ballantine Books, 1976).
9. D. H. Meadows *et al.*, *The Limits to Growth* (Universe/Pan, 1974).
10. Barry Commoner, *The Closing Circle: The Environmental Crisis and Its Cure* (Cape/Bantam, 1972).

Chapter Seven   The United States Since 1920

1. Robert E. Lane, *Political Ideology* (Free Press, 1962).
2. In *The Grapes of Wrath* (Penguin, 1970).
3. D. K. Adams, *America in the Twentieth Century* (C.U.P., 1967) p. 215.
4. Andrew Sinclair, *A Concise History of the United States* (Thames and Hudson, 1967) p. 200.

BIBLIOGRAPHICAL ESSAY

This bibliography is primarily intended for the non-expert general reader. Books also available in paperback are indicated with an asterisk.

There are any number of competent textbooks on modern American history. Four that deal primarily with the twentieth century are: Frank. B. Freidel, *America in The Twentieth Century* (Knopf, 4th ed. 1976); Arthur S. Link and William B. Catton, *American Epoch* (3 vols., Knopf, 4th ed. 1967); George E. Mowry, *Urban Nation* (Hill and Wang, 1965); and, for a more radical interpretation based on economic factors, Gabriel Kolko, *Main Currents in Modern American History** (Harper and Row, 1976).

Many of the books on the 1920s are impressionistic and not a few are plain flippant. The style was set by Frederick L. Allen, whose *Only Yesterday** (Harper, 1931) is an entertaining chronicle of the high-jinks of the Jazz Age. The same sort of material was moulded into a more definable shape by John D. Hicks in *Republican Ascendancy** (Harper and Row, 1960) and by William E. Leuchtenburg in *The Perils of Prosperity** (Univ. of Chicago Press, 1958). The economy of the twenties is ably explained in George Soule, *Prosperity Decade* (Holt, Rinehart and Winston, 1947). The ballyhoo of the wealthy is superbly portrayed in F. Scott Fitzgerald's *The Great Gatsby** (Scribner/Penguin) and the privations of the blacks are movingly described in Richard Wright's autobiography *Black Boy** (Harper and Row/Longman). The literature of the twenties, the era of Fitzgerald, Hemingway, Faulkner and others, is placed in its social context by Frederick J. Hoffman, *The Twenties** (Free Press, 1965). One book that makes an attempt to pull together many of the strands of the period is Andrew Sinclair, *Prohibition, the Era of Excess* (Little Brown, 1962; Four Square, 1965).

An excellent anthology of writings by contemporaries about the 1920s and 1930s can be found in Isabel Leighton (ed.), *The Aspirin Age** (Simon and Schuster, 1968). The moment of transition between the two decades is caught, analysed, and only a little caricatured in J. K. Galbraith, *The Great Crash** (Houghton Mifflin, 3rd ed. 1972/Penguin).

The classic work on the Depression is Arthur M. Schlesinger Jr's (so far) three-volume study under the overall title *The Age of Roosevelt*. The three volumes, all published in the USA by Houghton Mifflin (and in Britain by William Heinemann Ltd. but now out of print), are entitled *The Crisis of the Old Order** (1957), *The Coming of the New Deal** (1959), and *The Politics of Upheaval* (1960). There are many excellent short biographies of Franklin D. Roosevelt. One of the best (though it does not deal with the war years) is William E. Leuchtenburg, *Franklin D. Roosevelt and the New Deal** (Harper and Row, 1963). A biography that deals with both the New Deal and the war periods is the two-volume set by James McGregor Burns entitled *Roosevelt: the Lion and the Fox** and *Roosevelt: The Soldier of Freedom** (Harcourt Brace Jovanovich, 1963 and 1973). For a primarily economic treatment of the 1930s, see Broadus Mitchell, *Depression Decade* (Holt, Rinechart and Winston, 1947). The hardships imposed by the Depression upon the American people are excellently recounted in Dixon Wecter, *The Age of the Great Depression** (Watts, 1971) and poignantly (if over-sentimentally) portrayed in John Steinbeck's novel *The Grapes of Wrath** (Penguin/Pan). First-hand memories of the Depression have been collected in Studs Terkel, *Hard Times** (Avon, 1975). Of the many book-length memoirs of the period, one with a judicious combination of sentiment and hard fact is Frances Perkins, *The Roosevelt I Knew** (Peter Smith/Harper and Row). The story of Eleanor Roosevelt is told in her *Autobiography* (Harper and Row, 1961) and in Joseph P. Lash, *Eleanor and Franklin** (NAL/Deutsch) and *Eleanor: The Years Alone** (NAL/ Deutsch).

There are many narrative histories of American foreign policy. For the period covered in this book the reader might like to refer to the later chapters in Thomas A. Bailey, *A Diplomatic History of the American People* (Appleton—Century—Crofts and Prentice—Hall, 9th ed. 1974). A book that deals almost exclusively with the twentieth century is Foster R. Dulles, *America's Rise to World Power** (Harper and Row, 1955). Another is Richard W. Leopold, *Growth of American Foreign Policy* (Knopf, 1962). A brilliant and unusual interpretation can be found in William A. Williams, *The Tragedy of American Diplomacy** (Dell, 2nd ed. 1972). A more orthodox interpretation is George F. Kennan, *American Diplomacy** (Univ. of Chicago Press, 1970), a collection of essays that includes the famous 'Mr. X' article.

Anybody with a special interest in the making of US foreign policy from the 1920s to the 1940s will want to read Henry L. Stimson and McGeorge Bundy, *On Active Service in Peace and War* (Harper, 1948; reissued by Octagon, 1971). American policy before, during and immediately after the Second World War has been carefully described in a number of books by Herbert Feis; America at the outbreak of the war is also the subject of several works by Robert A. Divine, notably *Roosevelt and World War II* (Johns Hopkins, 1969). Perhaps the most rewarding way of understanding the war from the US point of view is to read Robert E. Sherwood's reconstruction of Harry Hopkins' papers, *Roosevelt and Hopkins: An Intimate History* (Harper and Row, 1950). For a recent biography of Hopkins see Henry A. Adams, *Harry Hopkins* (Putnam, 1977). Life in the United States during the war years is evocatively described in many of the essays in J. Goodman (ed.), *While You Were Gone* (Simon and Schuster, 1946 Da Capo Press, 1974). The most authoritative work on American life and politics during the war years is John M. Blum, *V Was For Victory* (Harcourt Brace Javanovich, 1976).

For the foreign policy of the United States since 1945 see John W. Spanier, *American Foreign Policy Since World War II** (Praeger, 6th rev. ed, 1973/Nelson) or Walter LaFeber, *America, Russia, and The Cold War* (Wiley, 1967). For thoroughgoing 'revisionist' history (which tends to emphasize the more imperialistic and aggressive aspects of US policy) see David Horowitz, *From Yalta to Vietnam** (Penguin, rev. ed, 1967) and, on the more specific question of the relationship between the atomic bombs and the origins of the Cold War, Gar Alperovitz, *Atomic Diplomacy* (Simon and Schuster, 1965/Secker and Warburg, 1965). For the detailed testimony of a participant in post-war policy making, see Dean Acheson, *Present at the Creation* (Norton, 1969/Hamish Hamilton, 1970) as well as appropriate passages in the two volumes of memoirs by President Harry S Truman entitled *Year of Decisions** and *Years of Trial and Hope** (Doubleday/NAL). American involvement in Vietnam has been the subject of much comment by journalists and pamphleteers but, as yet, little comprehensive analysis. A brilliant and witty account of an anti-war rally is provided by Norman Mailer in *The Armies of The Night** (NAL/Penguin). The role of the US Government in Vietnam was analysed by David Halberstam in a book entitled (with ironical reference to the Kennedy and Johnson 'whiz kids' who were responsible) *The Best and The Brightest** (Fawcett World, 1973/Pan, 1974), and was revealed in detail in Neil Sheehan *et al.*, *The Pentagon Papers** (Bantam, 1971). Henry A. Kissinger in mid career at the State Department was the subject of a readable narrative by Marvin and Bernard Kalb entitled *Kissinger* (Little, 1974/Hutchinson, 1974). For a hostile analysis, see Roger Morris, *Uncertain Greatness* (Quartet 1978) and for a psychiatric interpretation, see Bruce Mazlish, *Kissinger* (Basic Books, 1976). The first volume of Kissinger's own memoirs have been published as Henry A. Kissinger, *The White House Years** (Little Brown/Michael Joseph with Weidenfeld and Nicolson, 1979).

For an accessible and attractive picture of the Truman and Eisenhower eras, see Eric F. Goldman, *The Crucial Decade — and After** (Vintage). President Eisenhower's two volumes of memoirs are pretty dull but some first-hand insight into the Eisenhower White House can be gleaned from his chief aide Sherman Adams in a book entitled

Firsthand Report (Harper, 1961). Two of Eisenhower's former speech writers wrote memoir-biographies: Emmet John Hughes, *The Ordeal of Power** (Dell and Arthur Larson, *Eisenhower: The President Nobody Knew* (Scribner, 1968/Leslie Frewin, 1969).

Many revealing insights into the mind of Richard M. Nixon can be gleaned from his books *Six Crises* (Doubleday, 1962); the first crisis is the Hiss case and the sixth is Nixon's defeat by Kennedy in 1960. An entertaining if hair-raising insight into the activities of the House Un-American Activities Committee is contained in the edited transcripts of some of the HUAC's more notorious hearings in Eric Bentley (ed.), *Thirty Years of Treason** (Viking, 1973). For a lively biography of Joseph R. McCarthy, see Richard Rovere, *Senator Joe McCarthy** (Harper and Row, rev. ed. 1973). A stimulating symposium on McCarthy can be found in Allen J. Matusow (ed.), *Joseph R. McCarthy** (Prentice–Hall, 1970). The broader perspective is presented in David Caute, *The Great Fear* (Simon and Schuster/Secker and Warburg, 1978). Many of the most perceptive and provocative books on the 1950s tended to be written at the time by sociologists. See, for instance, David Riesman *et al.*, *The Lonely Crowd** (Yale University Press), C. Wright Mills, *The Power Elite** (OUP, 1959), William H. Whyte, *The Organization Man** (Cape, 1957/Penguin 1964), and Vance Packard, *The Status Seekers** (Longman, 1960/Penguin, 1971).

The best books on President Kennedy are still the earliest to appear. Two lengthy biographies by men who worked closely with JFK first appeared within a couple of years of his death – Theodore C. Sorensen, *Kennedy* (Harper and Row, 1965/Hodder) and Arthur M. Schlesinger Jr., *A Thousand Days** (Fawcett World, 1975). For an insight into the way in which Kennedy became president, see Theodore H. White, *The Making of The President 1960** (Atheneum, 1961; NAL/Cape, 1962). On JFK's death, you might imagine that everything that can be said was said in William Manchester's book *The Death of a President** (Harper and Row, 1967) and the *Warren Commission Report* (New York Times–Bantam, 1964) but fresh evidence now seems likely to surface from time to time. For the Kennedy era and mystique, see also Arthur M. Schlesinger, *Robert Kennedy and His Times* (Houghton Mifflin/Deutsch, 1978). On Lyndon B. Johnson the student will want to read LBJ's own memoirs entitled *The Vantage Point** (Popular Library, 1972/Weidenfeld and Nicolson, 1972) alongside studies by Eric F. Goldman, Hugh Sidey, Louis Heren and others. For an attempt to understand the mind of the man, see Doris Kearns, *Lyndon Johnson and the American Dream* (Harper and Row, 1976/Deutsch, 1976).

The political radicalism of the 1960s is well captured in Jack Newfield, *A Prophetic Minority* (NAL, 1966/Blond, 1967). On race relations, one of the best books was Louis E. Lomax, *The Negro Revolt* (Harper and Row, 1962) though it was written too early to take account of the more dramatic developments of the era. The frustrations that can impel a man to rebel are movingly evoked in Alex Haley (ed.), *The Autobiography of Malcom X** (Ballantine/Penguin). In addition to Malcolm, other black leaders of the 1960s put their thoughts in print. See, for example, Martin Luther King, *Why We Can't Wait** (NAL), Stokely S. Carmichael and Charles V. Hamilton, *Black Power** (Vintage) and Eldridge Cleaver, *Soul on Ice** (Dell, 1970/Cape, 1969). The student movement left in its wake innumerable printed ephemera but has been the subject of few book-length studies (except by outraged opponents). The best background study of the American university and college scene in the 1960s is in Christopher Jencks and David Riesman, *The Academic Revolution** (Anchor, 1969). Other aspects of the radicalism of the 1960s each had their landmark texts. The first major expression of the women's movement was Betty Friedan, *The Feminine Mystique** (Dell, 1975 ed./Penguin) while the most widely quoted of later books was Kate Millett, *Sexual Politics** (Avon, 1971/Hart-Davis). The problems of public poverty amid private affluence were analysed with elegance in J. K. Galbraith, *The Affluent Society** (Houghton Mifflin, 3rd ed. 1976/Penguin) and with more bite by Michael Harrington in his influential book *The Other*

America* (Macmillan, 1970 ed.). For an insight into the 'soft' side of the radicalism of
the 1960s — hippiedom and yippiedom rather than confrontation politics — see, for
example, Jerry Rubin, *Do It!** (Simon and Schuster/Cape, 1970) or Tom Wolfe's
account (written as though undergoing a permanent LSD trip) of Ken Kesey and his
Merry Pranksters in *The Electric Kool-Aid Acid Test** (Bantam, 1969). For the most
menacing aspect of sixties radicalism, see Hunter S. Thompson, *Hell's Angels** (Bal-
lantine/Penguin). An outstanding collection of all the divergent strains of the radicalism of the 1960s is assembled between the pages of the edited transcript of the Chicago
trial of various leaders arrested during the disturbances there in the summer of 1968;
this was issued as Judy Clavir and John Spitzer (eds.), *The Conspiracy Trial* (Bobbs,
1970/Cape, 1971).

As disillusion with the radicalism of the 1960s set in, Americans began to take stock
of themselves by reading books like Richard M. Scammon and B. J. Wattenburg, *The
Real Majority** (Coward, 1970). Major tracts of the anti-growth movement included
Paul R. Ehrlich, *The Population Bomb** (Ballantine, 1976 ed.), D. H. Meadows *et al.*, *The
Limits to Growth** (Universe/Pan), Barry Commoner, *The Closing Circle** (Bantam,
1972/Cape), and E. F. Schumacher, *Small is Beautiful** (Harper and Row/Sphere).
For an outstanding evocation and analysis of America in the 70s, see Christopher
Lasch, *The Culture of Narcissism** (Warner, 1979). There are few books on Nixon's
presidency as a whole but several on its beginning — notably the T. H. White
volume on the 1968 election and Joe McGinniss' exposure of the electoral techniques
of the Nixon people in *The Selling of The President 1968** (Pocket Books/Deutsch). There
are already even more books on Nixon's downfall, the most famous so far being the
two volumes by the *Washington Post* team who helped to pursue the early Watergate
clues; these are Carl Bernstein and Bob Woodward, *All the President's Men* (Warner
Books, 1976 ed./Secker and Warburg) and Bob Woodward and Carl Bernstein, *The
Final Days* (Simon and Schuster, 1976/Secker and Warburg, 1976). Several of the
Nixon people, including Kissinger, have published memoirs of this period. Richard M.
Nixon's *Memoirs** (Warner/Sidgwick and Jackson, 1979) cover the whole period of his
presidency. Jimmy Carter's *Keeping Faith* (Collins, 1982) gives his version of the later
1970s. For a critical assessment of the role of the American presidency in modern times,
see Arthur M. Schlesinger Jr., *The Imperial Presidency* (Houghton Mifflin, 1973/Deutsch,
1974).

Any reader with a head for statistics will find a mine of information in the annual
Statistical Abstract of the United States and the *Historical Statistics of the United States* (recently
updated to cover the whole period from Colonial times until 1970). These are published
in Washington by the Bureau of the Census and provide the source for most of the
figures cited in this book. For a critical guide to some of the literature of modern
America, see Tony Tanner, *City of Words: American Fiction 1950–70* (Cape, 1976).

INDEX